Coordinating the Communication Course: A Guidebook

Coordinating the Communication Course: A Guidebook

DEANNA L. FASSETT
SAN JOSÉ UNIVERSITY

JOHN T. WARREN
SOUTHERN ILLINOIS UNIVERSITY, CARBONDALE

BEDFORD / ST. MARTIN'S
Boston ◆ New York

For Bedford/St. Martin's

Publisher for Communication: Erika Gutierrez
Developmental Editor: Mae Klinger
Associate Production Editor: Kellan Cummings
Production Associate: Samuel Jones
Senior Marketing Manager: Adrienne Petsick
Copy Editor: Virginia Rubens
Permissions Manager: Kalina Ingham Hintz
Art Director: Lucy Krikorian
Cover Design: Billy Boardman
Composition: Achorn International, Inc.
Printing and Binding: Haddon Craftsmen, Inc., an RR Donnelley & Sons Company

President: Joan E. Feinberg
Editorial Director: Denise B. Wydra
Director of Development: Eric T. Appel
Director of Marketing: Karen R. Soeltz
Director of Production: Susan W. Brown
Associate Director, Editorial Production: Elise S. Kaiser
Managing Editor: Shuli Traub

Library of Congress Control Number: 2011932029

For information, write: Bedford/St. Martin's, 75 Arlington Street, Boston, MA 02116   (617-399-4000)

ISBN: 978-0-312-62345-6

"To live life fully is to live it as if it were an act of criticism."
  — Bonnie Marranca, "Acts of Criticism"

"The academy is not paradise. But learning is a place where paradise can be created. The classroom, with all its limitations, remains a location of possibility. In that field of possibility we have the opportunity to labor for freedom, to demand of ourselves and our comrades an openness of mind and heart that allows us to face reality even as we collectively imagine ways to move beyond boundaries, to transgress. This is education as the practice of freedom."
  — bell hooks, *Teaching to Transgress: Education as the Practice of Freedom*

In memory of John Thomas Warren (1974–2011)

Preface

As colleagues, friends, and coauthors who have been course coordinators for a combined 16 years, we have had many conversations—at conferences, on the phone, and via email—reflecting on the role. We've delved into its challenges and rewards, its crucial importance to the success of both introductory and advanced communication courses, and its ways of contributing to the discipline. We've worked to troubleshoot common challenges, like organizing new instructor orientation, ensuring consistent grading across multiple sections, balancing coordination responsibilities with other aspects of the academic life (such as research and teaching), and advocating for course needs in the face of budgetary concerns. And we've closely examined the process of learning how to coordinate effectively, first while learning the role ourselves, and later while mentoring others in the role. As introductory communication course coordinators, we learned the role in much the same way as many of our colleagues: from on-the-job experience, from talking to predecessors and mentors, and from combing books and journals for advice and insight—in effect, "the hard way." Discussing this process of learning to effectively coordinate communication courses inspired us to write the guide you hold in your hands—a current, comprehensive resource for people like us—essentially, the book we wish we had been able to read when we first began, and the book we wish we could have consulted as we navigated the role of coordinator over time.

We wrote *Coordinating the Communication Course: A Guidebook* in order to draw together the best practices, regarding every aspect of the coordinator role, as well as the wisdom of colleagues in the field, and that of educational luminaries. And we also sought to represent the diversity among the various iterations of the coordinator role at different institutions, and the many different courses one may organize, whether public speaking, human communication, interpersonal communication, or another introductory or advanced course.

As well as providing a resource guide for effective coordination, we hope this book helps our readers achieve a healthy, productive balance between coordination responsibilities, other academic and teaching responsibilities, and personal goals. This role is known for a certain degree of burnout, but we feel it doesn't necessarily need to be this way, and we hope this guide acts as a key element in a support network that helps coordinators avoid burnout and raise colleague and administrator awareness of what the role entails.

This book is divided into three parts, each centering on an essential aspect of coordination: continuity, professional development, and advocacy. All three of these parts are grounded in the principle that program vision is central to overall success; thus course vision is a recurring theme and topic throughout

Coordinating the Communication Course: A Guidebook. With the content grounded in this strong foundation, we discuss all the topics crucial to the coordinator role.

Starting in Part I, we dive into the essentials of creating continuity across multiple sections of a communication course. In Chapter 1, we begin with an extended discussion of the coordinator role in all its different iterations and then explore the meaning of effective coordination and how you can learn to be an empowered coordinator. In Chapter 2, we tackle program vision: its foundations and constituent parts; ways in which to understand it; techniques for articulating it clearly to stakeholders; ways in which it contributes to program strength; and tools for a dialogue about this vision. In Chapter 3, we provide advice on understanding assessment constructively, helping colleagues with assessment, designing meaningful assessment, and the impact of assessment. The final chapter in this part includes guidance on using common syllabi and common grading expectations to create continuity across sections. It covers how to find the right balance of structure and flexibility depending on the instructional environment; clarifies the elements of a common syllabus in-depth; and offers strong models of syllabi, assignments, and grading rubrics from real coordinators at diverse institutions.

In Part II, we move on to professional development and discuss how coordinators can help improve the quality of instruction through training and development, making changes to the course, fostering awareness about student diversity, and utilizing new technology. First, in Chapter 5, we consider a coordinator's role in hiring, evaluating, and dismissing instructors. Chapter 6 goes on to discuss training and development for novice instructors — from training and development objectives to different orientation strategies, and techniques for continued training and learning *after* orientation. We include sample syllabi for new instructor training and support courses in this chapter. In Chapter 7, we offer advice on professional development opportunities for more experienced instructors. We address ways in which coordinators can draw on the experience of veteran instructors for the benefit of all, while still providing these instructors with opportunities to keep current in terms of disciplinary and instructional advances. Chapter 8 guides coordinators who wish to make changes in their course to help it better adhere to program vision — whether the course needs extensive change or smaller tweaks. It also provides tools for adapting to outside change that may influence a program's ability to adhere to its guiding principles. In Chapter 9, the last in this part, we discuss responding to students' needs in today's learning environment. This chapter concentrates on the significance of the growing diversity of student populations and on the prevalence of technology in the classroom, and what these factors mean for the coordinator.

Part III completes the picture with in-depth coverage of advocacy. Chapter 10 concentrates on self-advocacy and on what coordinators can do to make sure their colleagues understand, recognize, and take into account their work as they seek professional goals such as promotion or a reorganized class load. In Chapter 11, we provide advice on research — how coordinators can conceive of research in relation to their role, how course coordination can inform research, and how

coordinators can make time for research. This relates closely to our aim of facilitating balance between coordination goals and other personal and professional
academic goals. Finally, in Chapter 12, we discuss campus advocacy—that is, how
the coordinator can be an effective advocate for students, instructors, the course,
the program, and the discipline itself, even in difficult financial times.

Each chapter includes practical techniques necessary for successful coordination, as well as how the day-to-day concerns relate to the health of the course
and program in a broader sense, and what constitutes effective coordination
in context. We don't shy away from providing advice on common coordination
challenges—from resolving grading conflicts to making changes in a program to
bring it more in line with course vision, and dealing with the financial hurdles
of reduced budgets. Whenever possible, we end a chapter with a list of recommended readings, culled from foundational books, essays, and journals. We feel
these readings are valuable extensions of chapter topics.

This guide is the second in the Bedford/St. Martin's Professional Resource
Series for Communication, following in the footsteps of Elizabeth Natalle's excellent *Teaching Interpersonal Communication: Resources and Readings*. The series was
conceived specifically for instructors seeking best practices for instructing, managing, and developing a course. We are honored to contribute to this series and
impressed with the editorial team's firm belief that textbook publishers should
attend to the needs of both students *and* professors. Thus, *Coordinating the Communication Course: A Guidebook* not only offers time-tested advice on every aspect
central to effective coordination, but also provides guidance on seeking balance
and thriving in this unique role.

We are grateful to all those involved in the writing and production of this
book: Joan Feinberg, Denise Wydra, Erika Gutierrez, Karen Schultz Moore,
Mae Klinger, Shuli Traub, Kellan Cummings, and Sam Jones. Mae, especially,
routinely went above and beyond the call of duty, and we are thankful for her
well-timed and well-phrased input.

A special thanks goes to the reviewers who provided valuable feedback at several
junctures during the development of this guide: Richard N. Armstrong, Wichita
State University; Marcia S. Berry, Azusa Pacific University; Mardia Bishop, University of Illinois; Audry Bourne, North Idaho College; Melissa Broeckelman-Post,
California State University–Los Angeles; Denise Gorsline, Minnesota State University Moorhead; Jennifer Hallett, Young Harris College; Heidi Hamilton, Emporia State University; Richard G. Jones, Jr., Eastern Illinois University; Sherry S.
Lewis, UT El Paso; Joseph P. Mazer, Clemson University; Lori Norin, University
of Arkansas–Fort Smith; Brandi Quesenberry, Virginia Tech; Cynthia Duquette
Smith, Indiana University; Blair Thompson, Western Kentucky University; Beth M.
Waggenspack, Virginia Tech; and Samuel P. Wallace, Dayton University.

We also wish to thank our colleagues around the country who shared their
wisdom, techniques, and course materials for this book: Jonny Gray, Southern
Illinois University, Carbondale; Heidi Hamilton, Emporia State University; Kurt
Lindemann, San Diego State University; Geri Merrigan, San Francisco State
University; Elyse Pineau, Southern Illinois University, Carbondale; Jason Teven,

California State University, Fullerton; Blair Thompson, Western Kentucky University; and Kristen Treinen, Minnesota State University, Mankato.

Finally, our ability to achieve meaningful balance in our lives, in and beyond · the classroom, is made possible by our families; for this, we are forever indebted to Ed, Zachary, Gina, Elias, and Isaac.

CODA, FOR MY FRIEND JOHN T. WARREN (1974–2011)

This guide is the result of a meaningful collaboration between me and my good friend and longtime intellectual co-conspirator, John Warren. John and I frequently worked together, sharing our successes and struggles — not only the intellectual challenges surrounding communication in our lives, but also the practical matters of how to teach communication to others, especially as course coordinators and GTA supervisors. What we did not know when we began working together on this project, and what I am heartbroken to share here, is that this book would be our last collaboration, our last public conversation about teaching and learning. John died quite suddenly in April 2011 of complications from advanced esophageal cancer, just eleven days short of his thirty-seventh birthday. While he leaves behind a wealth of published insights, his most important collaborations were with his partner Gina: their young sons, Elias John and Isaac James. I hope that in these pages and those of his other works, the artifacts of their father's life, they will one day know him for who he was: a warm, caring, insightful, critical, compassionate, and loving explorer, someone who wanted to better understand the world around him, and to make that world not only more sensible to others, but also more just and more humane.

Deanna L. Fassett, 17 April 2011

Contents

I

Creating Continuity

1

The Course Coordinator's Role

A Day in the Life of the Course Coordinator

It is a Monday deep into the fall semester. You get to the office early to review what you have planned for the week: finish grading presentations from your afternoon class, return your review of a manuscript to an editor who's expecting it, meet with a series of graduate students who have questions regarding their application to candidacy, revise a manuscript of your own for submission, and look over the materials for an upcoming faculty meeting. As coordinator of the introductory communication course, you have the responsibility of observing your Graduate Teaching Associates (GTAs), offering input regarding proposed changes to the campus general education assessment process, and revising the syllabi for the courses you teach and supervise so that they are electronically accessible. It's more than usual, but no more than you can handle. Just as you begin to prioritize these tasks in order of importance, the phone rings. You're speaking with the department chair, who has just learned from an irate student that one of the instructors you supervise has been screening a profanity-laced YouTube video to illustrate a point about audience analysis. It's only Monday morning, and already you're forced to reprioritize your plans for the day and the week, your upcoming staff meeting, and even summer orientation. You pause to consider the ways in which your position as course coordinator is uniquely challenging.

* * *

This day-in-the-life scenario speaks to the diverse responsibilities of the course coordinator — known to many as the "basic course director" or "TA supervisor" — and the numerous potential challenges these responsibilities bring. On days when you are tugged this way and that, it can be hard to remember what the value of this assignment is; but being a course coordinator, though challenging, is one of the most important leadership roles you can assume as an academic. As a course coordinator, in addition to your role as a faculty member (i.e., your research and publishing, the curriculum you develop, the interactions you have with students, and your participation in department, college, and university governance), you are responsible for the professional development of your sometimes-graduate-student colleagues, the accomplishment of meaningful learning in your discipline, and, as a result, the future relevance of academic study in communication. We typically think of disciplinary leaders as people who run for office in our professional organizations, and we typically think of department and campus leaders as chairs and deans, but make no mistake — the decisions you make as a course coordinator shape not only the experiences of other instructors or students you encounter; they help to set the agenda for what constitutes the academic study of communication. Fortunately, while

3

extremely demanding days such as the one described above do occur in the life of the course coordinator, they are balanced by the days (sometimes, in fact, the very same day) when you feel appreciated, vital, capable, and proud of the work you do. This book will help you navigate the many responsibilities of the coordinator role, and this first chapter will introduce the role and elaborate on the assistance this guide can provide.

DIFFERING ROLES AND RESPONSIBILITIES OF THE COURSE COORDINATOR

There are many different paths to becoming a course coordinator, as well as many different visions of just what this role entails. Though the title itself seems to suggest the duties of the position — a course coordinator coordinates or supervises the development and delivery of curriculum across multiple sections or classes of a given course — for example, public speaking or introduction to communication studies — this can vary widely from one discipline, institution, or department to the next.

It is perhaps most common for a course coordinator to be a "basic course director." In this role, the coordinator works in one of two models. In the first model, the course director works exclusively with GTAs, managing sometimes 50 or more sections of an introductory course like public speaking or introduction to communication (dubbed "hybrid" by some in the field), which includes interpersonal, intercultural, and small-group communication, among other areas, depending on the college or university. This model is common in large graduate programs in the Midwest and around the United States. In such large programs, like the one at Southern Illinois University at Carbondale where co-author John Warren directs the introductory course, the course director has little occasion to work with part-time or adjunct faculty; she or he would, instead, have the responsibility of supervising many "stand-alone" or GTA-led sections (where the students experience the GTA as the primary instructor of the course). However, it is also possible that a course coordinator might offer one or more large lectures of an introductory course and then supervise GTAs in "break-out" sections, where GTAs do not teach the course, but instead lead students in supervised practice of concepts and skills from the course. It is also possible, in some programs, for course coordinators to work with undergraduate students as teaching assistants or graders.

In a second model of course direction, the coordinator may never work with GTAs; rather, she or he supervises a staff of part-time or adjunct faculty who teach courses for the department. This configuration is more common at smaller campuses, liberal arts schools, and community colleges and may entail a title like "lead instructor" or perhaps no formal title at all. Here the course coordinator must draw together a diverse group of instructors (both in terms of interest and experience) to create continuity across sections of a given course. In some parts of the country, it is common for many of these part-time faculty members to teach multiple courses across multiple campuses, creating additional challenges for the course coordinator.

Finally, a large number of programs are, in recent years, just beginning to explore course coordination as a means of assessing educational effectiveness; in these programs, there may be little organized coordination, and what exists, if anything, may fall under the auspices of a chair, dean, or division head or occur as a result of voluntary efforts on the part of full- or part-time instructors.

Our own experiences with the introductory course do and do not map cleanly onto these models. For example, coauthor Deanna Fassett serves as her department's GTA supervisor, which means she works with each new cohort of graduate student public speaking teachers; she is, therefore, as her department has conceived of this role, one of the public speaking course coordinators, alongside the department chair and the department director of assessment. The three work to demonstrate to themselves, to their instructors, to their campus community, and, however indirectly, to larger state-based funding mechanisms that students enrolled across these dozens of public speaking sections are receiving a meaningful — and comparable — experience. In this way, she does supervise GTAs, but she also works with other instructors, part- and full-time, of the introductory course. Moreover, in addition to her role as GTA supervisor, she has also coordinated her department's critical thinking course and an upper-division general education writing workshop (initially approximately three sections a year and now closer to 30 sections a year). For these assignments, she rarely worked with GTAs; instructors for these courses are typically part-time lecturers (some with joint appointments in other departments) and, though less often, full-time, tenure-track faculty. By contrast, John has, in his role as the introductory course director at two research institutions (Bowling Green State University, 2001-2004, and Southern Illinois University, 2008-present), supervised approximately 30 to 50 graduate teaching assistants annually.

In this era of increasing scrutiny from outside constituencies (from the state legislature, to accrediting agencies, to campus funding allocation committees, to parents and students themselves), it is becoming common for departments to develop oversight (often in the form of assessment plans and protocols) of not only general education courses, but also core and graduate offerings. In these instances, the course coordinator works to review course offerings for continuity and efficacy; she or he also often assumes or shares responsibility in assuring others that students are mastering essential and relevant learning outcomes. In this way, course coordinators might also supervise full-time, tenured, and tenure-track faculty in a communication theory course, an introduction to graduate studies in communication course, or other advanced offerings.

In other words, course coordinators may supervise a range of different courses in communication studies (i.e., these courses may exist in different areas of the discipline, like public speaking or interpersonal communication; may serve as general education or major coursework; may involve introductory or advanced exposure). They may work with a variety of different types of instructors (e.g., they may or may not work with GTAs, tenured professors, or adjunct faculty, in large or small numbers). They may take on additional responsibilities at the intersections of course coordination and campus governance or service (e.g., they may play a role in campus assessment initiatives, sit on the student fairness or other academic senate operating committees, serve on department curriculum committees, and so forth). They may execute coordinating functions as part of another administrative assignment, such as when a chair or division head communicates learning outcomes to instructors of a given course or reviews syllabi for consistency against some college or program template. Finally, course coordinators may have purposefully sought this role (as some of us do when we pursue "Basic Course Director" positions in *Spectra* or *The Chronicle of Higher Education*), or they may have found this role thrust upon them (as, for example, service toward tenure or promotion, or because staffing limitations have meant assuming responsibilities they wouldn't ordinarily choose for themselves).

COURSE COORDINATION CONFIGURATIONS

There are many different possible course coordinator configurations, each affording a unique structure and set of enabling and limiting circumstances. First, a course coordinator may or may not also serve as a GTA supervisor. Further, in this role, she or he may or may not have the ability to make personnel decisions, as sometimes these are made by a graduate coordinator, department chair, or program director. Depending on departmental culture, this coordinator may or may not teach a support course for instructors or hold regular staff meetings. And, where these offerings/opportunities exist, they may be provided by another instructor. Generally speaking, however, formally titled course coordinators (e.g., "Director of the Core Curriculum" or, more commonly, "Basic Course Director") have this aspect of their role acknowledged in some way as part of their course or workload. For example, in many large doctoral programs like John's, this assignment may include a course load reduction, from, for example, a 2/2 load (teaching two courses in the fall and two in the spring) to a 2/1 load (teaching two courses in the fall and one in the spring). Or, in programs like Deanna's, assuming the role of GTA supervisor is addressed through reassigned time: Each semester, she teaches a course entitled Teaching Associate Practicum, which is, in effect, biweekly staff meetings. In this way, her role in coordinating the public speaking course and supervising the department's GTAs is characterized, for purposes of tenure and promotion, as part of an instructional assignment (and not as service toward campus or departmental governance, which, on many campuses, is less consequential for tenure).

A second type of configuration may be much less formal, in that the coordinator may be performing this as a service to her or his department; by this, we mean that the department does not acknowledge the course coordinator role through course release or reassigned time. In these cases, coordinators are typically supervising fewer instructors and/or they are not called upon to provide as much explicit mentoring (as they might for GTAs). For example, this coordinator might supervise instructors' efforts in the department's upper-division gateway course. Or instructors might take turns or rotations as course coordinator to make sure the department distributes assessment workload evenly. In this way, maybe even a third of a given department might be serving in a course coordination capacity, especially where a department is deeply invested in providing general education curriculum to the college or university. For example, in Deanna's department, there are an assessment coordinator, three public speaking course coordinators, one coordinator for each of the general education course offerings (i.e., critical thinking, argumentation and advocacy, intercultural communication, and writing in the discipline), and a series of informal coordinators of core courses for majors (i.e., people who are associated with the development and continued success of these courses, who remain available to mentor faculty new to teaching the course). In John's department, the chair supervises most of the courses except the introductory public speaking course that John directs and the multisection intercultural communication and performance studies courses, each of which has a faculty member who assumes that service responsibility for the department.

A third configuration might be more common at smaller campuses or at community colleges where instructors are part- or full-time faculty. In these configurations, the course coordinator may supervise instructors who may vary considerably in terms of preparation, experience, interest, and status; or in some programs, it is perhaps more accurate to say that the coordinator, though she or he may not carry this title, is a model for her or his colleagues, providing sample syllabi and assignment rubrics, facilitating assessment activities (if any), and making herself or himself available to colleagues for their questions. The responsibilities of this assignment will vary considerably from campus to campus, depending on state, campus, and department expectations for coordination and assessment.

In any event, it is highly likely that your department or program delivers multisection courses in one of two formats — each shaping, to some extent, your role as coordinator:

1. Separate, distinct, stand-alone sections: Where instructors (whether full-time, tenure-track faculty, part-time adjunct faculty, or GTAs) teach independent sections of a large, multisection course. Even where there is a course coordinator, students are typically responsible to their instructor (irrespective of academic rank/status) and unaware of other supervisory figures.
2. Large lecture with attached or "break-out" sections: Where an instructor teaches dozens or hundreds of students in a large lecture hall setting, often relying heavily on electronic media (e.g., anything from PowerPoint to YouTube clips) to bring course content to life. Application and assessment of whether and how well students have learned concepts (whether speeches, essays, group work, and so on) occurs in sections typically taught by teaching assistants. In this case, students typically understand that the instructor of the course is in charge, even when they interact primarily with the teaching assistant. Here the students benefit by more than one instructional voice helping them learn. They may also understand that they are, ultimately, responsible to the faculty member who

teaches the large lecture; however, they may also struggle with authority in this dual-instructor role (for example, by relying on the teaching assistant to mediate in disputes with the instructor, by complaining to the instructor regarding a grading dispute with a teaching assistant, and so forth).

As well as understanding its current structure, it is important to learn about the history of your particular program. It may be that your program has been satisfied with the content and delivery of a given coordinated course; however, it is also possible that the program for which you're now responsible has a history of significant change. For example, from time to time, programs change the nature of their introductory course, from the human communication course to public speaking (or vice versa), or from attached sections to stand-alone sections. As you work with your colleagues, with other instructors, and with students to shape and adapt the mission of this particular program and course, it will help you to know what others have tried, what motivated those changes, and how those actions fared. This will give you useful insight into your institution's and your department's organizational culture (their receptiveness to change, the degree to which those units are open to outside influences like changing administrators or disciplinary developments, and which offices or individuals function as gatekeepers for any changes you might want to make).

WHAT CONSTITUTES EFFECTIVE COORDINATION?

What constitutes effective coordination often depends upon whom you ask. Moreover, most of us probably take up this question only when we assume a position where others will evaluate us on our coordination skills (i.e., in the tenure and promotion — or retention — process), or when we need to evaluate someone else for those skills. Different vantage points can be helpful not only in imagining the complexity of the course coordinator's responsibilities, but also in educating the people with whom we interact about their own roles in supporting our work. Further, taking all these vantage points together helps us cultivate a more nuanced understanding of what constitutes effective coordination.

Students' Perspective

Students' perspectives on coordination will vary depending on their maturity, the content of the course, and how it is configured. For example, graduate students and advanced undergraduates are typically more sensitive to departmental roles and responsibilities and may understand not only an individual instructor's rank or status, but also the chain of command for particular concerns. For example, these students are typically more aware that disputing a grade involves first a conversation with the instructor who assigned the grade; then, if the instructor is a GTA, his or her supervisor; then the department chair; and then the ombudsman's office. If students are enrolled in a break-out section with a GTA, they may understand that the faculty member teaching the lecture has some oversight responsibility for the sections associated with the course. While most students enrolled in stand-alone sections of coordinated courses are unlikely to have given much thought to the issue of what counts as effective co-ordination, they are likely to be very concerned not only with whether their peers have similar workloads but with whether their instructor is engaging, appro-priately challenging, and prepared. Students' comments about an instructor's grading (oddly easy or unduly harsh), whether she or he is following the syl-labus or course calendar, whether the class does or does not read/follow the textbook, and so forth, tell you not only about a particular instructor, but the extent to which this instructor's actions are consistent with her or his peers' and what you have established. In this sense, students' comments, sometimes in your office but far more often in their evaluations of the course and instructor, can illuminate your strengths and limitations as a course coordinator.

Instructors' Perspective

In general, instructors teaching the coordinated course will be concerned with clear and consistent communication regarding the department's, college's, or university's expectations regarding this course; they can also reasonably ex-pect support for their instruction (both the conceptual aspects of teaching this particular curriculum and the technical aspects of teaching, like access to in-structional technology). These needs will vary, though, in relation to a given instructor's familiarity and experience. For instance, GTAs, who are relatively unfamiliar with how universities administer large multisection courses, are likely to experience the course coordinator as an employer (as well as a mentor, an instructor, and other possible roles); they will also often need and seek more guidance regarding how to teach than a more experienced instructor. Effective coordination for this group will mean consistency — especially in the modeling of particular practices and behaviors — and developing reasonable policies that cut across all instructors' sections. These instructors will need careful explana-tion and frequent feedback.

Part-time and adjunct faculty, because they have more experience and be-cause they may be spread thin across multiple campuses (with many different kinds of coordinated courses with different coordinators and different expecta-tions), give rise to a different vision of what effective coordination entails. This group, while more experienced than GTAs and often more frazzled than full-time faculty, still needs exposure to professional growth and renewal activities; because of the nature of their role, they are unlikely to have much support in learning the state of the art, whether regarding course management systems or disciplinary approaches to intercultural communication. It will also be more important to provide these instructors with consistent reminders regarding your particular program expectations (as these — from attendance/participa-tion policies to how to communicate campus evacuation procedures — will vary from your campus to the one where they teach at night or on weekends). If you can establish them, regularly scheduled assessment meetings provide a good opportunity to elicit feedback on how the course is functioning for these faculty; and, as with GTAs, students' evaluations can be instructive as well, if you have access to these instructors' personnel files.

Finally, tenured and tenure-track instructors will illuminate different qualities of effective coordination. While helping all instructors cultivate their best teaching skills in a climate of openness and academic freedom is part of your role as coordinator, this group may, at times, pose challenges to your authority as course coordinator because they are, in general, very knowledgeable about college or university policies and procedures. However, this group can also become a real asset to your coordinating repertoire, helping you read and negotiate campus culture, understand past practices in your department and program, and find resources (whether financial, instructional, or emotional) for your work. In this sense, we can see that other people's perceptions of our work — the "whom we ask" — are integral in our own growth as course coordinators.

Colleagues' Perspective

Your colleagues can be a resource to you as you learn what constitutes effective coordination. Here it is helpful to include in the definition of *colleague* not only the instructors discussed above, but also those outside your course, program, school, and even your field who have comparable experience to share. You might find guidance and inspiration from people who engage in research that has great potential for your program and niche of the discipline. For example, reading articles in your field (from *Basic Communication Course Annual*, *Communication Education*, *Communication Teacher*, and so on) can help you identify and pursue new directions for your course or for helping your instructors teach it; there is also a wealth of resources outside of our field, both the inspirational, like Parker Palmer's (1998) *The Courage to Teach* or Paulo Freire's (2003) *Pedagogy of the Oppressed*, and the practical, like Marilla Svinicki and Wilbert McKeachie's (2011) *Teaching Tips* or Anne Curzan and Lisa Damour's (2006) *First Day to Final Grade*. Moreover, you can find support at professional conferences, whether at the regional or national level or even in more specialized meetings like the Basic Course Directors Conference. In this way, part of effective coordination is putting aside time for what likely helped draw you into this discipline in the first place — reading and developing scholarship that influences how others learn what is important about communication.

Effective course coordination is about staying connected to your communities of peers. If they are available to you, it may be wise to speak with your predecessors, to learn what they feel are the mission, the strengths and the limitations of the program and course, as well as where they succeeded and struggled in coordination. Even your more cynical colleagues can help here; while they might suggest that good coordination is a matter of not drawing the attention or ire of other offices on campus (e.g., the ombudsman's office, the bodies and groups that assess general education curricula on campus, etc.), their comments can help you read the culture of your department or institution and their expectations for you. For some, though thankfully not all, successful course coordination is akin to being seen (working hard) and not heard (asking for resources). Understanding this set of expectations will help you negotiate the ways in which others will formally evaluate your performance in this role.

Supervisors' Perspective

For your continued success at your institution, it is essential you be aware of your supervisors' expectations for your work as a course coordinator. While your responsibilities as course coordinator are most likely only one aspect of your appointment, others' evaluation of your work will figure in your review, tenure, and promotion. Your department chair (or other immediate supervisor, perhaps a dean or a director) may feel that effective course coordination is measured by both the absence of complaints from faculty and students regarding the course and consistently high teaching evaluations (and reasonably low GPAs) across all sections of the course. It often helps to connect with these supervisors frequently, but strategically, about your and your instructors' strengths, limitations, and needs; in this way, you are able to sustain a dialogue with these influential colleagues about what does and should constitute effective course coordination.

Completing the Definition of Effective Coordination

All of these individual perceptions form *functional* definitions of effective coordination and are, at least to some extent, reasonable expectations, but all are incomplete. In our experience, in its most elemental sense, effective course coordination entails coherence and consistent quality across however many sections of a given course exist in a given semester, over the course of an academic year, and for the tenure of the coordinator. One way to think of this is to imagine your responsibility as creating continuity across those sections: Your attention and regard for instructors, students, and course content make possible comparable experiences for the individuals involved in the course. Comparable does not mean "the same," but it does connote a certain consistency, diligence, and mindfulness about the quality of this teaching and learning experience. In this sense, continuity is not only, or even primarily, about consistency, but rather is a reflection of an ethic of care and community that helps us take seriously the learning and growth of all the people — instructors and students — who participate in this course.

Enacting effective course coordination entails the capacity to envision both the role and the course as an open system nested within and influenced by an array of other systems. By this, we mean that the course itself does not stand alone; what occurs there is a function of many shifting and complex factors. For example, the course as a system is constituted by the efforts of the individual instructors teaching the course. It is also built through the policies of the course coordinator or other influential parties — policies such as whether to require certain course materials or the availability of certain technology resources (e.g., a common management system or digital video recording equipment). The sociocultural exigencies surrounding the campus and its surrounding community — whether a national tragedy like the events of September 11th, 2001; deep, statewide budget cuts to education in the wake of a global recession; or a campus decision to deny an organization such as the American Red Cross access to students because of discriminatory practices — will necessarily affect even the most mundane operations of the course. Finally, the individual and familial lives of students (for instance, whether many students work full-time in addition to attempting a full-time load, or whether they are struggling to pay bills because of layoffs, loss of child or elder care, and so forth) will influence the shape and mission of a coordinated course. Course coordinators must not only attend to the smaller details (such as when and whether and where they'll hold staff meetings), but also see these in the context of the larger goals of the course for the institution — i.e., the role of this course's curriculum in the larger general education mission of the college or university (for example, the ways the course does and does not support students' development as active, critically engaged citizens) and whether the course is relevant to students' lives and struggles.

HOW THIS BOOK CAN HELP YOU COORDINATE MORE EFFECTIVELY (OR BETTER UNDERSTAND WHAT COURSE COORDINATION ENTAILS)

As many of us who have already served as course coordinators know, we often learn this role through trial and error. While there are resources available to the course coordinator, including the annual Basic Course Directors Conference and the journal *Basic Communication Course Annual*, most of us develop our expertise through the school of hard knocks — that is, on the job. If we are lucky, we find mentors who are interested in and willing to help us through the thornier aspects of our responsibilities, but more often, we start as untenured or part-time faculty looking to draw as little attention to ourselves and our course or program as possible.

This book functions as an orientation to and support system for course coordinators in communication studies and other related fields as they enter and negotiate (or renegotiate) their responsibilities. This resource is structured around three core principles: continuity, professional development, and advocacy.

Continuity

Continuity refers to the coordination of multiple instructors across multiple sections of what can be a high-profile introductory course; it suggests the importance of assuring all stakeholders that students are learning what the instructors purport to be teaching. Furthermore, continuity entails more than a technically efficient, mechanistic process; it reminds us that we are all — instructor, student, and coordinator alike — individuals, with unique combinations of strengths and limitations, interests and abilities. Achieving a community-oriented, caring continuity with an increasingly diverse group of people (in terms of ethnicity, gender, sexuality, age, ability, faith, economic status, and so forth) is the responsibility of the course coordinator, who must learn to build and adapt her or his vision for the course or program so that it is inclusive, meaningful, and effective.

Professional Development

A focus on *professional development*, on working and growing with instructors — whether full professors, part-time lecturers, or GTAs — is essential to ensuring excellence across multiple sections of an introductory course. Professional development helps strengthen teaching, shore up and encourage participation in the vision of the course or program, align instructors' perceptions, create avenues for the coordinator to learn about the health and well-being of the course across multiple sections, and create a solid foundation for the health of the discipline.

Advocacy

Finally, *advocacy* refers to what may be both the most richly rewarding and deeply frustrating aspect of course coordination: communicating the strengths and needs of the coordinated course to the administrative bodies assigned to assess its effectiveness. While advocacy includes, for instance, efforts to recertify the introductory course for general education credit, it also includes learning to advocate for the students and instructors of those courses — to elicit, value, and act on information the coordinator learns from her or his staff. Perhaps most important, when a course coordinator learns to advocate for her or his own needs — for example in the review, tenure, and promotion process — she or he not only advocates for her or his vision and professionalism, but also those of her or his colleagues and discipline.

CONCLUSION

Though the principles of continuity, professional development, and advocacy will guide the advice herein, we imagine many different possible readers of this book. The first, perhaps most avid, readers are those who have just learned that they will be course coordinators in the immediate future. But we also imagine that some of you are reading because you would like to better understand just what goes into the supervision of a multisection course — perhaps because you are an instructor who teaches in one or more such courses, or perhaps because you are curious to learn whether this is a challenging and meaningful career path for you. Faculty who supervise graduate teaching associates or assistants in large lecture courses, administrative professionals (such as department chairs) who would like to learn more about the organizational challenges of course coordination, and course coordinators in other, related fields (e.g., composition, sociology, women's studies, etc.) will find the attention to continuity, professional development, and advocacy relevant for their own work.

One of the challenges associated with writing a book of this sort for so many possible readers is that we will necessarily fail in meeting all of your varying expectations. As we write, we imagine we are communicating with people who have always wanted to be course coordinators, who relish the mentoring role it entails, and who hold positions in the Basic Course Division of the National Communication Association. But we also imagine less sanguine readers, perhaps people who did not set out to become course coordinators but who found that this was a means to an end; if you're in this group of readers, we are assuming that while you might not be thrilled about becoming a course coordinator, you are interested in learning what you can and in doing your best. It is possible that we are also writing to instructors in these coordinated courses, to people who would like to better understand the method to what might sometimes feel like chaos and explore why we structure these sorts of activities in the ways we do. While it is impossible to meet the needs of all the possible readers this work might encounter, it is our hope that we can, in working to guide the novice course coordinator, help others better understand the purpose and function of this organizational process in our academic lives.

In what follows, you can expect to acquire a heightened awareness of all the different benefits, challenges, and opportunities to being a course coordinator. You can also expect to learn some strategies for success in meeting this responsibility. To be fair, there are good reasons why someone might want to shy away from taking on a role as a course coordinator. With each new issue of *Spectra*, it feels as though tenure-track "basic course director" positions are becoming fewer and farther between, replaced by part-time, contract, and adjunct faculty positions. Though public speaking and introduction to communication studies constitute the heart of our discipline and help to make possible doctoral programs, research reassigned time, and so forth, many established academics would prefer that their department's course coordinator be seen and not heard. We can see this mirrored, to some extent, in our collective willingness to describe our foundational courses, variously, as "the basic course" and course coordinators as "basic course directors." These language choices reflect, however unconsciously, a lack of status or prestige associated with this assignment (for a discussion of the dangers in referring to courses and coordinators as "basic," see Fassett and Warren, 2008). Nevertheless, course coordination is one of the most important roles a faculty member can assume in her or his career, and it is worth considering the benefits of this assignment.

There are many benefits to being a course coordinator. In addition to the extrinsic motivators, such as, perhaps, course release or reassigned time (and, so, greater autonomy in one's schedule) or additional travel support or credit toward academic assignment or service for tenure and promotion, there are intrinsic benefits as well. This can be a very important leadership responsibility within a department or program: As a course coordinator, you review and facilitate changes to your college or university's curriculum, you mentor faculty of varying degrees of experience, and you assure your colleagues in your department and across the campus that you are engaged in a meaningful endeavor. Moreover, there is a certain amount of pride you can assume in being a "go to" person—someone people depend on during difficult situations (such as when an instructor needs counsel regarding a difficult grade challenge). You also garner credibility from colleagues in your discipline who respect you for being someone who champions the heart of our discipline and who mentors and nurtures graduate students and faculty to a career in teaching that heart. Think of the people you respect most in our field; it is likely that each of these educators has occupied, at one time or another, a substantial role with respect to our most foundational courses. Most of us remember our own first GTA supervisors fondly; who we are as teachers is, in large measure, the result of their careful attention and guidance. Finally, it is absolutely essential that you explore the ways in which this role can grow and change with you; it is not necessarily a distraction from your "real" research, but rather a fertile garden for you to make real what you have learned from your investigations of communication. As we reflect on our colleagues who coordinate large, multisection courses, we see that they have drawn strength and purpose as coordinators from their research trajectories, drawing into their courses lessons suggested by their own cutting-edge research in power and privilege, environmental rhetoric and social justice, service learning and ethical professional communication.

You need not commit to course coordination for the remainder of your career for this to be a meaningful adventure. While there are course coordinators who make this work their mission for 30 or more years, there are many others who assume a rotation of three or six years. Even a three-year term can be a boon to a program or course; as a coordinator, you are a visionary, and this is your opportunity to bring your vision, your expertise, to this collective enterprise. Your insights, even years after you are no longer the course coordinator, leave a lasting impression on the course, program, department, and discipline. And you may find that, as you find ways to create congruence between your intellectual interests and your work as a course coordinator, this responsibility grows on you.

Perhaps the most significant responsibility of your leadership as a course coordinator is your role in determining what your discipline is, is not, and should or can be. In effect, you help to define what counts as knowledge in communication in the readings you assign, what count as essential communication skills in the assignments and activities you require, and what counts as rigor, depth, professionalism, accountability, and ethics for the discipline and for your college or university. Moreover, you shape the people who will assume leadership roles in the future — the students in these classes who will assume responsibilities in their families, schools, occupations, and government offices, and the instructors, often graduate students, whose work will define and extend the power and presence of communication scholarship in and beyond the academy.

In what follows, we will help you explore the sorts of opportunities and challenges you'll face as a course coordinator in what we hope is a systematic and thoughtful way that helps you make choices that are congruent with your values and mission as an educator and a leader. As a course coordinator, you occupy a significant leadership position, one where it will be important to build, sustain, and revise a mission that includes all kinds of students and instructors and drives them to pursue their best work. In Chapter 2, we will discuss how you can develop and share this vision to shape the course(s) you coordinate.

REFERENCES

Curzan, A., & Damour, L. (2006). *First day to final grade: A graduate student's guide to teaching* (2nd ed.). Ann Arbor, MI: University of Michigan Press.

Fassett, D. L., & Warren, J. T. (2008). Pedagogy of relevance: A critical communication pedagogy agenda for the "basic" course. *Basic Communication Course Annual, 20*, 1–34.

Freire, P. (2003). *Pedagogy of the oppressed: 30th anniversary edition.* New York, NY: Continuum.

Palmer, P. J. (1998). *The courage to teach: Exploring the inner landscape of a teacher's life.* San Francisco, CA: Jossey-Bass.

Svinicki, M., & McKeachie, W. J. (2011). *Teaching tips: Strategies, research and theory for college and university teachers* (13th ed.). Belmont, CA: Wadsworth, Cengage Learning.

RECOMMENDED READINGS

Basic Communication Course Annual

Currently in its 23rd volume and edited by David Worley of Indiana State University, this journal is an excellent resource for introductory communication course directors. Because authors include graduate teaching associates, as well as part- and full-time faculty and course coordinators or directors, there is a broad range of articles addressing topics related to the administration, instruction, and assessment of introductory communication courses. Back issues of the journal are available through American Press, but it is also possible to find many of the volumes online.

Hugenberg, L. W., Gray, P. L., & Trank, D. M. (Eds.). (1993). *Teaching and directing the basic communications course.* Dubuque, IA: Kendall/Hunt Publishing.

While somewhat dated, this book is an excellent collection of articles representing foundational understandings of course coordination in the discipline at the height of publication and interest in the topic. While chapters address the needs of graduate teaching assistants or associates, this volume addresses course coordination more broadly, from multiple perspectives (e.g., the administrator's perspective, the part-time faculty member's perspective, and so on) and in relation to multiple topics (from assessment of students' learning to effective teaching methods to student needs and evaluation of faculty of different rank).

Vangelisti, A. L., Daly, J. A., & Friedrich, G. W. (Eds.). (1999). *Teaching communication: Theory, research and methods* (2nd ed.). Mahwah, NJ: Lawrence Erlbaum Associates, Inc.

An excellent resource for both communication instructors and communication course coordinators alike, this text is a collection of readings that represent a coherent disciplinary perspective on communication education — i.e., how to best teach communication as a field of study. Comprehensive coverage of topics ranging from "how-to" skills (e.g., creating a new course, teaching different content areas within communication studies, engaging in different teaching methods) to conceptual understanding of professionalism in the discipline (e.g., joining the discipline in general and as a course coordinator, becoming involved in assessment and evaluation activities, pursuing consulting assignments) makes this a useful resource not only for locating provocative and helpful reading excerpts, but also for developing a complex and nuanced "big picture" sense of introductory courses as foundational to the discipline.

2

Program Vision

An Unexpected Opportunity

This is your first meeting with the new dean of the college; she was, prior to this appointment, a professor of environmental studies in a more prestigious institution in your state. During this meeting, she asks you about your research background as well as your impressions of campus culture. When you mention your role as course coordinator and GTA supervisor for the human communication course required of all undergraduates, she is curious, and she wants to know more about what that entails and how that position works within your department. This may be an opportunity, you think, to garner support from the dean — if not tangibly, in terms of financial support for your pre–academic-year orientation efforts, then perhaps in terms of greater awareness and connection and the construction of a strong foundation for future conversations about more specific needs. This is your opportunity to articulate what it is you do and why it matters, to your department, to your university, and to her.

* * *

When you accepted the role of course coordinator (or if/when you do choose to take on this role), you inherited (or will inherit) a vision for your program. By vision, we mean a philosophy, an organizing logic that helps to establish, clarify, and nurture what matters (and minimize, or eliminate what is less important). When you became coordinator, this inherited vision became your vision, to some extent; the more flexible your institution, the greater your capacity for negotiating, altering, and developing this vision so that it is congruent with your values and expertise, the strengths of the instructors who teach this course, and the needs and challenges of the students who commonly enroll in this course. Further, when you became a course coordinator, you became a leader and a champion — not only for that particular course or content, but for your program or department and your discipline. Your program vision is your opportunity to draw your colleagues together in common purpose, creating continuity across what might be a broad array of sections; it is also your opportunity to define and advocate for both your program and discipline.

We find it helpful to think of program vision as a set of values. In our own programs, we work toward sustaining communities we enjoy being a part of. As teachers who, for many years, were the only instructional communication scholars in our departments, and as researchers who write frequently on issues of power, privilege, and social justice in the classroom, we wanted to create a space where we could discuss these issues without our colleagues' feeling as though they must also embrace critical, social justice-oriented approaches to communication instruction in order to succeed. Together we contribute to communities where we are, more often than not, collegial, committed to one another's success, and willing to explore professional development opportunities; collectively, we hold each other accountable for a vision of teaching that is reflective of, aware of, and speaks directly to sociocultural circumstances and that is attentive to issues of power and privilege, even if that looks somewhat different for each of us. Our visions do not have to be your community's vision, but you should know what that vision is, be capable of articulating it to others, engage with it critically, and be able to negotiate it if necessary, in order to most effectively coordinate your program.

Understanding program vision and being able to explain it concisely to others can help strengthen campus perceptions of particular departments or programs and faculty as leaders, communicate clearly to others how communication curricula are vital, and affirm for students that the work they undertake in college is challenging, meaningful, and carefully designed with their needs in mind. It can also help a coordinator prepare her or his promotion dossier as well as better understand her or his responsibilities and weather the challenges they sometimes bring. In this sense, program vision functions as an organizing logic for your program or course, helping you build congruence between your own and your colleagues' values and actions.

THE FOUNDATIONS OF PROGRAM VISION

Multiple sources can inform the organizing logic behind a program. First, program vision may, in many ways, fit into and be shaped by significant institutional structures. For example, one way to realize program vision for many introductory communication courses is to participate in first-year-experience programs, which work to promote retention and graduation rates for all students, but especially students from historically marginalized groups (for example, students who are the first generation in their families to pursue college, students who are working class, students of color, LGBTQ [Lesbian, Gay, Bisexual, Transgendered, and Queer] students, international students, and students who have disabilities). In this sense, the vision of your coordinated program or course may help strengthen the mission of your department, college, or university. Whether one is at an HBCU (Historically Black College or University), a rural community college that serves students from across a large geographic region, or a large metropolitan university with a commitment to its surrounding communities, large, multisection courses usually complement these comprehensive missions.

Disciplinary commitments may also help form the foundations of program vision; this can include a sense of what contemporary communication theory means and how we should share it with introductory communication students. Increasingly, programs are reacting to and shaping themselves in relation to socioeconomic exigencies—for example, becoming programs that explicitly prepare students for effective business/professional communication or civic engagement. And as critical theory and cultural studies gain greater currency in communication education, instructional communication, and intercultural communication, some programs have adopted visions where students, instructors and administrators work toward social justice, advocacy, and peace studies.

Further, a program coordinator will play a significant role in shaping her or his program's or course's vision. Not all coordinators imagined that they would become course coordinators or GTA supervisors; this means they do not have what we might think of as a conventional instructional or "basic course" background for this role. Instead, as a course coordinator, you might bring with you expertise in performance studies, environmental rhetoric, interpersonal communication, or some other area of our discipline. Our own GTA supervisor when we were in graduate school, Elyse Pineau, is a performance studies scholar; her work as a coordinator included explicit attention to the body, to experiential, performance studies–informed engagements in the classroom, and beautifully crafted, poetic lectures at the start of each orientation on what it means to be a teacher-scholar — someone who does not fracture her or his identity between what she or he teaches and what she or he studies. Other course coordinators and GTA supervisors introduce new elements into a program's or course's vision — gifts that only they could bring, based on their particular interests as researchers and learners.

Similarly, community college course coordinators have much to offer the campuses where they provide leadership. Faculty at community colleges are often familiar with the communities they serve, as former community college students or members of the local neighborhood themselves. Their link to the community can become an essential part of building a foundation for success. Not only is this an important part of recruiting both teachers and students, but it also helps in creating commonly understood examples for class or generating assignments that students of all walks of life will find meaningful. While an introductory communication course at a research institution may be taught by a GTA who is from the other side of the world, a community college has the unique ability to draw from community resources and, in turn, invite the community to become the foundation or heart of the course. Further, given that adjunct instructors are often industry professionals, students may learn skills that will serve them perhaps more explicitly in local and regional employment.

KEY ELEMENTS OF PROGRAM VISION

For some, the process of learning (and shaping) a program's vision is relatively clear; for example, you might be someone who has had time to learn a particular department culture, teach in a given course or program, and interact with colleagues regarding their experiences with and expectations of the course coordinator role and this particular course. For others, though, it might seem like a daunting process. For example, someone who joins a department specifically to be a course coordinator and/or GTA supervisor may need to learn the various cultures that surround her or him while simultaneously searching out the lockshop for keys, checking the public transportation routes to campus, and finding affordable housing. While the first group may feel they understand

and can articulate the vision of this program or course (though they may not yet feel ownership of or responsibility for this vision themselves), the second group may not feel they have enough understanding of the nested communities and their expectations surrounding this course to advance a new or revised vision. In either case, it may help to have a better understanding of what constitutes a program vision, including common values and goals, and the methods through which we can implement these. It is also worth noting that, as a coordinator, you may feel as though you are somewhere in between these two different groups. For example, you may be familiar with campus and community, but your role as course coordinator may be foreign not only to you, but to your colleagues as well; with increasing emphasis on accountability and assessment in postsecondary education, many programs are working to develop or discover models of coordination that suit their students and themselves. In such cases, reading your colleagues for their sense of what course coordination entails may be tricky, requiring the sensitivity and tenacity of a private investigator.

Common Values

A program vision, as a set of values that helps to organize and coordinate a group of people toward some common end or purpose, serves to create both community and continuity. As you reflect on the community you're charged with coordinating—whether a large, multisection public speaking course or a small core course in the major—what are the beliefs and goals that draw this group together? For example, do you and your colleagues share an interest in pedagogical innovation, exploring the possibilities of teaching online or in Second Life? Or are you drawn together because of your care and regard for students' acculturation to university life, prompting your participation in first-year programs that introduce students to communication studies as part of living and learning cohorts? You are likely to feel some kinship as a result of common understandings of communication studies, of the importance of general education courses or core courses in the major, of your students' interests and needs, of your collective strengths and limitations as a faculty member, or some combination of these. It is also important to note where you and your colleagues do not see eye to eye, in part so as to create opportunities for substantive dialogue regarding your purpose and work together, but also so you can determine whether any particular values are harmful for your community. For instance, an overly competitive faculty can create a hostile learning environment for students that works against dialogue and positive communication.

Common Goals

Part of the program vision are those outcomes community members agree to work toward together. These goals might include contributing toward campus graduation and retention rates, pulling together to offer enough sections of a given course to meet college or campus need, introducing students to particular curricula (for example, an emphasis on public speaking or small-group communication) or experiences (for example, service learning opportunities), gathering for professional development activities or assessment discussions, and so forth. In inventorying the different aspects of program mission, consider whether and where your values as a community are in line with your collective goals; finding and engaging in dialogue about places where there is a disconnect between these two will help strengthen not only the program vision, but colleagues' investment in it.

Generating positive goals built from your values can yield a program and series of courses that enable learning and produce the conditions that make learning meaningful and fun for both faculty and students. Identifying your collective hopes and desires for the course and instituting them across multiple sections enable you to build a foundation for your program that is driven by vision and not just by the practicalities of your daily interactions on the campus.

Implementation

To some extent, developing a program vision is very similar to developing course learning outcomes (CLOs). While students could learn from teaching that is not informed by specific CLOs, everyone, both teachers and students, stands to gain from understanding how particular tasks and assignments (whether assessment meetings, instruction in a common management system, or the percentage of a course grade dedicated to public speaking activities) serve larger lessons about communication. In this sense, the coordinator, as a leader, must consider the ways in which the activities of that course or program either support or undermine the community's values and goals. Some of the ways course coordinators implement program vision include (but are by no means limited to) curriculum development and textbook selection; orientation, staff meetings, and support courses; professional development activities, including guest speakers; and one-on-one mentoring or "water-cooler" conversations. In each of these settings, course coordinators articulate, enact, and develop or adapt program vision.

Curriculum Development and Textbook Selection. Curriculum development — the lessons, concepts, experiences, and activities that constitute a particular course — is a significant way in which course coordinators help implement program vision. Course coordinators often help to determine (usually along with state, campus, or accrediting agency guidelines, and often with the input of course instructors and relevant supervisors) the content of a coordinated course, including course concepts and degree of mastery, the amount of public speaking, timed testing, or written words. Coordinators who work with large numbers of relatively inexperienced instructors (as is often the case with GTA supervisors) will also often "spell out" finer details within the curriculum as well, such as the use of Turnitin.com to detect plagiarism, the structure and scope of instructors' feedback (through a structured grading rubric), or whether instructors are to allow for late work. Coordinators may also play a significant role in the structure and role of a course; for example, coordinators may pursue restructuring of a coordinated course from large lectures to multiple, stand-alone sections, or from the human communication course to public speaking (and sometimes even back again).

The choice of students' readings in coordinated courses is also an important aspect of the course coordinator's role. While she or he may not have exclusive authority to select a particular text or texts (she or he may, for example, make this selection with a committee of colleagues or students), she or he is usually instrumental in identifying which books are most appropriate for the course. There are many factors to consider when choosing a course text — including, for example, its approach to content and skills, the reputation of the author(s), or its affordability — but significant among these should be whether it fits the values of the program/course and enables students' achievement of program/ course goals. For instance, Southern Illinois University recently moved to a new textbook based on instructors' desire to include more of a focus on activism and civic engagement in their courses. Such a focus builds both from the department graduate area in rhetoric and the critical approach endorsed by the faculty. In this way, even the course text selection is part of a programmatic effort that builds a meaningful vision.

Orientation, Staff Meetings, and Support Courses.   Certainly not all programs have the ability to offer extensive training; for example, programs with few or no full-time faculty may provide little formal mentoring. There are ways to build collaborative spaces for dialogue, though, through more flexible formats like brief staff meetings or online discussions. If, however, your job is to supervise GTAs, you may have greater control in designing and implementing support programs to aid teaching and learning in coordinated courses, including orientation programs, staff meetings, and support courses that often accompany GTA programs. Because these meetings typically address the needs of new instructors, they offer an opportunity to mold current and future instructors of the course. Certainly program vision should influence the tenor and tone of these meetings, fully preparing instructors to assume their role in shoring up the vision or mission of the course/program (including, where appropriate, suggesting changes and adaptations). If a given course foregrounds civic engagement and service learning, it would be reasonable for instructors to expect the coordinator to help them better understand and implement effective pedagogy associated with this value set and learning outcome. Or if one of the course objectives is to help students critically master certain kinds of new media (e.g., PowerPoint, Desire2Learn or other learning management systems, podcasting or Second Life, etc.), then training activities should include opportunities for instructors to master these skills as well. These activities play a significant role in creating continuity across multiple sections of a course, and in the interests of continuity and perceptions of course coordinator integrity, it is important that the course coordinator model or practice the values she or he hopes instructors will engender in their own students.

Professional Development Activities.   Course coordinators can reach out to more experienced instructors of a course through professional development activities. Some of these activities may appear overtly instructional, as in sessions for how to learn new disciplinary approaches for a given topic or skill, or survival strategies sessions for how to effectively respond to students' written work in a public speaking class; or they may appear more administrative, such as assessment meetings where instructors discuss what is and is not functioning well in a given course. These activities may also take the form of guest speakers who help invigorate pedagogy by taking up socially significant issues facing instructors — for example, issues concerning work-life balance, resilience in the face of furloughs, engaging millennial students, or the effects of social networking media in/on the classroom. While such activities may occur in centers for faculty development or instructional support (i.e., outside the department), it may serve a coordinator well to explore with her or his colleagues the links between the work of a given course and what is happening within the department in thesis or dissertation defenses, job interview presentations, forensics and debate events, and other opportunities.

One-on-One Mentoring. Another place where program vision takes shape is during one-on-one mentoring. While perhaps the most common example of course coordinators as mentors is consulting with GTAs or other relatively inexperienced instructors (e.g., troubleshooting how to adjust the course calendar because of a sick day, or adjusting an assignment or exercise so that it better meets the needs of a group of students), this mentoring may take a variety of different forms. For example, the department chair or other leaders who hire part-time faculty may, in an interview, help a prospective instructor understand the vision of a particular course. Even what may seem like a very technical meeting, such as when a coordinator and instructor meet to discuss the features within PowerPoint that can make lecture slides accessible, can help to shore up and sustain program vision (in this case, that instructors and program leaders are committed to teaching all students, including students who have disabilities that affect their learning). While perhaps not mentoring in a formal sense, water-cooler conversations can also reinforce (or undermine) program vision. Whether these conversations consist of the coordinator speaking with instructors in the copy room about how she or he responds to student work or the ways in which the assessment meetings are (or are not) meaningful, these moments help to constitute program vision and instructors' investment in it. That our mundane actions and utterances as instructors and coordinators can affect, however subtly, the success of a coordinated course is a reminder that we should take care that our actions and our espoused values align.

Whether you have recently inherited coordination of a course, find yourself in a position to take a course or program in a new direction, or are attempting to build some continuity across sections of a course for the first time, you may find it helpful to discuss with others their histories with and expectations of you and the program. In order to work together as a team, in order to create continuity and community across all sections of a given course, you will need to understand your colleagues' common values, goals, and past experiences with and strategies for implementation.

UNDERSTANDING PROGRAM VISION FOR INTRODUCTORY COURSE SUCCESS

It may be tempting to believe, at least initially, that there isn't much of a vision for something as routine as a course like public speaking. This is especially true if your colleagues tend to think of introductory courses, whether public speaking or the human communication course (a mixture of communication theory, interpersonal communication, intercultural communication, small-group communication, and public speaking), as natural, inevitable, and relatively stable and enduring over time. As one of our colleagues put it: "There's no vision — I just keep doing what the guy before me did."

Just as it is unwise to spend an inordinate amount of time crafting a vision that does not complement your program, department, or students, it is equally unwise to assume you have no vision at all. There is a vision (or many and sometimes conflicting visions) for this course, however opaque, and many curricular decisions will be informed by it. For example, the values that organize your course and program will shape which people will teach the course, the sorts of books and assignments they engage in with students, policies regarding incompletes or waivers, and even whether or not you assign instructors to "smart" (technology-enhanced) classrooms. Moreover, even if you're part of a program that has been around for generations, where it seems as though all you have to do is "hold the line," or a program where your authority is limited, where you might not be invited to make staffing decisions or provide instructor evaluations, your colleagues and supervisors will rely on this vision to build their impression of the work you do, as will students. They may see your program as vital to both discipline and campus, and your work as a meaningful and substantive contribution, or they may see it as staid and tired, something that might not merit their continued support. Your understanding of your vision and mission as a course coordinator will affect your reputation — as an individual and for your program.

UNDERSTANDING PROGRAM VISION FOR COORDINATOR SUCCESS

The responsibilities of course coordination can sometimes be unreasonably demanding, disrupting plans and bleeding over into other, perhaps more overtly rewarded aspects of academic life, like teaching, research, and publication. This suggests the importance of establishing clear, though permeable, boundaries around your work as a course coordinator, as appropriate for your peers', supervisors', students', and your own expectations of this role. Understanding your program's vision is one of the keys to better navigating these expectations successfully.

In particular, your own success as coordinator depends, in large measure, on your ability to create both congruence with and boundaries between you and your responsibilities. Congruence will strengthen your integrity, in that you will feel as though you are making a difference, making choices that are consistent with your values. On a day-to-day basis, this involves having conversations about teaching and learning that you think are purposeful and engaging and sharing aspects of your research interests with your colleagues that extend and enrich your collective conversations about pedagogy (and having conversations about pedagogy that speak back into your research interests, so you don't feel as though your intellectual curiosity and your teaching are pitted against each other in a zero sum game). This also includes receiving authentic, formative feedback about your performance that helps you understand what you do well, and not just where you might not be meeting others' expectations.

Boundaries help you avoid the feeling of being swallowed whole by your role. Though not all of us need help protecting time for our writing or our families, some of us most certainly will. We would suggest that this varies according to the nature of the coordinator's responsibilities. Some course coordinators — particularly those whose responsibilities are limited to an assessment report at the end of the semester, or making sure faculty have ordered from a list of approved textbooks — can compartmentalize their duties. But those of us who work with GTAs or other relatively inexperienced instructors (or who are new to this assignment) may find it easy, as many teachers risk doing with course preparation or responding to student work, to go "all in" — to allow concerns from the office to spill over into evenings, weekends, and other personal spaces. Often it is not possible to build totally impenetrable boundaries (because of emergencies, sudden staffing changes, or other unforeseen circumstances), but permeable boundaries may help us achieve a kind of dynamic equilibrium in our role. On a day-to-day basis, these permeable boundaries may include setting aside regular blocks of time for writing or returning emails and voicemails, building a structure for staff meetings or support course sessions that includes time for troubleshooting issues of common interest (issues that might otherwise require you to engage in multiple, individual consultations), and developing a mentor program that helps new and more experienced faculty work together to answer each other's questions.

What informs your approach to congruence and developing boundaries is your program vision. On the one hand, your vision may set a high standard, but on the other hand, this vision, by challenging you to model your collective goals and values, helps you make decisions, from staffing to time management. It is absolutely a challenge to articulate and get others to embrace a particular program vision (even sometimes when they help to develop it), but this process is time well spent, as it can help you avoid considerable difficulties in the future. When you and your colleagues are aligned along a particular vision, then you can rest easier knowing that people are working toward a common goal. Moreover, with this vision, you are no longer alone when it comes time to select (or dismiss) instructors, you have a guide for making policy decisions or structuring assessment activities, and you have a rationale that helps organize your curriculum.

Program vision can also make a frustrating or scary day a whole lot easier to take. Deanna's goal in working with GTAs, for example, is to help them learn not only how to teach, but how to teach well (in a discerning, intentional way) for as long as they'd like to continue teaching. This aspect of a vision — this one way, among many, that she understands her role in program vision — helps her assign Parker Palmer's (1998) *The Courage to Teach* as part of staff meetings. It helps her remember that she is a model for GTAs of someone who will teach for the rest of her life. While it would be disingenuous for her to pretend to be calm when she's frazzled, or casual when she's panicked, she doesn't serve them or herself by allowing her wellness to deteriorate to a point where she is easily frazzled or panicked. Despite how it may feel sometimes, abject panic is not a necessary component of an academic's life. In this sense, the program vision helps her remember to take good care of herself, so that she can help both students and colleagues take good care of themselves. In a similar vein, John rereads his tattered copy of Donald E. Hall's (2002) *The Academic Self: An Owner's Manual* each fall as he prepares for orientation. Such a book enables him to refocus his vision, to build his energy toward both teaching and course direction in a manner that feels empowering.

In a more formal sense, learning and actualizing a compelling program vision are also helpful to the course coordinator during the review, tenure, and promotion process. While part of this process is a matter of listing what you have done during a particular period in review (everything from the classes you taught, to your participation in campus governance and other service commitments, to your published work — if appropriate), essential to your successful evaluation is your ability to share with readers not only your accomplishments but also your reasoning behind them. Admittedly evaluative processes like review for tenure and promotion vary from one campus to another, but what unites them all is, to some extent, this quality of intentionality. In developing your academic profile, it is important to show others (whether a department or university committee; a dean, director, division head, or provost; or some other evaluating body) that you are engaged in a program of work that makes sense, that makes the most of your expertise and serves your students, your discipline, and your program, college, or university. A compelling vision, one that draws strength from and lends depth to your own career trajectory, helps you make the case that your academic assignment and your work as a campus leader or researcher are mutually informing. Articulating this vision in such a way that someone else can appreciate the value of your work is key to the evaluation and promotion process.

LEARNING AND EVALUATING PROGRAM VISION

So, understanding program vision can help course coordinators on a variety of fronts, but how exactly do we go about understanding the mission of a particular course? Though as supervisors of what are generally large numbers of sections and equally large numbers of instructors, very rarely do any of us start from scratch, it may be that, despite having some sense of how the program worked before, we don't inherit a clear and comprehensive sense of the mission or vision of our program. Or, if we do feel solidly versed in our program's identity, we may lack a sense of how successfully it is working for those it is meant to serve. Even in cases where a program has yet to implement any organized coordination of courses, we must explore our colleagues' understandings of the course and its role as part of vision development. To illuminate these areas, we must examine and learn the program vision and then take stock of our program, evaluating its strengths and limitations and the expectations that surround it (which is more than a matter of what others think we can or should be doing, but also includes our own sense of what we'd like to achieve in this role).

You might approach your analysis from the intersections of several interdependent systems: your university mission; your college mission; your department mission; the goals of your campus general education oversight body (i.e., your college or university's understanding of what general education is/should do); the history of your course — its position in your school and department or program curriculum and how it has developed over time; and research perspectives on your particular course as published in your discipline (e.g., how articles in *Communication Education* approach the teaching of public speaking or intercultural communication, whatever the content of your course). Your colleagues are a wealth of information about all of the above; even if they cannot provide the factual or official perspective on these matters, they are in a good position to offer their own perspectives on, impressions of, and experiences with your work. As the saying goes, take these with a grain of salt.

Learning one's program is, at the outset, a little like playing an organizational detective (in Goodall's [1994] sense): We must investigate, at least to some extent, the history of the program (i.e., how it came to be, who started it and to what end), its function within other institutional missions (e.g., university, college, division, department), how the program has evolved under and in relation to past coordinators and chairs, and the public perception (colleagues' perspective, students' perspective, administrators' perspective) of the program. As a coordinator, you're looking to better understand the solvency of the program:

- In general, is this program in pretty good shape? What kind of reputation does it have — with students, instructors, colleagues, administrators? Is it cohesive? Or have you inherited a program that is in disrepair? Are there compliance issues (for example, with college or university policy or general education requirements) you must address?
- How do instructors feel about this course? Are they excited to teach it, or do they feel it's a burden? Are instructors qualified to teach this course? Do they seem satisfied with their responsibilities? Do they feel as though they're "heard" by you or other department leaders?
- Are students reporting meaningful learning experiences in this course? It may help to know whether students consider this class to be overly easy or hard, and whether they perceive any teachers to be particularly fair or unfair. When they share their perspectives on assignments, are they seeing their work in this class as meaningful and relevant? Or are there aspects of the course that aren't working, or aren't working with particular segments of your student population?

- What is the history of this course in terms of its approval or support? If this is a general education course, has it sailed through past recertifications, or will you need to take corrective action? Has this course come under fire from any offices on campus (for example, have other departments begun to lobby for your piece of valuable "GE real estate")?
- What resources are available to you as coordinator? Are you able to enlist the help of your department chair, dean, division head, campus assessment or other offices, or colleagues? Do you have a support staff? For what responsibilities might you employ student assistants?

This inventory of questions can help you enter this new responsibility with a realistic sense of the program's strengths and limitations. It is wise to watch and wait until you better understand the culture of your program; this way, you can strengthen and, where appropriate or necessary, modify the program.

Part of what you are looking to do, with this sort of investigation, is determine where to begin. For example, if you find that instructors are frustrated with the course because they believe the required course textbook isn't relevant for or accessible to their students, this could be an opportunity for you to review, as a group, your program vision and review textbooks that would be a better fit in realizing that vision. As a coordinator, this decision not only reveals you to be an advocate for students' learning and instructors' expertise and a willing dialogue partner about issues related to the delivery of this course, but it also affords you an opportunity to revisit, and possibly revise, your program's vision. Or, for example, if, in your review of students' evaluations of their instructors, you learn that students have serious concerns about the textbook (or that they don't understand the relevance of a particular assignment or activity, or that they perceive the class to be too easy), then this may be an occasion to discuss these perceptions with instructors, to consider why students may feel this way and what options you have, collectively, for addressing it.

Another technique for analyzing and evaluating program vision is to think of this vision or philosophy in terms of metaphor. For example, you may see yourself as "holding the line established by my predecessors" or "shepherding students and colleagues toward social justice," or you may hear such a metaphor spoken by colleagues or administrators. Examining your metaphors can help you both conceptualize your vision and interrogate it. When you think about your particular program, what metaphors come to mind? Rigorously examine the metaphors that resonate with you for your program and your role in it. For example, if you see yourself as "holding the line" your predecessors established, what is the line you're holding? How does this metaphor position you as course coordinator in ways that are congruent or divergent from your values and commitments? Do the values implicit in your use of your metaphor drive you and your instructors toward some teaching methods instead of others? What are the consequences of this vision for the discipline, for the department, for the program, for instructors, for students, for you? Use the answers to these questions to put a fine point on what you feel is most central to the course and to help scrutinize the metaphor that you, or others, may have been taking for granted.

ARTICULATING PROGRAM VISION

As a course coordinator, you have the responsibility of articulating your program vision to a number of different constituencies, including students, GTAs and other instructors, colleagues who teach in other areas of your discipline or in other fields of study, administrators (from your department chair, to your dean, division head or provost, to college or university review, tenure, and promotion committees), supervisory groups (such as an accrediting group or general education course recertification committee), and perhaps even the general public. In large measure, this is a matter of the same sorts of audience analysis you're already likely teaching your students in some form or another. This is to say that how you articulate your program vision is a function of what your audience members (whether students or administrators) know, need, and expect.

In this endeavor, it helps to remember some advice you may have learned in composition classes when you were a student. An effective message is a function of aligning your purpose (your message or goals), your audience (the people you would like to change or influence with that message), and your voice (how you will shape that message so that your audience will find it compelling) (Elbow, 1998). How you articulate program vision to students enrolled in a section of the coordinated course that you are teaching is likely to be different from how you articulate this vision to the instructors you supervise (and, further, you may articulate this vision differently in a routine staff meeting than you might at orientation or in an assessment meeting) or how you articulate this vision in your first meeting with the new dean. Each audience has a different investment in your program and your role, each will require different kinds of explanations, and each has a different reason for inquiring into what it is you do.

It can be helpful to shape program mission in different ways for different people, depending on your relationship with them and their degree of interest or investment in the course or program. For example, Deanna coordinates the multiple-section public speaking course with her department's assessment coordinator (who is, generally speaking, interested in the quality of students' learning in all courses in the department, general-education–related and otherwise) and with the department chair. When discussing the purpose and mission of this course, they typically do so in the same terms as the general education oversight committee on their campus; this helps them focus on whether or not students are mastering the learning outcomes associated with the course. To this end, one way to understand our course vision is that it helps students become ethical and engaged speakers on issues of social significance. However, when Deanna works with GTAs, many of whom are engaged in research pursuits at the intersections of communication, instruction, and critical theory—what we have termed "critical communication pedagogy" (Fassett & Warren, 2007)—she finds it more helpful to explore this same vision in terms of power and privilege. To this end, one way to understand the course vision is that it helps students better understand the relationships of power and privilege implicit in advocacy with respect to prevailing social issues. And when Deanna shaped this program vision for the colleagues who reviewed her dossier for promotion to full professor, she underscored the importance of this course in helping retain and graduate university students from historically marginalized groups. In this way, she was able to help readers of her dossier understand that the course is a form of activism, one that helps the university succeed in its strategic planning goals of access and inclusion. These are all ways in which an awareness of audience might productively shape program mission.

John has engaged in similar shaping of program vision for different audiences, especially as he has served in that capacity for two very different programs and campuses. At Bowling Green State University, for instance, not all students are required to take the introductory communication course, and, because of this, his articulation of the purpose of the course focused on the needs of the students who typically enrolled in it. With primarily business and education students, the course needed to resonate with those departments and programs and to emphasize communication skills and contexts as appropriate. At Southern Illinois University, all students must take the introductory communication course. In this case, a closer match to the general education mission was necessary. Further, the way John articulated his work in his tenure and promotion materials at each institution differed. At BGSU, he framed his supervision efforts as teaching and service, while at SIU, he demonstrated that his work as coordinator spanned his assignment in all areas — teaching, research, and service.

PROGRAM VISION AS A SOURCE OF PROGRAM STRENGTH

It is important to build and maintain bridges between your program and others on campus; further, you'll want to work toward nurturing the support of your supervisors. Here, program vision serves as a source of strength, a basis from which you may act in the interests of your program or course, on behalf of yourself, your instructors, and your students. This will mean helping administrators and other campus decision makers understand the purpose and wisdom of your program vision (i.e., the rationale behind your actions — why your program does what it does). While, in part, this is a matter of sharing this vision as a compelling advocate, working toward goodwill and mutual understanding, at times this will also mean engaging in the sometimes uncomfortable act of asking for what you deserve.

As academics, especially in lean budget years, we learn not to ask for too much, to do increasingly more with less. This is a survival strategy that makes some sense in that we encourage the impression that we are thankful for what we have, that we are hard workers and appreciate the privilege and autonomy that attend our role as academics. That said, you will probably find yourself in need: For example, some of your instructors may not have offices; some may have been moved to offices in different quarters on campus, not all of which have phone lines; or the GTA office may be beyond filthy — not because the GTAs themselves are mistreating it, but because it hasn't had regular maintenance in a decade or more; or you've been putting a lot of time and effort into running an orientation each August before school begins and you need to be compensated accordingly. In each of these instances, a galvanizing program vision will be a source of strength.

Though the connection between program vision and a grimy office may seem thin, it may help to consider how someone's office conditions are an indication of status and respect. Deanna still recalls her surprise at the original conditions of the GTA offices in her department: peeling and overlapping multicolored paints; dark, silty grime on all surfaces, but especially on the window blinds and shelves; loose ceiling and flooring tiles; collections of obsolete computing equipment; and impressive piles of yellowed visual aids and other student work.

At that time, as an assistant professor, she did not fully understand what she could and could not ask for from her department; for years, with the help of the GTAs, during each orientation they cleaned what they could, mopping floors, dusting the blinds, wiping down the phones and desks, and shredding and re-cycling student work they didn't absolutely need to keep. However, it became increasingly difficult for her to ask these instructors to do the work of the cus-todial staff, as well as to ask them to keep "making do" when there were prob-lems in those offices that were the university's responsibility to repair.

In the end, what helped her effect change to those offices wasn't making an aesthetic argument, or challenging administrators' sense of commitment, but rather helping a variety of people (from facilities offices to our office manager and all points in between) to understand that one of their responsibilities is to help students (both graduate students and the undergraduates they teach) understand the power of communication to create our social worlds. Students and teachers, on witnessing and tolerating learning spaces in disrepair, come to question whether the institution values them and their work. (You may be wondering what she would have done if her argument hadn't worked. She was of three minds: approach the faculty and GTA unions about safety issues; seek donations through personal and alumni contacts; and/or launch a guerrilla renovation with whatever she could find: Super Glue, garage sale wall cover-ings, or perhaps even a little paint here and there. And if you work in a pro-gram where a large number of faculty have no offices at all, perhaps this helps you conceptualize how you might work toward creating some kind of space for instructor-student meetings.) Fortunately, communication educators, as adept rhetoricians, are often well positioned to argue effectively.

Perhaps the best time to negotiate for what you think you or your program might need is prior to assuming the role. You would be wise to ask around, connecting with colleagues who are employed in similar roles at similar institu-tions; find out—delicately—the nature of both their compensation and their workload. Because positions develop organically at each campus, course coordi-nators' and GTA supervisors' roles and responsibilities may look very different.

Even within the same university system, this will be the case. For example, San José State University typically runs more than 35 stand-alone sections of public speaking, most staffed by part-time faculty and GTAs; Deanna super-vises approximately 15 GTAs at any given time, and she serves as one of the three cooperating course coordinators. Further, she is able to require GTAs to enroll in a support course and then continue in biweekly staff meetings for as long as they continue in this role. The enrollments in the support course constitute her as a GTA supervisor for approximately 20% of her workload. However, at San Diego State University, our colleague Kurt Lindemann supervises approximately 80 sections of an oral communication class that includes both communication theory and public speaking. He provides four repeating lectures a week to students, who then participate in two section meetings each week with a GTA. Though he and Deanna are both GTA supervisors in the eyes of the California State University, Kurt effectively supervises nearly 30 GTAs each semester. He does not meet with GTAs in staff meetings; however, they do participate in orientation and other professional development activities.

This is within one university system; we will find variation across the country not only in the nature of the responsibilities associated with these roles (i.e., what constitutes workload), but also what each of us has negotiated locally in terms of compensation for taking on this assignment. These differences can vary across the country. For instance, John supervises about 50 independently taught sections of public speaking each semester at Southern Illinois University. His teaching load is normally two courses per semester; however, in the fall he teaches a support course for all new GTA public speaking instructors. In the spring, his load is one course — he receives a release for his supervision work. Community colleges and smaller public and private colleges and universities will reveal still greater variety in configurations of and compensation for this role.

Depending on the relationship you have with key administrators, it is possible to ask for additional travel support, improved office conditions (e.g., painting, furniture, blinds), additional research and teaching resources (e.g., a research assistant, coding software, a subscription to *Basic Communication Course Annual* or other books/journals), course release or other workload reconfiguration (for example, release from undergraduate advising or departmental service), stipend for work that goes above and beyond the call (e.g., coordinating an orientation), and so forth. It is, however, still possible to ask for these things once you have become a course coordinator, which is why it is important to cultivate your relationships with colleagues and supervisors so they see your efforts with this course as essential and integral to their mission. The burden of proof, so to speak, will rest with you for explaining what it is you want, how much it will cost, why it matters (i.e., what problem it will alleviate or what benefit it will bring), and how everyone will suffer to some extent if you don't have it. Remember, you are advocating for yourself, but you're also advocating for a community; you have to get your instructors and their students what they need, and this will mean assertiveness.

It is particularly essential that you maintain an effective working relationship with your department chair (or other immediate supervisor) and departmental office manager (or other support staff); these people are, in turn, able to help you work with various campus offices as appropriate. When you have questions, whether about how an instructor files for family leave or how to negotiate jury duty, these are the people who will make your life a lot easier. If these people understand the value of what it is you (and the instructors you supervise) do, they will be similarly galvanized by this direction and focus, becoming your allies in working toward this vision.

DIALOGUE AND VISION

It can be common to feel isolated as a course coordinator, as though you alone are responsible for the successes and failures of a particular program. We risk this further when we use language like "your vision" or "your instructors." This language does help inspire feelings of ownership in course coordinators, but it can come at the cost of remembering the many people who participate in the collaborative development and maintenance of a program vision. There is considerable value in working toward continuity and community in a dialogic fashion. We hear the term *dialogue* frequently these days, often in situations where people simply mean to suggest that multiple people participate in discussion. However, dialogue is not a matter of voices standing in relation to one another, but rather, as Buber (1970/1996) would suggest, a process of active engagement, of standing in the tension between holding one's own ground and remaining genuinely open to the other (Spano, 2001). Dialogue foregrounds understanding, but it may also mean inviting dissent. This is a tall order, of course, especially for someone who is new to course coordination and the responsibilities that role entails, and we don't mean to suggest that this is an ideal we can adhere to on most days. Yet, dialogic communication—everyday communication that aspires to dialogue, that invites people to share their values, goals, and experiences with one another—is something we can strive toward, and it can make a significant difference in the lives of our colleagues and teachers, our students, and ourselves. Working collectively, through consensus and conflict, toward a program vision that people commit to and respect will improve the odds of nurturing a vibrant, vital, and responsive program.

Attending to program vision in this way returns benefits for all—for students and teachers, campus leaders and administrators. Further, the discussions and efforts at dialogue you achieve within your community (and, to some extent, between your community and others on campus and in the discipline) will help you develop the structure you need to understand and respond to challenges your program may face. A significant challenge in recent years, for faculty members in general and course coordinators in particular, has been demonstrating to others that their courses and programs are effectively helping students learn. Engaging in dialogue as a community concerned with one another's individual and collective success will help strengthen not only a sense of program vision and identity, but also that program's effectiveness.

REFERENCES

Buber, M. (1970/1996). *I and thou*. New York: Touchstone.

Elbow, P. (1998). *Writing with power: Techniques for mastering the writing process* (2nd ed.). New York: Oxford University Press.

Fassett, D. L., & Warren, J. T. (2007). *Critical communication pedagogy*. Thousand Oaks, CA: SAGE Publications.
Goodall, Jr., H. L. (1994). *Casing a promised land: The autobiography of an organizational detective as cultural ethnographer.* Carbondale, IL: Southern Illinois University Press.
Hall, D. E. (2002). *The academic self: An owner's manual.* Columbus, OH: Ohio State University.
Palmer, P. J. (1998). *The courage to teach: Exploring the inner landscape of a teacher's life.* San Francisco, CA: Jossey-Bass.
Spano, S. J. (2001). *Public dialogue and participatory democracy: The Cupertino Project.* Cresskill, NJ: Hampton Press.

RECOMMENDED READINGS

Morlan, D. B. (1994). The history and development of the basic course. In L. W. Hugenberg, P. L. Gray, D. M. Trank (Eds.), *Teaching and directing the basic communications course* (pp. 1–8). Dubuque, IA: Kendall/Hunt Publishing.

Morlan offers readers a trajectory of how introductory communication courses have developed over the decades since their inception. While his writing does not specifically encourage any approach to program vision, having a historical perspective on the purpose and functions of introductory courses will help you contextualize your own program's role in the communication studies discipline.

Fassett, D. L., & Warren, J. T. (2008). Pedagogy of relevance: A critical communication pedagogy agenda for the "basic" course. *Basic Communication Course Annual, 20*, 1–34.

While we might include this particular writing under advocacy, it seems appropriate to include it with respect to a chapter on vision, as it represents our own efforts to "read" the discipline—our collective disciplinary efforts in administering introductory communication courses and make recommendations we feel will improve the status, focus, and direction of such programs. While you may not wish to pursue any of the recommendations in this piece, we hope it provides you with fodder for how you learn and develop the vision associated with your own program.

Williams, G. (1996). (En)visioning success: The anatomy and functions of vision in the basic course. *Basic Communication Course Annual, 8*, 26–57.

An excellent reading for course coordinators on how to conceptualize vision with respect to introductory communication courses, with a particular emphasis on how to engage in participatory leadership toward group ownership and implementation.

Wulff, D. H., Nyquist, J. D., & Abbott, R. D. (1991). Developing a TA training program that reflects the culture of the institution: TA training at the University of Washington. In J. D. Nyquist, R. D. Abbott, D. H. Wulff, & J. Sprague (Eds.), *Preparing the professoriate of tomorrow to teach: Selected readings in TA training* (pp. 123–134). Dubuque, IA: Kendall/Hunt Publishing.

A case study of how to develop a coordinated course (in this case, one that relies on GTAs) in light of institutional culture and mission. The program at the University of Washington is particularly noteworthy for its continued influence on the preparation of future faculty in the discipline of communication studies.

3

Meaningful Assessment

Put to the Test

Each semester, you gather instructors of your public speaking course together for a discussion of how well they feel they are achieving the stated learning outcomes of the course with their students. Full professors drag their feet none-too-subtly, frustrated that they have been to dozens of these meetings; part-time faculty participate fully, in hopes of gleaning meaningful teaching strategies and establishing reputations as team players; and GTAs, especially new ones, sit quietly and watch, worried that they might say the wrong thing or ask an irrelevant question. This is, however, a meaningful exercise for you, as you have to prepare a report for the Board of General Education on your campus regarding the successes and struggles of these instructors in helping students achieve learning outcomes from choosing socially significant speech topics to crafting compelling theses and distinguishing between plagiarism and academic honesty.

* * *

Too often, academics think of assessment as an unfunded mandate. At Deanna's university and the community colleges that articulate most commonly with it, faculty commonly point to WASC (Western Association of Schools and Colleges — the accrediting body), or groups that govern general education or assessment on campus, or even the legislature as the source of our discontent. (At John's school, colleagues similarly bemoan the North Central Association of Colleges and Schools and the Illinois Board of Higher Education.) Many academics meet these offices' requests for information — about the degree to which students are learning what we say we are teaching them — with frustration and defensiveness: Are they saying we're not doing our jobs? How do they expect us to gather this information without additional resources? How are we supposed to teach (research, serve on committees, read dissertations/theses, etc., etc.) and prepare all these assessment reports?

These are all fair questions, but they speak to an adversarial vision of assessment that is not entirely fair. If we think about just what it is that we do as educators — we engage students in particular kinds of content, facilitate the acquisition of skills, and engender certain ways of thinking — then it can be reasonable to ask whether and how we know the effects or outcomes of our efforts with students. Assessment entails all the efforts we undertake to understand what our students are and are not learning and how to better improve the learning process. In general, these efforts can include our own and our students' reflection and self-assessment of strengths and limitations (e.g., what a student can now do as a result of a particular lesson or course and how confident she or he feels in this knowledge), our use of pre-/post-tests and other measures of student learning (e.g., using the PRCA-24 to measure students' communication anxiety, or collecting instructors' impressions of how many students in a given class met a particular learning objective and what they feel might help improve that percentage), and even, at times, our recollection and review of the grades and feedback we provide to students (e.g., when instructors learn through discussing their experiences with a particular assignment that students appear to routinely struggle with source citation or construction of a thesis statement). Further, assessment is not only a collaborative process of better understanding and addressing the learning needs of our students (and, to some extent, our colleagues), but also an opportunity for strengthening and advancing our program vision and demonstrating our relevance as a program and as a discipline.

UNDERSTANDING ASSESSMENT CONSTRUCTIVELY

We find it helpful to introduce assessment to instructors in this way: Assessment is not another hoop through which we must jump in increasingly tight budgetary times, but rather an opportunity to better understand whether and how (and with whom) we are successful in the classroom and to communicate the value of those endeavors with other groups of leaders and decision makers. Good teachers often ask themselves whether students are learning course content; that is why they design assignments and examinations and other forms of formative and summative assessment (if they design an examination well, and if they interpret their findings carefully, they can better discern which concepts students still don't understand by the end of the unit, mid-term, or semester). In this way, grading can be a common form of assessment for the individual instructor; we are able to use students' responses, whether oral or written, as an indication of how effective our efforts as instructors have been.

That said, using grading exclusively as a form of assessment can be problematic, as it may be possible for students to pass an assignment while still not fully mastering all learning outcomes for that assignment or course. (Further, an instructor may use assignments in layered ways to address multiple course-learning outcomes, making it difficult to discern students' mastery of an individual learning outcome from a particular assignment.) For more information on developing common grading expectations as part of course continuity, refer to Chapter 4. It is helpful to use a variety of different assessment activities in order to develop a more comprehensive picture of students' learning in a particular course or program.

Assessment Activities

Assessment activities are significant to building and adjusting the vision or rationale of the coordinated course. These activities may take many different forms — for example, structured discussion of how instructors feel students are meeting learning outcomes, perhaps in regularly scheduled face-to-face meetings or in a virtual forum like a wiki or blog; the creation and distribution of reports that synthesize program strengths and limitations; and so on—making them flexible to different program needs. Schedule these activities in such a way as to invite instructors into dialogue with one another about their experiences in the course, and assessment can become a means of finding consensus or identifying frustration with particular aspects of the course (whether regarding the nature of the speeches instructors assign or the clarity of a required learning outcome from the campus general education office).

Further, in your efforts to gather data, it is important to remember that university communication is not one-way: You are gathering data not only to satisfy another office on or off campus, but also to build an argument for how the course ought to run or, perhaps, the way the university understands this course, in particular, or approaches general education overall. If you and your colleagues are looking to shape the course in ways that are more critical, more humanizing, or more meaningful for students' learning, then assessment will help you develop your case.

This suggests the importance of designing assessment activities and procedures that are meaningful within your community (that is, your nested community of state, university, college, discipline, division, department, and course). This is, again, a matter of reading your campus culture, as campuses can often serve as the last outposts of the paradigm wars. For example, you may find that a given campus committee will accept only statistical patterns as assessment data or believes that activities like service learning or contemporary theories that appear unrelated to public speaking are not legitimate ventures for your course or program. Increasingly, campuses are moving beyond pre- and post-test data to include narrative data, inviting departments to propose how others should measure their success; but it may be that you need to include different kinds of data to demonstrate the effectiveness of your community's efforts.

Modeling

When you are feeling especially frustrated about assessment as an added responsibility to your already full plate, it may also help to think of assessment in terms of another responsibility effective educators take very seriously: modeling. Generally speaking, when we want to encourage a particular behavior or way of thinking in our students, we model it with them; we might think of this as showing them our best possible example, or, better still, how we have woven this concept or skill into a way of being. Assessment is a means of encouraging ourselves to plan intentionally for relevance; many of us hope our students will become mature learners, and this quality of intentionality will lead them to reflect on their mistakes, helping them make good choices. Assessment is a means for us to do the same. Just as we might model for our students the importance of previewing the relevance and direction/scope of the day's lecture as we teach them to give introductions in a public speaking class, we can also model for them and for each other the importance and value of self/program assessment.

AN EFFORT AT MEANINGFUL ASSESSMENT

When we were in graduate school, we thought assessment was basically grading — what instructors did to determine what concepts and skills students were learning and where they were still struggling. Particularly, we developed an interest in how we might use daily learning objectives (framed with the ubiquitous TSWBAT — "the students will be able to . . .") to make sure that we targeted and aimed each lesson plan toward helping students successfully complete a larger assignment (a more comprehensive assessment item, like a speech or a research paper). Now, we realize that, while this is assessment, it barely scratches the surface of what we had to learn about assessment in our years as professors. While no doubt imperfect, our departments have each come a long way in designing, implementing, and sharing assessment activities, and we share our experiences here as examples of the different ways we must work collaboratively to gain insight into students' learning.

Deanna's department assesses every class it offers, though in slightly different ways for different oversight groups, internal and external. Appointed coordinators supervise the general education courses (whether introductory or advanced) and play a role in the assignment of faculty to teach the course, the nature of assessment activities, and campus oversight of these courses. These coordinators hold assessment meetings (sometimes face-to-face and sometimes online, depending on the coordinator) and assign instructors structured reflection questions regarding how well students have performed with particular learning outcomes; they then use these sources of instructor data to develop brief end-of-the-semester assessment reports. These reports form the basis of each course's recertification application. Recently they reconfigured the department committee assignments so as to constitute a combined curriculum and assessment committee. This committee evaluates new curriculum proposals, but also helps the assessment coordinator supervise assessment activities across the department; instead of being course coordinators and also members of standing committees, course coordinators are now able to earn "credit" or relief from other service assignments for taking on this role.

While Deanna's program had a long history of assessment with general education courses, they are now becoming more comfortable with assessing all graduate and undergraduate offerings. They have adopted a similar model for these courses, assessing particular departmental learning outcomes (one or two per year during a five-year review cycle). The assessment coordinator organizes this process, using Survey Monkey and online wikis to collect data from instructors and then presenting an analysis of this information to the faculty at an end-of-the-semester meeting, where they are able to discuss where they are pleased and where they are frustrated by their efforts and students' learning. At the graduate level, they follow a similar process, where the assessment coordinator gathers data on one or two learning outcomes and the graduate program coordinator analyzes the data and prepares a brief end-of-the-semester report.

Often, what Deanna and her colleagues learn from these meetings is invaluable. For example, they recently assessed all public speaking sections for how well students are mastering the first learning outcome for the course: "Students will be able to identify and assess socially significant and intellectual topics, then compose and deliver extemporaneous oral presentations (using note cards or key-word outlines) on those topics." In this meeting, as a community, they struggled with whether end-of-term grades alone are sufficient to indicate whether students have mastered a particular outcome, especially when a student might still pass the class with some instructors when she or he hasn't yet fully mastered extemporaneous speaking. They also struggled with the way this outcome, authored by a university-level committee, has drawn together many different elements. For example, as a community, they find it difficult to ensure they are gathering data regarding several different elements, such as the nature of students' topics, their evaluation of their peers' topics, the quality of their delivery, and whether they prepared note cards or outlines (and of what quality). Perhaps the most valuable parts of these meetings are when they discuss "best practices": How does one help students learn which topics are or are not socially significant (and according to whom)? What strategies does one have for helping students rely on their notes less? By sharing their "on-the-ground" efforts and ideas, instructors not only help one another better meet these learning outcomes, but they help the coordinator complete her or his assessment report. In short, in these assessment meetings, Deanna's colleagues are mindful of the data they cite to support their impressions of how students are faring in courses; interrogate the intention and meaning of the services they have been commissioned by the university to provide; and learn from one another how best to teach these particular students with this particular content.

John's department assesses the courses that participate in the University Core Curriculum every five semesters, per university policy. Assessment includes a detailed portfolio with quantitative and qualitative measures of how the course meets its goals and mission. The portfolios are then reviewed by the Core Curriculum committee, which provides feedback and recommendations to the department to implement over the next review period. The previous assessment report is the ground from which they begin the next review: How has the program incorporated lessons from the previous assessment, and how have those changes affected student learning? While this process functions as a formal assessment of the course, each supervisor continues to monitor courses between formal reviews. A large measure of this routine monitoring occurs in the support course John offers each fall to new instructors.

ASSISTING COLLEAGUES WITH ASSESSMENT

One of a course coordinator's most important responsibilities is to create continuity across multiple sections of a course, which means she or he must assume some responsibility for assessment of that course; that said, assessment is a collaborative process. For assessment to be effective in a coordinated course, *all* instructors must feel welcome to share their experiences. This is more achievable if instructors understand not only the vision and purpose of the course, but also the meaning and value of assessment.

One of the challenges in supporting a broad array of different instructors, with varying levels of commitment and expertise, is helping to facilitate their development as educators; course coordinators must strive to respect the individuality of each teacher while also seeking common ground across multiple sections of the same course. This way, instructors can play to their own strengths in the classroom, while students across different sections have comparable experiences. The key here is "comparable" — as in, not exactly the same, but similar enough. Not only is it not possible for all instructors to be the same, even if they were to share similar philosophies on teaching (a focus on social justice, on preparation for civic engagement, on professional preparation, etc.); they no doubt draw from a variety of different teaching methods, materials, experiences, examples, and vocabularies. The challenge here is to strike a balance between continuity and creativity.

Part of how you achieve this balance as a course coordinator is to create opportunities for instructors to engage each other in dialogues and discussion regarding the purpose and value of an education, the role of this particular course in students' lives or in the university's mission, and so forth. This sort of open discussion gives rise to shared examples and resources — questions people might never have voiced in more formal (e.g., assessment-oriented) meetings, opportunities to observe one another's classrooms, and so forth. In other words, staff meetings and other similar occasions (like brown-bag discussions or professional development seminars) serve a centrifugal function: They draw your diverse group of faculty into the same orbit. Just as planets orbit around the sun in a similar fashion, they also have their own unique trajectories; this is a helpful way to think about continuity across multiple sections.

For example, in recent assessment meetings, Deanna's colleagues have surfaced a series of questions that continue to inform collective and individual conversations about the public speaking course, and more specifically, the learning objective regarding extemporaneous delivery of a socially significant speech, mentioned above. These questions productively unsettle assumptions about the social significance of student speech topics (for example, do students and instructors have similar understandings of this term? To what extent are our differences in opinion cultural?); about power and control in the classroom (for example, must instructors "approve" student topics in order to ensure their social significance, or might instructors introduce the same sorts of questions from assessment discussions to their students as a means of forming a common understanding of course expectations?); and about teaching methods (for example, how might instructors model social significance in their own selection of examples?).

As one of the course coordinators, Deanna must attempt to invite discussion between colleagues of varying experience and commitment to the course in such a way as to encourage growth and appropriate risk-taking (for example, in the form of trying new assignments or teaching methods) without becoming overly directive in terms of which teaching methods individual instructors should use. Often these meetings continue into the hallways and offices, where she meets with instructors (and where instructors meet with one another) to discuss new ideas and options for particular instructional challenges. As a co-ordinator, Deanna may find herself meeting with a GTA who has very little ex-perience but considerable enthusiasm to discuss what she or he heard in the meeting and what relevance that discussion might have for her or his work in the classroom; and then she might meet a day or two later with a part-time faculty member to learn more about a strategy she or he has had success with over the years, but that Deanna never thought to try herself because it always seemed like a stretch to her comfort zone. In this way, assessment meetings can be a learning moment for all who participate in them.

Your challenge as a course coordinator is to create enough structure to en-sure continuity without this structure becoming stifling to the growth and passion of the people (whether full professors or graduate teaching assistants) teaching the course. In addition to the structure of regular staff meetings, you could consider common course texts (or a listing of "approved" course texts), a common syllabus and/or series of assignments, and the development of a common course pack or repository of instructional resources (e.g., PowerPoint slides, software, videos, board games, etc.). See Chapter 4 for more information on developing a common syllabus.

DESIGNING APPROPRIATE ASSESSMENT

How you decide what structures to implement has a lot to do with the purpose and function of the course you're coordinating. For example, if your course draws people into the major and prepares them for all that follows, then it might be essential that all instructors be on the same page, if not in terms of teaching methods, then certainly in terms of what constitutes preparation for that major (the essential readings, concepts, experiences students will need). Further, if you supervise a general education public speaking course that has a series of assessed learning outcomes (e.g., that all speeches will be socially significant, that students will participate in 100 minutes of timed testing, that students will prepare full-sentence outlines), then it is important that all in-structors of that course agree to meet those learning outcomes. Again, there is still some freedom within this structure; for example, the requirement that stu-dents experience 100 minutes of timed testing does not mean that they must all take the same standard multiple-choice test (individual instructors' strengths and limitations can shape the sorts of examinations students experience; there are many possible types of effective examination designs).

Similarly, the instructors you supervise will shape, to some extent, the rela-tionship between structure and freedom regarding assessment of this course. For example, less experienced teachers or instructors who do not receive a lot of professional development support may benefit by more structure at first, so that your decisions can help to scaffold their own efforts to learn to teach. For example, with GTAs or other less experienced instructors, course coordinators often use a common or template syllabus (see Chapter 4), helping these new teachers understand what is (and is not) customizable about this document. More established professors, on the other hand, may bristle at unnecessary structure, feeling that these rules or guidelines are threats to their academic freedom. Again, coordinators must work to achieve what can be a fine balance between the structure all sections need for continuity and the freedom instructors need for creativity and fulfillment.

Cooper and Simonds (2011), in their book *Communication for the Classroom Teacher*, help the developing instructor learn that her or his choice of teaching methods is a function of the instructor's strengths and limitations (is she or he a strong lecturer?), the students' needs (do they learn better from small-group work or from large discussion circles?), the lesson objectives (teaching credibility may require different teaching methods than teaching vocal delivery), and the context (this can mean the context of the lesson; the context of the class period — whether this is the first class before a holiday or the class immediately following some community or campus incident — or the context of the room — as in whether the seats are movable or the room is too warm). This illustrates the importance of context in our discussion of structure and freedom with respect to a coordinated course. Assessment activities across these multiple sections must make space for instructors' diverse teaching methods, strengths, and limitations, helping to create a dialogue across and about the many different ways teaching may be effective.

For instance, John's assessment of his program's introductory course is tricky given the diversity of instructors and the freedom the program makes possible in the teaching of public speaking. The assessment process in the Core Curriculum Office prefers not only courses that are identical in structure but also methods and outcomes that are easily quantifiable. However, part of John's (and his department's) mission is to teach both masters and doctoral students how to design and implement their own pedagogies in their classrooms. In this way, the final exam in a class or the specifics of the second speech can be wildly divergent in form and in purpose from one section to another. The portfolio option from the Core Curriculum Office enables John to articulate connections and patterns across the various iterations of the course, demonstrating that the strength of the introductory communication course at SIUC is in its diverse approaches.

METHODS FOR ASSESSMENT

Assessment is another way of describing data collection — something that many of us, as researchers in one form or another, know and appreciate. In graduate school, we learn that our research questions are influenced by our paradigm, by our epistemological and ontological commitments. What we take to be truth or some form of actionable reality and what we take to be people's capacity for agency will shape not only the kinds of questions we ask but also how we ask them. Moreover, while our paradigm will shape the kinds of research questions we ask, it does not necessarily dictate our choice of research method. Ideally, we should choose the research method or combination of methods that is best capable of answering our question; assessment, as a form of data collection, is similar. If, as a course coordinator, one needs to understand how students are performing across 80 different sections of a course, it does not serve her or him to complete in-depth individual interviews with each student, no matter how fond one might be of this method (though there may be some value to sampling and interviewing some students, depending on just what it is that one is hoping to learn and/or show to others). Fortunately, there is no single "right" way of assessing a course. We appear to be entering a climate in higher education where, at least on some campuses and in some departments, we are able to determine our own most useful means of learning where we are and are not effective with students.

In writing this section, we struggled with word choice; we first tried on *measures* and then *instruments* to refer to methods we might use for assessment. Neither word captured our intent, which was to explore how assessment is a matter of feeling out, as a coordinator (or as part of a program or department), the means to answering our questions about students' learning. The methods we use may be quantitative or qualitative, and, within these large umbrella categories, of many possible varieties. What is important is to choose methods that will bring you insight and with which you and your colleagues have (or can acquire) some facility.

Finding Data Collection Tools

It may be helpful for you to consider, in building your assessment plan, whether there are already methods or tools available to you. For example, if it is part of your course's vision to help reduce students' public speaking anxiety, you might want to use an instrument like the PRCA-24 (Personal Report of Communication Anxiety) or PRPSA (Personal Report of Public Speaking Anxiety) as a pre-/post-test. Or, if it serves your course to document and assess students' efforts to integrate material across all their general education courses, then it would be wise to explore electronic portfolios. Coordinators who supervise large lecture format communication courses may find it helpful not only to explore global assessment of students' learning in the course (through, for example, common examinations), but also students' participation and attention during class time (through, for example, the use of response pads or "clickers," which can help you assess students' understanding of concepts as a lecture develops). Or coordinators who favor the use of a course learning system, like Blackboard or Desire2Learn, may find the quiz, rubric, and blog functions useful in measuring or understanding students' learning. Just remember that there are many possible assessment tools available to you, from colleagues on campus and in the discipline, through the campus center for teaching and learning, and from textbook publishers.

Building Data Collection Tools

For some learning outcomes, you might be best served by developing your own data collection tool or process. For instance, if you are interested in learning not only the degree of students' communication anxiety but also their perceived sense of self-confidence and their past experiences with public speaking, then you should consider developing your own instrument that combines, for example, the PRCA, the SPCC (Self Perceived Communication Competence instrument), and your own questions.

You may find it helpful to explore how the assignments you use function to meet the course learning outcomes. For example, John asks introductory course instructors to assign a "communication analysis paper," a six-to-eight-page essay that not only reminds students that communication is written as well as oral, but encourages them to build connections between their classroom learning and their experiences in the world. Instructors are able to shape the assignment toward their own ends, but the central purpose of strengthening and evaluating students' written analytical skills is consistent across their diverse iterations. This particular assignment illustrates how to build a measure (in fact, many of us wouldn't think of a paper as a "measure") that can document students' learning while also being flexible enough to match different instructors' experiences and interests. The assignment helps assess students' use of course concepts, the sophistication of their description and analysis of communicative events, and their critical thinking/ethical practices. The analysis paper has proven useful even as the course has foregrounded public speaking. In their most recent assessment, John's department noted a drop in writing quality and analytical ability, prompting both coordinator and instructors to frame and prepare for this assignment in ways to help students better acquire these skills.

Amassing a Variety of Measures

If, after your survey of available assessment tools, you find that there isn't really any one method that helps address all learning outcomes for your course (or all the important questions you and your colleagues have about teaching and learning with respect to this course), know that it is not only possible but common to develop something that uniquely suits your program. Further, this may involve a collection of different kinds of measures. It is likely that your course is grounded in several learning outcomes; each may require a different type of assessment. For example, you might best measure one outcome by a pre-/post-test, while you might best assess another by reviewing a random sampling of students' written work. In such cases, building and implementing a repertoire of assessment methods will result in the most helpful and useful data collection. Know that, in most cases, you needn't assess all outcomes each semester or even each year; you can develop an assessment plan that shows how you will gather and review with instructors (and other department leaders, as appropriate) the data for each outcome on a timetable.

THE POWER OF ASSESSMENT

While we are often motivated toward assessment activities by groups of others, whether agencies or campus communities or people who we suspect may not really understand what we do as educators, it is important to remember that we do not "serve" them. We serve our own interests: our professional judgment about the needs of our students, ourselves, and our society. If we assume that others dictate our assessment activities for us, then we will have abdicated our agency in the teaching and learning process. Yet if we design assessment activities that are meaningful to us, then the power of assessment rests with us and not with outside forces beyond our control. We can assert authority in the assessment of coordinated courses by designing assessment processes that extend our disciplinary conversation about teaching and learning. In addition, such work may help us seek promotion and tenure (and other forms of job security), and also builds our reputations as people who care about the foundations of our field. Further, we can empower ourselves through assessment by ensuring that we use what we learn to strengthen our courses, departments, programs, and campuses.

Assessment as Research

Assessment is a form of research that relies on research methods, and, as such, it is worth noting that the data you gather as coordinator need not reside entirely with your program, college, or university. Part of building congruence between your research interests as an academic and your professional responsibilities as a course coordinator entails exploring the ways in which assessment opportunities might give rise not only to creativity and insights, but to fruitful collaborations with colleagues, and also to publication. This is not to suggest that all manner of data you collect for your school's general education oversight committee or department's program review will be in line with your research interests, but perhaps there are ways you might bring these two seemingly disparate areas together. You might find this easiest to do if you are someone who already researches at the intersections of communication and instruction; in this area of our discipline, you'll find many outlets for manuscripts that help colleagues in our field better understand how to teach communication or that lead to new insights regarding communication in the classroom — outlets such as *Communication Education*, *Basic Communication Course Annual*, and *Communication Teacher*. However, even a cursory review of other prominent journals in our discipline, from *Communication and Critical/Cultural Studies* to the *Journal of Applied Communication Research* to *Text and Performance Quarterly* (in particular, their special issues on dis/ability and performative pedagogy) will show published work regarding communication and pedagogy. Considering where and how you're able to strike a productive tension between your particular disciplinary expertise and your work as a course coordinator may result in some wonderful and heretofore unexpected opportunities.

Assessment as Advocacy

Another important quality of assessment we should remember as we reenvision it as intentional, as something that emerges from and helps us respond to our own programmatic needs, is that it may be foundational for advocacy. College and university structures misleadingly suggest that communication between supervisory bodies and individual programs or courses is unidirectional—i.e., these are the requirements, so go fulfill them. However, the sort of data collection you engage in as a course coordinator may also inform those supervisory groups, helping them understand where their policies and procedures are helpful, at best, or untenable, at worst. For example, you may discover that students in your introductory human communication course do not have writing skills sufficient to the learning outcomes the university proposes; this insight can prompt a discussion about how best to improve those writing skills, whether to require introductory composition as a prerequisite to the course, or whether to amend the learning outcomes (or assignments that help demonstrate students' mastery of certain learning outcomes).

At its core, effective assessment helps course coordinators discern what students and instructors need; this helps them advocate for those constituents with other offices on campus, arguing for extended writing or communication center hours, better instructional technology (whether an ADA accessible learning management system or digital recording and storage of public speeches and debates), or even offices that have working phone lines, rudimentary computing equipment, or clean floors. Effective assessment practices, in all their forms, give rise to the data that function as support for your cause and your community.

Where we share these data with instructors (and perhaps, at times, with students), we can also nurture and sustain a community that shares responsibility in the coordination of this course. As these community members assume ownership for whether and how students are learning, for the course/program vision, they will come into a flexible and shifting alignment, creating continuity across multiple sections and multiple approaches to teaching. A prism for this process of balancing structure and freedom is the common course syllabus, which we'll address in the next chapter.

REFERENCE

Cooper, P. J., & Simonds, C. (2011). *Communication for the classroom teacher* (9th ed.). Needham Heights, MA: Allyn & Bacon.

RECOMMENDED READINGS

Avanzino, S. (2010). Starting from scratch and getting somewhere: Assessment of oral communication proficiency in general education across lower and upper division courses. *Communication Teacher, 24,* 91–110.

Avanzino provides a model of one communication program's efforts at assessment—across their program and in relation to general education. While it may not mirror your own program exactly, it does provide guidance you can use in considering how to build and implement a comprehensive assessment plan.

Backlund, P., & Arneson, P. (2000). Educational assessment grows up: Looking toward the future. *Journal of the Association for Communication Administration, 29,* 88–102.

Though not specifically written for course coordinators, this is a succinct and useful article that contextualizes communication studies assessment efforts within a larger backdrop of recent developments in higher education assessment.

Docan-Morgan, T. (2007). Writing and communicating instructional objectives. In B. Hugenberg, L. Hugenberg, S. Morreale, D. Worley, & D. Worley (Eds.), *Basic communication course practices: A training manual for instructors* (pp. 25–41). Dubuque, IA: Kendall Hunt Publishing.

A lucid, concise, and engaging account of how to develop and communicate with students' instructional objectives, this is a useful reading not only for a course coordinator, but also for instructors of any degree of teaching experience.

Suskie, L. (2009). *Assessing student learning: A common sense guide* (2nd ed.). San Francisco, CA: Jossey-Bass.

Suskie provides readers with both a process and a toolkit for assessment activities that can serve a broad array of functions in higher education. Of particular value is her attention to the development of program- and course-specific measures, including exams, assignments, and rubrics.

Walvoord, B. E. (2010). *Assessment clear and simple: A practical guide for institutions, departments, and general education* (2nd ed.). San Francisco, CA: Jossey-Bass.

Another excellent volume in an excellent and easy-to-digest series in higher education assessment, this is a comprehensive guide to assessment activities in higher education that includes clear and empowering definitions of assessment. While Walvoord does not write specifically to communication studies faculty, she speaks directly to our interests and needs by providing guidance in assessment of both disciplinary and general education courses.

4

Creating Continuity through Common Syllabi and Grading Expectations

Syllabus Oversight(s)

Your department chair calls you into his office, pleased to inform you that your course has passed through the assessment recertification process with flying colors. But as you smile and offer a happy sigh of relief that you no longer have to think about assessment for a while, the chair bursts your bubble: "The committee had some feedback for us; they made a list of syllabi that didn't seem to be on the same page as the rest." Frustrated, you pick up the notes and review the names of a handful of faculty whose syllabi were not accessible for students with disabilities, did not include the learning objectives for the course, indicated they would grade on attendance when, by policy, they can only grade participation, and so forth. The final remarks of the committee, while still positive, hold an undertone of disappointment: "We feel confident that these syllabus oversights are indicative of previous lapses in organizational oversight, and we expect the materials we receive in the next recertification period to reflect a shared and consistent mission." You know there are other departments on campus clamoring for a share of the precious allotment of general education units, and it is important for you to demonstrate how this course, the one that helps to sustain your graduate program and employ many of your alumni as part-time faculty, is beyond reproach.

* * *

A common or shared course syllabus is one useful way to establish and sustain continuity across a large multisection course. Many of us, as individual instructors, are aware that the syllabus functions as a contract with our students, spelling out our expectations, helping students understand what they can expect to learn from the course, and so forth. A common syllabus can help a course coordinator work with instructors to identify and clearly communicate common grading expectations, helping to ensure that an A in one class looks similar to an A in another instructor's class. Moreover, where a course coordinator works with a large number of relatively inexperienced instructors, her or his use of a common syllabus can help shelter those instructors, through clear policies (whether regarding grade challenges or attendance policies), from unwarranted student complaints. While seeing the syllabus as a contract can be helpful to us—our students and ourselves—in that it reminds us of our shared responsibilities, there is a more nuanced and constitutive understanding of the syllabus that can serve our purposes here. For example, the syllabus does not just identify contact information or deadlines for assignments; it also helps to constitute or create the relationship between an instructor and her or his students. The sorts of information we include and how we mediate that information in class, online, and in office hours shape us as helpful, professional, or approachable (as well as quirky, charming, earnest, passionate, or otherwise). Similarly, a common syllabus is not limited to procedural details, but rather, it works to constitute a relationship between instructors and a course or program, as well as between instructors and students.

A common syllabus is a document that often specifies, at a minimum, the learning outcomes for the course, the means of assessment (e.g., types of assignments, percentages of the total grade, revision opportunities), significant college or university and department or program policies, and a tentative schedule of topics/lessons. The common syllabus should identify any elements that must be consistent from one section of the course to the next. For example, must students complete a particular amount of timed public speaking or write a minimum number of words? A syllabus might also include the major assignments for the course and instructions for them, if it is important for those items to be consistent across multiple sections. For example, it may be necessary to specify an informative speech and a persuasive speech, if these are essential to meeting course learning outcomes.

THE COORDINATOR AND THE COMMON SYLLABUS

As a document that encourages connection across faculty, the common syllabus functions as an artifact that shows your collective efforts at implementing program vision. To the extent that you, as a coordinator, invite discussion and revision of the common syllabus, this document can draw instructors of different experiences and academic ranks into conversation about learning outcomes, curriculum, and policies. Further, as a coordinator, you can review instructor syllabi to better understand where your colleagues embrace or struggle with the program vision (for example, where they add their own framing thoughts about the value of particular learning outcomes or where they haphazardly or incompletely include certain elements of the syllabus). This is an imperfect process, but it can be illuminating all the same.

For example, in reviewing instructor syllabi, course coordinators can learn quite a bit by what instructors omit or implement inconsistently. We might find that some instructors do not consistently follow a department or course "syllabus template" (often this results in missing elements or in a document that is incompletely accessible to students who use screen readers), which may indicate a lack of familiarity with recent department or program guidelines (as can happen when we rush to hire a part-time faculty member, suggesting that both the department chair and the course coordinator need to work together to orient instructors to program expectations). Or we might find that an instructor does not state course learning outcomes or states them but does not outline assignments that are consistent with these outcomes; in these cases, it may be that the instructor is using assignments she or he has developed for another program or school, or it may be that she or he doesn't fully understand her or his role as someone who has been contracted by the general education body on campus to provide this instruction (instead of as someone who might teach public speaking or some other disciplinary content as she or he wishes).

In orientation of faculty, then, it is essential to help instructors understand not only which aspects of the syllabus are malleable and which are not, but also the rationale or logic that informs any of the common policies or syllabus expectations. This can be a matter of sharing the consequences for not upholding these commonalities; for example, on Deanna's campus, the general education committee that reviews the public speaking course can request a more frequent recertification interval (or deny recertification of the course outright) if individual syllabi do not consistently include general education outcomes and policies. However, to focus only on this punitive element misses the larger issue of whether and what students are learning and encourages a negative understanding of assessment as an unfunded mandate. Ideally, policies become such by being reasonable and meaningful; they do not fall from the sky, and they are not issued to us on stone tablets. Educators compose policies for reasons; if we concur with these reasons, then we should discuss them among ourselves and with our students, and if we don't concur, then, through discussion, we can seek change to policies that are or seem irrelevant.

As a coordinator, you will find it helpful to establish some guidelines for consistency in instructors' syllabi. For this, we would recommend preparing either a template syllabus, so instructors can see a model of what you expect, or a syllabus checklist that includes required or suggested elements, which can help heighten instructors' awareness of how other supervisory readers will review their syllabi. This can be especially helpful where some or all course coordination activities may occur outside a given department or program (for example, in a dean's or chair's office, as is sometimes the case in community colleges); further, it is important for communication faculty to author templates or checklists for communication courses, so be sure to contribute to these processes as you are able. It is also possible to hold a meeting (for example, as part of orientation, or as part of a course GTAs enroll in before beginning classroom instruction) where you help instructors develop their syllabi in the light of their own values and goals, as mediated by college or university or other policy. The approach you choose will depend on your program size, how essential it is for syllabi to cohere along common guidelines, and the support you receive in this task. But it is essential you clarify what you require of all syllabi for this course, what you recommend, and what is optional.

Because we both often work with GTAs and part-time faculty who have few supported and structured occasions for continued professional growth, we find it helpful to provide a template syllabus that is already in an accessible format (so instructors who aren't as technologically savvy can focus more on the content of the syllabus than, for example, on understanding Microsoft Word's instructions for levels of heading). We then review this syllabus with instructors (in orientation, if they are GTAs, or as they are hired into part-time assignments) so they can see what must be on each syllabus for our continued general education certification, as well as where they can include additional details and requests of their own.

STRUCTURE VS. FLEXIBILITY

The syllabus, whether for an individual instructor in a single course or for a community of instructors working toward a common goal, functions as the platform for our vision, for what we hope we and our students will achieve in a given semester. Well crafted, this document can strengthen program vision (in moments where instructors engage each other and their students in dialogue about what elements of the syllabus mean and why they matter), and it can help to create continuity and community across multiple sections of a course. To this end, for a common syllabus to be effective, a course coordinator must appreciate and respond to a delicate balance between structure and flexibility — between common goals and vision and an individual instructor's need for creativity and integrity. Most of us entered postsecondary education because we care deeply not only about our respective disciplines, but also about student learning; it is not surprising that we hold strong feelings about our own autonomy as instructors as well, caring equally about how we teach and how students learn at least as much as what they learn. All instructors, as a matter of academic freedom, should have the ability to make their syllabi their own, even — and perhaps especially — in large coordinated courses with common syllabi.

The degree to which an instructor has flexibility with the syllabus usually depends on her or his experience with the course. As coordinators, we use template syllabi that are, apart from unique instructor information (for example, instructor name, office hours, etc.), basically complete and ready for use. This template is accessible — i.e., it is electronically available to students, it is editable, and it takes advantage of updated software features to indicate levels of heading and to clarify links and images. It includes the catalog description and student learning outcomes for the course, identifies one path through meeting the student learning outcomes (e.g., it includes reading selections, specific assignments, and a course calendar), and identifies required university policies regarding academic honesty and resources for students with disabilities. First-semester GTAs in our programs have very little flexibility, at least initially; we usually tell them that they cannot remove anything from the syllabus, but they might add materials (e.g., motivational quotes, additional requests regarding student conduct — such as whether to turn off cell phones, or other advice). We recommend following the template syllabus this first time teaching the course, but we do offer to review instructor-proposed modifications. More experienced instructors may use the template, but they are welcome to make revisions to it, so long as it remains compliant with university, department, and general education guidelines. Yet another way to address flexibility within a structured common syllabus would be to assign a certain amount of discretionary points to each instructor so she or he feels empowered to make some significant pedagogical decisions and assess their success.

ELEMENTS OF A COMMON SYLLABUS

While syllabi vary somewhat from campus to campus in style and format, there are some common elements that are especially useful for the development of a common syllabus for a coordinated course. Perhaps the first consideration, however, is whatever local customs and guidelines shape syllabi on your campus. For example, at San José State University and a number of other Silicon Valley campuses, syllabi are called "greensheets" and have historically been printed on pale green paper; as strange as it may sound, when Deanna prepared her dossier for tenure and promotion, she printed copies of all greensheets on that pale green paper. There is a growing interest in sustainability on many campuses; in many cases, departments are reducing copy allowances, asking instructors to make their syllabi available to students electronically. It may be that a syllabus template is unheard of in your program; in such cases, it may be wise to tread lightly, moving in baby steps toward more coherence across sections, one element at a time. In any event, your students', colleagues', and supervisors' expectations should inform the development of a common syllabus.

All syllabi in Deanna's department have a consistent structure; though they vary in style and content, they all follow this same order: title, section, and instructor, a contact information grid, course catalog description, instructor Web site (or use of course learning system) information, required text(s), add/drop policy, grading and assignments, university policies, and meeting schedule. A similar structure is shared by all core curriculum courses at Southern Illinois University; all syllabi include specifics about the instructor, the objectives, the course description, course polices (including the appeal process), and a course calendar. We do not intend to suggest that this is exactly how all syllabi should look, but rather, that your common syllabus should develop in consideration of what is appropriate for your campus community.

The structure of a common syllabus is important not only because it evolves from others' expectations, but also because it contributes to creating and shaping those expectations in a reciprocal process. While a consistent structure can be helpful to a coordinator who must review dozens of syllabi for compliance with a particular guideline or requirement, it is also helpful to students, in that it encourages a preferred reading process from them as they encounter other syllabi in your department or on your campus. As a faculty member, Deanna initially bristled at the notion of a department template when it was first discussed in faculty meetings; it felt unnecessarily restrictive to her (interestingly, most of her concerns were aesthetic). However, later, she marveled at students' ability to read syllabi across multiple courses; they could readily find, for example, the grading policy for her class, because these policies — though somewhat different from class to class — appeared in generally the same location of all department syllabi. What she thought she'd lost, in terms of freedom, she was able to reassert through other means (changing fonts, adding material the template didn't explicitly call for, and so on), and students gained in terms of order, clarity, and consistency.

Essentials

If we think of a syllabus as meaningful communication between an instructor and her or his students, then among the most important elements of that document are those areas that facilitate communication between them. At a minimum, syllabi should include the following:

- Name of the course
- Section number (if appropriate)
- Instructor's name and contact information (including email address, phone number, mode of preferred contact, office location, office hours)
- Course meeting days, times, and location

Providing space on a template syllabus for any information that might help students and professors communicate more consistently and effectively with one another, especially in times of emergency, will limit gaps or missing information and confusion or frustration.

Policies

Often this portion of the syllabus is established for faculty by the academic senates on their respective campuses; it is wise to provide space on a template syllabus (or indicate as items on a syllabus checklist) for any policies that must appear on all syllabi at your college or university. Typically, these policies include statements regarding student conduct and academic integrity, emergency procedures, or resources available to students with disabilities. You may also need to include any policy your campus or department may have regarding attendance, adding or dropping the course, grade forgiveness and attempts to retake the course for an improved grade, and so forth. As a coordinator, you should also guide faculty to include any policies that govern all sections of this course.

Textbooks and Other Reading Assignments

Textbook selection can be, but is not necessarily, a complicated process. While you gain a measure of continuity from a shared set of readings across instruc-

tors and sections, you risk stifling individual instructors' creativity and autonomy in the classroom. Instructors, whether GTAs or full professors, often have
a keen sense of their students' needs and how best to meet them, and textbooks,
no matter how well written, are often fodder for dissatisfaction and complaint.
It may be that instructors have a full range of texts and other readings to choose
from; it may be that, as a department or course, they must choose materials
from among a menu of options; it may be that instructors must use a particular
text. Or it may be that experienced instructors may choose materials as they
wish, and GTAs must use a particular, common text. If instructors are able to
select their own course readings, then they should include these on the syllabus
(preferably in whatever citation format they expect their students to use, for
purposes of modeling). If you have, whether as a coordinator or as a member of
a selection committee, chosen a common textbook or other common materials,
then these should appear on the common syllabus template or checklist.

Learning Outcomes or Objectives

An element of each syllabus, individual or common, is a listing of what the student
can expect to learn during the semester. This list may include learning objectives,
often phrased as "The student will be able to . . ." (or some variant) followed by a
particular skill, or learning outcomes. The use of the phrase "learning outcome"
as opposed to "objective" has been very useful to our work as course coordinators;
while it can be easy for instructors to misinterpret objectives as goals they would
like to achieve with their students (e.g., "cover Chapter Two"), learning outcomes
are much harder to confuse: What will students be able to do at the end of the
course? Many instructors, in describing learning objectives or outcomes, find it
helpful to consult Bloom's Taxonomy, as it helps them remember a broad range
of skills they might cultivate in their students, from recall and translation to syn-
thesis and evaluation. Typically, overarching course objectives focus on the higher
levels of Bloom's Taxonomy, on integrative and complex skills.

For large coordinated courses, it is common for other committees or groups
on campus to develop some of these learning outcomes — for example, the group
that oversees general education. Often, in such cases, a given department has applied (however long ago) to provide a course that would help students master
those learning outcomes; in this sense, the department and the instructors of
the course are agreeing to teach toward those outcomes, but they do not "own"
the curriculum or goals/direction for the course. It is also common for particular programs, courses, or instructors to develop additional learning outcomes for
the course. These additional outcomes should evolve from the mission or vision
of your program. For example, if, in your course, you and your colleagues work
toward a critical, social justice–oriented understanding of communication and
public advocacy, then it would make sense for all sections of a course to include a
learning outcome that involves greater appreciation (through selection of speech
topics or course readings) of cultural diversity. Or if it is part of your collective
vision to better prepare students for business and professional communication,

then you might include an additional learning outcome that specifies a degree of student mastery of PowerPoint or other presentational software.

These learning outcomes, both the ones you develop and the ones you inherit from other offices on campus, will form the core of the assessment efforts you undertake with faculty. If you and your colleagues assert that these are the learning outcomes for the course in your charge, then you (and, to some extent, your colleagues) will be responsible for demonstrating that students are, in fact, learning what you claim they are learning.

Assignments and Examinations

Assignments for the course should follow from the stated learning outcomes for the course. For example, if the outcomes specify that students should deliver at least three speeches on topics of social significance, then syllabi for the course should reflect this, not only in the learning outcomes portion of the syllabus, but also in the assignments and the points these assignments are worth. If you and your colleagues who teach the course agree that a nuanced understanding of diversity (or mastery of presentational software) is a key focus within the course, then assignments should reflect this emphasis.

Where you are working with instructors who have little teaching experience or familiarity with the discipline, it may help to include assignment descriptions in the template syllabus, so that they have some direction in terms of how to sequence assignments for skills-building and achieving learning outcomes. For example, on Deanna's campus, all public speaking sections must include at least three extemporaneous speeches on topics of social significance; these must, collectively, account for at least 50% of the course grade, include at least one opportunity for revision in light of peers' or instructor's feedback, and full-sentence outlines. First-semester GTAs assign, in order, a demonstrative speech, an informative speech, and a persuasive speech, concentrating first on outlining, then research, then argument and persuasion. These assignments carry increasing point values, so that each speech is worth more as students' speaking skills improve. Deanna stipulates these points in the template syllabus, though she make it possible for GTAs to assign portions of each speech grade in accordance with material they address with their students (for example, assigning 10% of a speech grade to creating a compelling visual aid or engaging in an interview with an expert on the topic). A coordinator could absolutely resequence these speeches in other ways; what is important is choosing a narrative structure for your coordinated course that helps students and faculty navigate that course successfully. Later, GTAs may request or develop modified speech assignments, so long as they are still consistent with general education guidelines — for example, a speech of values or a tribute speech.

What is important for creating continuity and community across a broad array of sections is establishing any points of connection you, your colleagues, and your students need for success in achieving course learning outcomes. This will likely mean setting a certain number and type of oral and written communication activities, examinations, or readings; where you, your program, or other offices on campus require an emphasis on time or ratio of total course points, this will mean greater specificity. As with assessment, though, it is important to invite instructors to participate, as appropriate, in the discussion about the content, relevance, structure, and function of each assignment — of all assignments, but especially those that cut across all sections.

Grading

Grading may appear as part of an assignments and examinations section, or as a separate section in its own right. Here instructors should clarify the grading expectations for the course. This may include some instructions to students as to how to format their work for the course (for example, the use of APA citation), or information about how the instructor will evaluate students' work (for example, for the presence of a concise, compelling thesis — and what "concise" and "compelling" mean). For courses that enroll large numbers of first-year students, it may help to include a grade monitoring form, especially for sections where instructors do not use a course learning system like BlackBoard or Desire2Learn; this form provides blanks where students can track their progress in the course and compute their grades at regular intervals if they wish. As a coordinator, you may find it helpful to provide instructors with a common rubric for grading oral or written work. This may appear as a description within the syllabus or as an attachment to assignment instructions that helps students (and instructors) understand what constitutes an A, a B, and so on, or it may mean that you provide instructors with a template for how they provide feedback to students on oral or written work (specifying categories of attention in grading — for example, organization of ideas or compelling expression/delivery — and perhaps point values).

This is an area of the syllabus where the tension between structure and freedom may be most palpable. Where instructors have experience and insight, they should, to the extent you are able to engage them productively in this way, have influence on the direction and scope of assignments in the course, so long as they continue to meet the learning outcomes the course must satisfy to continue to be recertified by others. Here it may help to build "play" into the template syllabus, identifying a certain percentage of the overall course grade that each instructor might allocate according to outcomes that are specific to her or his section, or by providing a menu of options instructors might choose from to satisfy learning outcomes (so that there is no single "correct" way to develop the course).

Calendar

The course calendar functions as the spine from which the course develops in the direction of the learning outcomes. It should include deadlines for the major assignments of the course, as well as any smaller assignments or exercises (for example, smaller speaking exercises or engagements, rough drafts, visits to the library) that help prepare students for success on these larger tasks. It should show the narrative logic of the course — the story that helps the course hang together as relevant and meaningful for students; discussion topics should lead logically and purposefully from one to the next, and each reading assignment should build on the previous assignment. Significant dates should appear on this calendar, including known campus closures, significant department events (for example, the intramural speech and debate tournament), and the date and time of the final examination period. It may help to note (or ask instructors to note) a time frame (e.g., approximately one week) within which students may reasonably expect to receive feedback on their coursework.

Extra Credit

So that there is consistency across all sections of this coordinated course, it may help you to provide instructors with a specific maximum percentage of extra credit they should make available to students. Extra-credit opportunities may be excellent occasions, where well planned, for students to attend and prepare analyses of on- and off-campus speakers, participate in organized research in communication studies, or engage in other relevant learning (for example, by participating in workshops in the campus communication center). Where extra credit assignments map clearly onto course learning outcomes, they may be an integral part of the course. However, extra-credit opportunities must not interfere with the assessment of the course by making it attractive for students to pass over important assignments/assessment activities.

STRATEGIES FOR CREATING COMMON GRADING EXPECTATIONS

While it can be difficult, and perhaps impossible, to create truly common grading expectations across a diverse group of instructors, attempts to do so, where well planned, can function as a means to build continuity across a large multi-section course. Grades can be a common point of comparison for students enrolled in a coordinated course, and it can be a challenge for a course coordinator if students perceive an instructor to be much "easier" or "harder" than others (as such perceptions often give rise to complaints to the department chair and other offices on campus, classroom management challenges, and so on). Discussions regarding what instructors expect their students to be able to do on a given assignment, as well as what constitutes different levels of quality (from A to F), are occasions where a course coordinator can introduce any institutional or departmental expectations regarding grading, share any relevant research on grading for that particular subject matter or those assignments, and invite conversation about expectations that can help draw instructors of the course into alignment with one another. For example, orientation of new instructors or GTAs might include a session where they can screen or read student work against a rubric and discuss the feedback they might provide and the grade they might issue this student; this is even common practice during some community college interviews, where colleagues wish to gain insight into a prospective new instructor's approach to evaluation (see Chapter 6).

In addition to discussions about grading expectations, course coordinators might include any items related to grading that they expect to remain consistent across all sections of the course. For example, the common syllabus Deanna provides to GTAs includes instructions on submitting work to Turnitin.com, as well as a policy that indicates that the instructor will not accept late work except in cases of "extreme personal emergency," and a grade monitoring form. Each of these is an attempt to scaffold new GTAs through their first semester of instruction. The instructions for Turnitin.com help field students' questions about the process, and the service itself helps minimize instances of plagiarism; the late-work policy allows for humane treatment of students' unexpected crises but otherwise minimizes absenteeism on speech days (important on a campus where academic senate policy prohibits grading attendance); and the grade monitoring form encourages students' attention to their progress in the course and provides the instructor and students with a context for engaging in a productive conversation about assignments and course grades. The late-work policy is a relief to Deanna; over the years, it has drastically reduced the number of conversations she has needed to have with new instructors who have allowed so many "make-up" speeches that they cannot complete the remainder of the course content within the days remaining in the semester.

It is also possible to include language in a syllabus that gives instructors and students a common vocabulary for the quality of students' work. For example, in an upper-division writing course Deanna coordinated for many years, a number of the instructors still use the following language from the template syllabus:

> You should strive for five qualities in your writing: (1) Your writing should be COMPELLING (i.e., it should articulate a claim — make a point, be purposeful — and an audience for that claim); (2) Your writing should be COMPLETE (i.e., it should address all aspects of the assignment — it should be sufficiently developed); (3) Your writing should be COHERENT (i.e., your argument should logically progress from one paragraph to the next); (4) Your writing should be CONCISE (i.e., it should be richly developed but not meandering or repetitive); and (5) Your writing should be CORRECT (i.e., it should be free of grammatical, typographical, and source citation errors, as well as fallacious reasoning). I will look to these five criteria as I read and respond to your written work in this course. You should know that, while I will always read your papers for your argument, your paper is only as strong as the sentence-level choices you make to create it (in other words, never underestimate the power of careful proofreading).

While it was always vexing for Deanna, as a course coordinator, to know she could not guarantee that instructors would see eye to eye about the quality of students' work (that they might "let slide" aspects of students' writing she felt were crucial to their success in future courses and employment), this sort of statement gave rise to dialogue with one another about how each approaches these qualities with students, and later to common policies regarding a maximum number of errors in students' writing and a minimum number of peer-reviewed sources for each assignment.

Even where a course coordinator provides criteria for a given assignment (see, for example, the demonstration speech assignment instructions included for reference on pages 61–62)—where students can expect to earn a C if there are "no serious deviations" from the assignment requirements, a B if they are more than effective in meeting the assignment requirements, and an A if they meet the assignment requirements "exceptionally well"—it can be very difficult to draw instructors into alignment about particular grades without either spending considerable time together in holistic grading sessions or reducing the assignment to the presence or absence of particular qualities. We have sought a balance: While one cannot bring everyone into exact alignment, one can encourage open dialogue about grading expectations and can encourage instructors to remain consistent in their grading from one assignment to the next, so that students can earn an A or a B without feeling as though they are tracking moving targets. To encourage consistency in grading and to help instructors learn to provide substantive qualitative feedback to students, Deanna asks GTAs to use a common rubric. While not highly structured, this rubric does highlight aspects of assignments that are appropriate to their course text and program vision. This rubric, as well as the speech assignment to which it corresponds, and a related outline grading checklist, are included on pages 61–64 for reference.

SAMPLE: SPEECH ASSIGNMENT INSTRUCTIONS

Speech #1: Demonstration

Purpose of Assignment

The primary purpose of demonstration speaking is to help clarify a complex process, idea, or event for your audience. In other words, in this approximately five-minute speech, you are to demonstrate (or teach us) how to do something; what you choose to demonstrate can be as simple or as complicated as you like, so long as it has something to do with your culture. You are welcome to define culture broadly — i.e., in addition to your racial background or ethnic heritage, you might also consider your gender, sexuality, age, or other co-cultural affiliations (e.g., musician, skater, cheerleader, and so on). Keep in mind that effective use of visual aids will likely help your audience better understand and learn what you choose to demonstrate. Please explore your creative options (within the guidelines of common sense and university policy). Refer to the text as you see fit. Your grade will be based on the following:

Requirements

- Your topic should be informative and challenging to this audience.
- The speech should be **approximately five minutes**.
- Delivery is to be extemporaneous. Use up to four note cards. These are to be turned in following your speech upon your instructor's request.
- The introduction and conclusion should be fully developed.
- There should be a definite, logical transition bridging each component of the speech.
- Each main point should be clearly stated and developed.
- Use at least **one visual aid** according to the guidelines presented in the text.
- Adhere to the principles of clear explanation. Use organizers (signposts, enumeration, acronyms, slogans), emphasis cues, and figurative analogies. Also use definitions where appropriate.
- Be prepared to answer questions from the audience after the conclusion of your speech.
- A **typed, full-sentence** outline (following the correct format on the outline checklist) is required and should be submitted on the day of your

speech. The following elements are to be included and **labeled in the margin or where appropriate**:

- Organizational pattern
- Specific purpose and primary audience outcome
- Thesis statement
- Three functions of your introduction and conclusion
- Transitions between main points
- A reference list in APA format

- Your presentation skills should include:
  - Natural and conversational delivery
  - Appropriate oral style
  - **Extemporaneous mode** using speech notes (note cards or key word outline)
  - Effective vocal and physical delivery skills
  - Effective use of visual aids
- **Bring videotape** the day of your speech per your instructor's request.

Criteria for Evaluation

To receive a passing grade for this assignment you need to make an earnest attempt at meeting the above requirements. In other words, if there are no serious deviations from the above requirements, expect to receive about 70% of the possible points (C range). If you not only meet the minimal requirements but carry them out well, expect to receive 80–89% (B range). If you carry them out exceptionally well, expect to receive 90–100% (A range) of the possible points. Total points for the assignment will be weighted as follows:

Introduction	25 points
Organization	25 points
Development	25 points
Conclusion	25 points
Delivery	25 points
Total	125 points
(Outline:	25 points)

SAMPLE: SPEECH OUTLINE GRADING CHECKLIST

Speech #1: Outline Checklist

Rough Draft Due: _____ Outline Due: _____

I have attached this sheet to my final outline and have included my rough draft.

- ☐ 4 I have used **full, single sentences** (not paragraphs) on all components (you may use multiple sentences in the intro and conclusion).
- ☐ 3 I have included, prior to the introduction: Topic, Organizational Pattern, Specific Purpose, Primary Audience Outcome, and Thesis Statement.
- ☐ 3 My thesis statement is stated as a **single declarative sentence** that emphasizes the central focus or idea of my speech, and has been integrated into my introduction.
- ☐ 3 My introduction includes **Attention Getter, Psychological Orientation** (puts my topic in a context that is relevant to my audience), and **Logical Orientation** (establishes my credibility and previews my main points).
- ☐ 3 My conclusion includes **Logical Closure** (reviews my main points and summarizes my argument), **Psychological Closure** (connects to my introduction and reminds audience why my topic is relevant to them), and **Clincher.**
- ☐ 2 I have used the correct format for **numeration** and **indented** my points and sub-points properly (I, A, 1, a, etc).
- ☐ 2 I have included **full-sentence connectives** between each of my main points.
- ☐ 1 I submitted a rough draft of my outline.
- ☐ 1 I have taken the peer comments from my rough draft seriously and have made the necessary adjustments on my final outline.
- ☐ 1 I have **proofread** this outline for spelling and grammatical errors.
- ☐ 1 My points are **mutually exclusive**, and I have no more than five sub-points for each main point.
- ☐ 1 I have attached a separate APA style reference sheet at the back of my outline if I have cited any sources.

Outline: _____ /25

SAMPLE: SPEECH GRADING RUBRIC

Speech 1: Demonstration Speech

Introduction: Strengths: ?s/suggestions/not-so-strengths

Attention-getting material
_____ out of _____ pts

Thematic statement
_____ out of _____ pts

Preview
_____ out of _____ pts

Establishing credibility
_____ out of _____ pts

Organization: Strengths: ?s/suggestions/not-so-strengths

Logical organization
_____ out of _____ pts

Development: Strengths: ?s/suggestions/not-so-strengths

Appropriate development
_____ out of _____ pts

Conclusion: Strengths: ?s/suggestions/not-so-strengths

Summary/Review
_____ out of _____ pts

Closure
_____ out of _____ pts

Delivery: Strengths: ?s/suggestions/not-so-strengths

Effective extemporaneous
delivery
_____ out of _____ pts

       Total: _____ out of _____ points possible; Grade: _____
       Outline: _____ out of _____ points possible

Peer Feedback: _____ out of _____ points possible

SAMPLE COMMON SYLLABI

Perhaps one of the most useful exercises you can undertake as a course coordinator is to explore syllabi for other coordinated courses, from earlier iterations of the course you currently coordinate and from other, similar courses at other, similar institutions. These syllabi will illuminate how they have evolved from particular campus exigencies. To the extent you are able, speak with the people who played a role in creating these syllabi. It may be tempting for course coordinators, especially new ones, to assume that we have little to do with the shape and direction of a coordinated course — that it somehow exists outside or beyond us. But, as a review of course syllabi will show, course coordinators leave an imprint on the courses they supervise; their personalities and their expertise will shine through, even if it is only in small ways. Though a syllabus might feel like a technical document — a contract that stipulates deadlines and other formulaic bits of information — it also constitutes relationships. Earlier, we discussed the ways a syllabus shapes the relationship between students and teachers, facilitating communication and understanding between these two groups. Syllabi also constitute relationships between colleagues; through dialogue about elements of the course syllabus, instructors align along vision and mission. Moreover, the syllabus is one artifact that illuminates our efforts as scholars to define our discipline. In even our smallest curricular decisions, we identify for ourselves and our colleagues what is important about communication studies and how we might best teach and learn this discipline. Several sample common syllabi follow, and it may be useful to consider them in comparison with the structure and needs of your specific program.

SAMPLE: PUBLIC SPEAKING SYLLABUS #1

The syllabus that follows was developed by Heidi Hamilton, who directs the public speaking course at Emporia State University. At her institution, every instructor is required to use the same textbook, and they have agreed on a minimum number of speeches and a requirement that students give at least one informative speech and one persuasive speech, but the rest of the syllabus is up to each instructor's discretion. Note that she uses speaking groups to organize her students' speeches and that she provides guidelines for appropriate visual aids directly on the syllabus. Also note the clear articulation of exactly what will be assessed in terms of attendance and participation.

SP101: Public Speaking
Fall 2010

Dr. Heidi Hamilton
Emporia State University
Office Hours: 11–12 M; 11–1 T; 1–2 W; 11–12 F; and by appointment

Course Objectives

This course provides an opportunity for you to engage in the theory and practice of public discourse. The goal is to develop proficiency in public speaking skills through the understanding of audience, purpose, situation, organization, reasoning, and delivery.

Text. O'Hair, D., et al. *A speaker's guidebook: Text and reference*. 4th ed. Boston, MA: Bedford/St. Martin's, 2010.

Assignments. Each assignment will be explained in detail later. Total of 580 points possible.

Self-introduction presentation	50
Informative presentation	100
Persuasive presentation	100
Final major presentation	75
Humorous presentation	25
Quizzes (30 points each)	90
Homework; 1–2 minute speeches	45
Peer evaluations	45
Participation	50

***You are required to give all five presentations to pass the class. Failure to give even one of those presentations will result in an F in the course.

Grading. The following percentage grading scale will be used. Work that meets the minimum requirements of an assignment and is not lacking is deserving of a C. A higher grade is awarded to work that goes above or beyond those minimum standards. You must complete all assignments to successfully fulfill the course requirements. I will not use the plus/minus grading option.

A = 90–100   B = 80–89   C = 70–79   D = 60–69   F = 59 and below

Course Policies

1. Academic dishonesty: Academic dishonesty includes but is not limited to activities such as cheating and plagiarism. Any student who knowingly uses another person's work as though that work were his/her

own or any student who knowingly permits another student to use her/his work will be given a grade of F for the course and subject to discipline in accordance with the ESU Academic Dishonesty Policy.

2. Students with special needs: ESU will make reasonable accommodations for persons with documented disabilities. Students need to contact the Director of Disability Services and the professor as early in the semester as possible to ensure that classroom and academic accommodations are implemented in a timely fashion. All communication between students, the Office of Disability Services, and the professor will be strictly confidential.

3. No makeup presentations: You will be expected to deliver your presentation the day you are assigned. If you are uncertain which day you are speaking, you should come prepared to speak the first day of that assignment. Each student will be assigned to a speaking group that will remain intact for the semester. Each member of a speaking group will present according to the attached schedule. If you know you will be absent for an excused reason (athletic event, school sponsored field trip) for which I will be notified by the coach, adviser, etc., then you should contact me before speaking groups are assigned, so you can be placed in an appropriate group. Missed presentations (for any but the most dire circumstances) will result in failure of the course. If at all possible, if you believe you have a dire circumstance, you should contact me prior to class.

4. Late assignments: No late assignments will be accepted without prior arrangement with me. Prior does not mean five minutes before class. Prior consultation does not guarantee an extension. All late assignments will be reduced by 10% of the total per day (not per class); thus, late assignments cannot receive an A.

5. Tardiness: I start class on time, and I expect you to be there at the start of class. Walking in late disrupts the class and is a sign of disrespect to both me and the other students. If you are late on a speaking day, make sure to not walk in while another student is giving her or his speech. If excessive tardiness is observed, the formula of four tardies equals one absence will be applied.

6. All written assignments, including outlines, should be typed (1-inch margins, 12-inch font), and properly cited following the MLA or APA guidelines. Handwritten assignments will not be accepted. Please spell-check <u>and</u> proofread for spelling and grammar.

7. Cell phones: <u>Turn off</u> cell phones upon entering the classroom. There should be no text messaging, listening to music, etc. during class time. If any of this occurs, it will be noted, and will affect your over-all participation grade.

8. Occasionally, I may need to contact the class or an individual student via email. I suggest that you check your stumail account regularly. While I will reply to all emails confirming that I have received them, it is <u>your responsibility</u> to make sure that I receive your email (and any attachment that you might be sending with it). Assignments sent via email that do not arrive to me on the due date and are not in a readable format on the due date <u>will be regarded as late with the relevant point deduction</u>.

9. We will meet during the scheduled final examination period. Do not make plans to leave campus prior to the final. No early finals will be given. It is the policy of our department to follow the final examination schedule.

10. Visual aids: Visual aids may not violate any law or University policy (thus, no alcohol, no firearms or other weapons, etc.). They may not endanger fellow students; consequently no living visual aids will be allowed. Always check with me if you have any questions prior to your presentation day. I reserve the right to disallow the visual aid if there is no advance notice.

<u>Attendance and Participation</u>. Attendance is important, as public speaking assumes the existence of an audience to which one is speaking. Class members comprise that audience for other students. You will be expected to listen atten-tively and respectively to other students' presentations.

Additionally, this is an activity-centered class. Much of our learning will oc-cur through class discussions, exercises, and viewing experiences, which cannot be made up. My job is to offer you an enriching educational experience; your job is to be here to take advantage of it and to enhance the classroom experience for all of us. Thoughtful preparation, regular attendance, and active participation are strongly encouraged.

Attendance is a minimum requirement, and alone does not guarantee a good participation grade. The only excused absences are for campus-related activities for which I have received notification (for example, from a coach) or due to death or major illness for which I have received prior notification. Excessive absences, even if excused, can still negatively affect your participation grade.

Students who miss 20% (eight class periods) or more of our scheduled class meetings will not receive credit for the course. (A student may withdraw if the deadline for withdrawing from classes has not passed or, if that deadline has passed, will receive an F for the course.)

- To receive 50 points: You must miss no more than two class periods during the term. You should also illustrate your knowledge of the material from assigned chapters and actively participate in discussion without dominating discussion. In this case, soliciting responses from other students and asking questions are two ways to actively involve others. All students are expected to be on time with every assignment.

- To receive 45 points: You must miss no more than three class periods during the term. You should also illustrate your knowledge of the material from assigned chapters and actively participate in discussion without dominating discussion. In this case, soliciting responses from other students and asking questions are two ways to actively involve others. All students are expected to be on time with every assignment.

- To receive 40 points: You must miss no more than four class periods during the term. You should have read and have an understanding of the material. You will answer and raise questions. As with A work, your nonverbal behavior will be such that it is obvious to me that you are alert, interested, and prepared for class each day. All assigned homework must be completed.

- To receive 35 points: You must miss no more than five class periods. You must show a grasp of the material. You will answer and raise questions. As with A and B work, your nonverbal behavior will be such that it is obvious to me that you are alert, interested, and prepared for class each day.

- <u>To receive 30 points</u>: You must miss no more than six class periods. Participation will be low, but the high level of interest will still be evident.
- <u>Lower</u>: It is of course possible to receive less than 30 points if absences become excessive or participation does not exist or negatively impacts the class.

Outlines

As will be discussed in class and in the textbook, you should be writing your speech in outline form. If you do not have an outline the day that you speak, this indicates to me one of a couple of things: (1) You didn't write your speech, but instead you just stood up and made it up as you went along; or (2) You wrote your speech but then didn't practice at all (as you would have presumably printed your outline out in order to create your notes before you could practice). Your outline indicates to me how you constructed the speech and what you had planned to say. It is thus a crucial part of the grading process.

- If you don't have an outline at the time of your speech, 10% of the total presentation points will be deducted. If you don't get your outline to me by 5 PM the day of your speech, 50% of the total presentation points will be deducted.

Homework/One- to Two-Minute Speeches

The completion of a variety of short homework assignments is expected. Below is a listing of these assignments and their point value. Due dates are listed in the course schedule, and each assignment will be explained later.

Informative topic selection	5
Persuasive topic selection	5
Final topic selection	5
Graded impromptu speech	10
Classmate award speech	20

Tentative Course Schedule

8/18	Introduction to course	
8/20	Communication process & Ethics	Ch. 1 & 5
8/23	Your first presentation	Ch. 2
	Self-introduction presentation assigned	
8/25	Delivery	Ch. 17, 18, & 19
8/27	Outlining; Listening	Ch. 13 & 4
	Peer evaluation assignment explained	
8/30	Confidence; Impromptu speeches	Ch. 3
9/1	**Self-introduction presentations [A, B]**	
9/3	**Self-introduction presentations [C, D]**	
9/6	*Labor Day — no class*	
9/8	Informative speaking; organizational designs	Ch. 23
	Informative presentation assigned	
9/10	Informative speaking continued	
	Quiz #1	
9/13	Audience and situation analysis	Ch. 6
9/15	Audience analysis/narrowing your topic exercise	
	Informative topic due	
9/17	Research	Ch. 9 & 10
9/20	Supporting materials	Ch. 8
9/22	Structuring/organizing; oral citation exercise	Ch. 11 & 12; review checklist boxes in Ch. 8

***Extra Credit Opportunity: Bonner & Bonner Diversity Lecture, 7 pm		
9/24	Oral citation exercise continued	
9/27	Visual aids	Ch. 20, 21, & 22
9/29	Thesis statements; introductions; credibility	pp. 119–123; Ch. 14
10/1	Introductions continued; conclusions	Ch. 15
10/4	**Quiz #2**	
	Making verbal pauses "taboo" exercise	
10/6	**Informative presentations [C]**	
10/8	**Informative presentations [D]**	
10/11	**Informative presentations [B]**	
10/13	**Informative presentations [A]**	
10/15	*Fall Break — no class*	
10/18	Persuasive speaking	Ch. 24
	Persuasive presentation assigned	
10/20	Fact, value, and policy propositions	pp. 391–400
10/22	Reasoning	pp. 401–407
10/25	Persuasive organizational designs	Ch. 26
	Persuasive topic due	
10/27	Audience analysis exercise	
10/29	Language use	Ch. 16
11/1	Language use continued; podium use	
11/3	TBA	
11/5	**Graded Impromptus**	
11/8	Workshopping your persuasive presentation	

11/10	**Persuasive presentations [D]**	
11/12	**Persuasive presentations [A]**	
11/15	**Persuasive presentations [B]**	
11/17	**Persuasive presentations [C]**	
11/19	Special Occasion speaking	Ch. 27
	Final major presentation assigned	
11/22	**Quiz #3**	
11/24	*Thanksgiving break*	
11/26	*Thanksgiving break*	
11/29	Giving a classmate an award exercise	
	Final major presentation topic due	
12/1	**Award speeches** — exercise continued	
12/3	Workshopping your final major presentation	
12/6	**Final major presentation [B, A]**	
12/8	**Final major presentation [A, C]**	
12/10	**Final major presentation [C, D]**	
	Course evaluations	
	Humorous presentation assigned	
Final Exam — Humorous Presentations		
Thursday, December 16		**10:10–12**

SOURCE: Personal correspondence with Heidi Hamilton, December 13, 2010. Used with permission.

SAMPLE: PUBLIC SPEAKING SYLLABUS #2

The following is the common syllabus for public speaking from Deanna at San José State University, which is designed to provide a highly structured template for GTAs. Note the care with which the common syllabus represents the campus resources like Student Technology Services and the SJSU Writing Center. The common syllabus ensures that all students are informed about these resources no matter what material their instructor chooses to emphasize. Also note how the course schedule includes a column for Course Learning Outcome(s), ensuring a demonstrable link between CLOs and class work.

San José State University

Communication Studies

Comm 20, Public Speaking, Section xxx, Spring 2010

Instructor:	GTA
Office location:	HGH 25x
Telephone:	408-924-xxxx
Email:	yourname@someserver.com
Office hours:	Mondays and Wednesdays x:xx to x:xx AM, and by appointment
Class days/time:	Mondays and Wednesdays x:xx to x:xx AM
Classroom:	HGH/CL xxx
General Education Category	A1

Catalog Description

Speaking principles of rhetoric applied to oral communication; selecting, analyzing, adapting, organizing, and delivering ideas effectively.

Class Material Communication

Copies of the course syllabus, lecture material, and major assignments may be found on the class Blackboard site. You are responsible for regularly checking class materials and messages sent via the Blackboard announcements page.

Course Goals

Effective public speaking skills are essential for members of a democratic society. In this course, you will develop strategies for designing well-organized, researched, extemporaneous speeches on topics of social significance adapted to a diverse audience. The speaking engagements, in-class activities, small-group discussions, and speeches allow you to practice and critique your oral communication skills as well as observe and evaluate those of others. Readings, lectures, written assignments, and class discussions serve as resources for you as you develop your public speaking abilities and become more at ease when addressing an audience.

Course Learning Objectives

After successfully completing this course, you will:

L.O.1 Identify and assess socially significant and intellectual topics, then compose and deliver extemporaneous oral presentations (using note cards or key-word outlines) on those topics.

L.O.2 Engage in critical and analytical listening.

L.O.3 Analyze audiences, adapt oral presentations to diverse audiences, and use that information to accomplish the purpose of the speech.

L.O.4 Assume the ethical responsibilities of the public speaker, including basic understanding of the economic, legal, and social issues surrounding the access and use of information.

Required Texts and Readings

Sprague, J., Stuart, D., & Bodary, D. (2010). *The speaker's handbook* (9th ed.). Belmont, CA: Wadsworth.

Department of Communication Studies. (2009). *Communication studies course packet* (4th ed.). Mason, OH: Thomson Custom Publishing.

Kirszner, L. G., & Mandell, S. R. (2008). *The pocket Wadsworth handbook* (4th ed.). Boston, MA: Wadsworth Cengage Learning.

Other Equipment Requirements

One standard VHS videocassette.
One package of 4 × 6-inch index cards.

Library Liaison

The Communication Studies Department encourages vigorous and ethical research as part of information literacy for all of its students. For assistance in the library, go to the King Library Reference Desk and/or utilize the Communication Research Guide available on the Library Web site.

Classroom Protocol

If you arrive late to class on a speech day, please wait outside until you hear applause before entering. Please also be aware of your nonverbal behavior on speech days. It can be difficult to deliver a speech when your audience members are texting, writing notes, doing other homework, or chatting. Please be a good audience member and respectfully listen to speeches.

Dropping and Adding

You are responsible for understanding the policies and procedures about add/drops, academic renewal, and similar topics found on the SJSU Advising Hub Web site.

Assignments and Grading Policies

To receive full credit, all assignments should be typed, proofread, appropriately referenced, and turned in on the day they are due. Homework assignments count toward participation unless otherwise noted, and may be assigned without being listed on the class schedule at the end of this syllabus. In order to complete the three major speeches (demonstrative, informative, and persuasive) and their self-evaluations on time, you are required to turn in a hard copy in class and an electronic copy to turnitin.com by 11:59 pm on the due date.

Participation and Late Work Policy

Public speaking is an intensive, skills-building class for most students — a class that involves and evolves from our collective discussions and risk-taking. This means that it is in your best interest to attend and actively participate in each and every session. However, should an emergency arise, please do everything in your power to contact me prior to missing class so that we might try to make alternative arrangements. Please be aware that I will only accept late work in cases of extreme personal emergency; furthermore, such work may be subject to a 50% grade penalty or additional, elaborative assignments.

Assignments and Grade Monitoring Form

Speeches	Demonstrative	____out of 125 points
	Informative	____out of 150 points
	Persuasive	____out of 225 points
Outlines	Demonstrative Outline	____out of 25 points
	Informative Outline	____out of 50 points
	Persuasive Outline	____out of 75 points
Evaluations	Self-Evaluation 1 (500 words)	____out of 20 points
	Self-Evaluation 2 (500 words)	____out of 20 points
Responses	Demonstrative Responses	____out of 20 points
	Informative Responses	____out of 20 points
	Persuasive Responses	____out of 20 points
Tests	Midterm	____out of 50 points
	Final	____out of 50 points
Engagements	Engagement 1	____out of 20 points
	Engagement 2	____out of 20 points
	Engagement 3	____out of 20 points
	Engagement 4	____out of 20 points
	Engagement 5	____out of 20 points
Participation	Assignments, freewrites, etc.	____out of 50 points
Total		____out of 1000 points

Your final grade is based on the following point scale:

A = 1000–940 points	A- = 939–900 points	B+ = 899–870 points
B = 869–840 points	B- = 839–800 points	C+ = 799–770 points
C = 769–740 points	C- = 739–700 points	D+ = 699–670 points
D = 669–640 points	D- = 639–600 points	F = 559 and fewer points

Note: Please remember that in order to receive general education credit for this course, you must complete it with a grade of C or better.

University Policies

Academic integrity

Your own commitment to learning, as evidenced by your enrollment at San José State University, and the University's Academic Integrity Policy requires you to be honest in all your academic course work. I will uphold San José State University's policy on academic honesty, found at the Office of Student Conduct and Ethical Development Web site. Consequently, an instance of academic misconduct (e.g., plagiarism, cheating, taking credit for others' work, submitting work for another course as work for this one, etc.) will likely result in a failing course grade.

Campus Policy in Compliance with the Americans with Disabilities Act

If you need course adaptations or accommodations because of a disability, or if you need to make special arrangements in case the building must be evacuated, please make an appointment with me as soon as possible. Presidential Directive 97-03 requires that students with disabilities requesting accommodations must register with the DRC (Disability Resource Center) to establish a record of their disability.

Student Technology Resources

Computer labs for student use are available in the new Academic Success Center. In addition, computers are available in the Martin Luther King Library. The COMM Lab also has computers available for student use. A wide variety of audio-visual equipment is available for student checkout from Media Services.

Communication Studies Lab and Resource Center

Tutors for the lab are recruited from well-qualified communication studies graduate-level and upper-division students. The lab provides resources for enrichment and assistance for those enrolled in all Communication Studies classes. Lab hours vary by semester and are posted on the COMM Lab wiki.

Learning Assistance Resource Center

The Learning Assistance Resource Center is designed to assist students in the development of their full academic potential and to motivate them to become self-directed learners. The center provides support services, such as skills as-sessment, individual or group tutorials, subject advising, learning assistance, summer academic preparation, and basic skills development.

SJSU Writing Center

The SJSU Writing Center is staffed by professional instructors and upper-division or graduate-level writing specialists from each of the seven SJSU colleges. The writing specialists are well trained to assist all students at all levels within all disciplines to become better writers.

Comm 20, Public Speaking, Spring 2010 Class Schedule

This schedule is subject to change with fair notice. I will announce any changes in class.

Date	Description	Reading	Assignments	CLOs
1/27/2010	Introduction and course overview	Chapter 1		
2/1/2010	Ethics and overcoming fear	Chapters 3 and 4	Student info sheet	
2/3/2010	Listening and modes of delivery	Chapters 2 and 23	Engagement 1: Cultural Artifact	
2/8/2010	Planning and topic selection	Chapters 5 and 6		
2/10/2010	Audience Analysis and research	Chapters 7 and 8	Engagement 2: Audience Analysis	1,2
2/15/2010	No class meeting	Cancelled: Mandatory Furlough Day Due to Budget Cuts	Grammar worksheet due	

Date	Description	Reading	Assignments	CLOs
2/17/2010	Transforming ideas into speech points and organization Exam 1	Chapters 9 and 10 Exam 1	Demonstration Speech Topics due	
2/22/2010	Outlining	Chapter 11		
2/24/2010	Introduction, connectives, and conclusions	Chapters 12, 13, and 14		
3/1/2010	Speech 1	Demonstrative Speeches	Outlines and Peer Reviews	1,2,3
3/3/2010	Speech 1	Demonstrative Speeches	Outlines and Peer Reviews	1,2,3
3/8/2010	Speech 1	Demonstrative Speeches	Outlines and Peer Reviews	1,2,3
3/10/2010	APA citations Exam 2	Small Group Instructional Discussion (SGID) Exam 2	Self-Evaluations due	4
3/15/2010	Supporting Material, Language, and Style	Chapters 15 and 17	APA citation sheet due	4
3/17/2010	Attention and Interest and Credibility; Informative Strategies	Chapters 18, 19, and 21		

Date	Description	Reading	Assignments	CLOs
3/22/2010	Practice Sessions and Presentation Aids	Chapters 24 and 27	Engagement 3 due: Outlining Module from the Comm Lab, Informative Speech Topics due	4
3/24/2010	Vocal and Physical Delivery	Chapters 25 and 26	Engagement 4: Oral Interpretation	2,3
3/29/2010	No class meeting	Spring Recess		
3/31/2010	No class meeting	Spring Recess; Cesar Chavez Day		
4/5/2010	Speech 2	Informative Speeches	Outlines and Peer Responses	1-4
4/12/2010	Speech 2	Informative Speeches	Outlines and Peer Responses	1-4
4/14/2010	Speech 2	Informative Speeches	Outlines and Peer Responses	1-4
4/19/2010	Speech 2	Informative Speeches	Outlines and Peer Responses	1-4
4/21/2010	Motivational Appeals and Answering Questions Exam 3	Chapters 20 and 29	Self-Evaluations due	
4/26/2010	Persuasive Strategies	Chapter 22	Engagement 5: Sell it!	3

Date	Description	Reading	Assignments	CLOs
4/28/2010	Reasoning	Chapter 16	Persuasive Speech Topics due	
5/3/2010	Adaptation Exam 4	Chapter 28	<u>Proofreading guide due</u>	
5/5/2010	Speech 3	Persuasive Speeches	Outlines and Peer Responses	1-4
5/10/2010	Speech 3	Persuasive Speeches	Outlines and Peer Responses	1-4
5/12/2010	Speech 3	Persuasive Speeches	Outlines and Peer Responses	1-4
5/17/2010	Speech 3	Persuasive Speeches	Outlines and Peer Responses	1-4
5/24/2010	Finals	Final Examination		

SAMPLE: HUMAN COMMUNICATION SYLLABUS #1

The following sample is a common syllabus from Jason Teven at California State University, Fullerton. Notice that Jason's syllabus refers to the section instructor as "your instructor" as opposed to being written in the first person (in which the instructor is "I"). This subtly highlights the common nature of the syllabus, and its function in continuity across sections, for the student.

HCOM 100 — INTRODUCTION TO HUMAN COMMUNICATION, 3 units

Fall 2010, Days and Meeting Times of your class and LOCATION

INSTRUCTOR:

OFFICE:

PHONE:

EMAIL:

OFFICE HOURS:

TEXT

O'Hair, D., & Wiemann, M. (2009). *Real communication: An introduction.* Boston, MA: Bedford/St. Martin's. ISBN: 978-0-312-53616-9.

Course Description

This course is an introduction to the theory and practice of human communication. The focus of the course is on learning and practicing the skills needed to improve the quality of interpersonal communication in a variety of contexts, such as in relationships, groups, organizations, public settings, and diverse cultures. You are expected to practice skills in class and in everyday communication outside of class. This course fulfills the General Education requirement for the core competency of category I.A, Oral Communication.

This is a course in basic human communication — it comprises three major components of the communication field: interpersonal, small group, and public speaking. The basic public speaking aspect is designed to develop oral communication skills of students through the delivering of speeches, participating in group activities, completing assigned readings, and writing brief peer critiques. The interpersonal component will focus on the pragmatic aspects of relationships, including those relationships between friends, family, co-workers, and significant others.

Course Objectives

Through participation in assigned activities, students will achieve the following objectives:

- To develop an understanding of some of the basic concepts operating in the communication process and to develop an understanding of cultural awareness and cultural viewpoints.
- To increase students' "relational sensitivity." Only as we become more socially sensitive can we recognize the various conditions that help and/ or hinder the process of interpersonal communication.
- To increase students' "behavioral flexibility." Only as we become more flexible in our behaviors can we select the appropriate behavioral responses to specific communication situations.
- To increase students' awareness of their own behaviors in interpersonal settings.
- To develop and improve listening skills.
- To provide students with the knowledge, skill, and motivation necessary to become competent communicators.
- To enhance competence in managing communication anxiety/ apprehension.
- To analyze audience characteristics and adapt a topic appropriately for a particular audience.
- To distinguish between informative, persuasive, and special occasion speeches, recognizing the unique characteristics of each.
- To locate and analyze supporting material from Internet sources as to their usefulness and credibility.
- To encourage critical analysis of and ethical issues relating to communication in public settings.

Class Format

A course in communication requires *active participation* in class discussion and exercises. You must be present to be an active participant. Please be considerate of others and of your instructor so that all can enjoy a dynamic, engaging, and comfortable environment. CSUF's *Blackboard* system will also be utilized, so make sure you become familiar with how it operates and use it often.

Class Policies

Please carefully read the following class policies:

1. Attendance: Because this is a performance course, regular attendance is essential. Three or more absences will result in loss of points from the class participation portion of your grade (2 points per class period). On scheduled speech days, attendance is mandatory. Warning: A 10-point deduction from the student's speech grade will occur for every speech day that he or she misses.
2. Speeches are to be delivered on ***the assigned day***. Speakers who are absent on the assigned speaking day will receive a zero unless prior arrangements are made with the instructor. You are also required to provide evaluations of your peers' speeches. Participating as an audience member is a graded assignment.
3. PAPERS and WRITTEN EXERCISES: All assignments written out of class MUST be typed, double-spaced, in a 12-point font with one-inch margins on all sides. Your name, the course number, the instructor name, and the assignment name should be single-spaced and centered on a cover page. Papers will be due on the date specified in the syllabus. If an assignment is turned in late, the student will receive a 15% reduction (or a 1½ letter grade) per 24-hour period including weekends.
4. PLAGIARISM and ACADEMIC DISHONESTY: Plagiarism is defined as the act of taking the specific substance of another and offering it as one's own without giving credit to the source. Sources must be cited accurately and appropriately. Cases of plagiarism could constitute dismissal from the course with a failing grade.
5. STUDENTS WITH DISABILITIES: Please let your instructor and the Office of Disabled Student Services know if you have a disability that might affect your participation or study in this class. The instructor will keep this information in strict confidence. Your instructor will

work with this office to provide students with disabilities with reasonable accommodations.

6. No administrative withdrawals will be initiated by the instructor. If you stop attending class but do not officially withdraw from the class, your name appears on the ending roll sheet. Grades will be assigned based on the work completed.

7. HCOM 100 classes regularly participate in research or classroom assessment projects during the course of the semester. Feedback from students for the latter will help target areas of instruction that need improvement.

EVALUATION

Exams. Exams are designed primarily to assess comprehension, retention, and application of central ideas from readings and class (lecture and class discussion). There will be two exams: a midterm and a final. You will need to provide your instructor with appropriate documentation to make up an exam.

Speeches. You will be required to prepare and deliver at least two major speeches and several minor speeches throughout the semester. Each individual speech will be graded on your research, content, organization, and presentation. You must submit a typed outline of your speech to your instructor **before** your presentation.

Activities. There will be a number of in-class activities that you will participate in. These may take the form of group activities, impromptu speaking, homework assignments, or planned or unannounced quizzes. Any quizzes will always be administered at the beginning of class ONLY. Points for participation may be earned by completing in-class exercises. In-class activities usually cannot be made up, at least not for full credit.

Application Papers. The reaction paper is your opportunity to (1) analyze what you have learned from an activity assigned by your instructor, (2) integrate concepts from class to elaborate on your explanation of the experience, and (3) illustrate your growing communication competency through your analysis and your written communication. Each paper must be two to three pages. Successful completion of reaction papers will facilitate your reflection on your progress toward accomplishing the learning goals of this course. Each reaction paper is worth 15 points for a total of 30 points possible.

Guidelines to Follow for the Major (and minor) Speeches

Object Speech. For this initial assignment you are to bring in something from home (your residence hall or off-campus) and introduce yourself and your object to the class. Your presentation should be about **1–2 minutes** long, and you may use one side of a 4 × 6 note card. No formal outline is required for this first introductory speech.

The object may be a personal collectible, a photo of a friend, or anything that has personal importance to you. Each student will go to the front of the class and explain what relevance it has in her or his life. Other information that you may and should include are where you found or obtained the object, special things about it, and so on. All in all, the item should reveal something about you — an interest and/or an insight for us in getting to know you.

This assignment also serves as an icebreaker for the class. Have fun with it! DUE DATE: _____ (In-class exercise — Counts 5 points)

Informative Speech Using a Visual Aid. Choose a topic for this speech that lends itself to presentation using a visual aid. The speech must be informative and include at least **four sources** of information listed on your speech outline. Provide a **typed** outline that follows the format of the sample outline at the end of the syllabus. This speech should demonstrate good organizational skills and audience adaptation skills. (Counts 100 points)

Persuasive Speech. You must choose a controversial topic for this speech and take a position either in support or in opposition. For example, you could choose to speak about why the electoral college must be abandoned. You must cite at least **five sources** in this speech, sources that meet the tests of reliability and credibility. (Internet sources may be used, but be sure to evaluate them very carefully.) Prepare a **typed** outline that follows the format of the sample outline. This speech should demonstrate good persuasive arrangement, as well as appropriate use of logical and emotional appeals. (Counts 100 points)

GRADING

Plus/minus grading will be used in the final grades for this course. The following table indicates the number of points and the percent of total possible points associated with each grade.

Grade	Percent of total possible points	
A+	98–100	(490–500 points)
A	93–97.9	(465–489 points)
A-	90–92.9	(450–464 points)
B+	87–89.9	(435–449 points)
B	83–86.9	(415–434 points)
B-	80–82.9	(400–414 points)
C+	77–79.9	(385–399 points)
C	73–76.9	(365–384 points)
C-	70–72.9	(350–364 points)
D+	67–69.9	(335–349 points)
D	63–66.9	(315–334 points)
D-	60–62.9	(300–314 points)
F	59.9 or below	

You must receive a C or better in the course (i.e., 73% or higher, which means 365 points or more) for it to fulfill the general education requirement for oral communication.

GRADING (Cont'd): Record Your Scores:

Point Values	Possible	Earned
Midterm Exam	100	_____/100
Informative Speech	100	_____/100
Persuasive Speech	100	_____/100
Final Exam	100	_____/100
Application Papers _____ (15) + _____(15) =	30	_____ / 30

Other written assignments; Attendance, Any quizzes, Exercises; Object, Classmate, Impromptu Speeches; Participation, etc.	70	_____ / 70
TOTAL	500	_____/500
		Final Letter Grade:_____

Tentative Course Outline for HCOM 100 (Section #__), FA '10

Reading Assignments: The chapter to be covered on the designated day should be read prior to class.

DAY	ACTIVITY /TOPIC /ASSIGNMENT DUE	READING ASSIGN
Aug. 24	Syllabus / Introductions: The Course and the Instructor / Begin Ch. 1	
26	Ch. 1, "Communication: Essential Human Behavior"	Ch. 1
31	**"Object Speeches"** / Conclude Ch. 1 / Begin Ch. 2	
Sept. 2	Ch. 2, "Perceiving the Self and Others"	Ch. 2
7	Conclude Ch. 2 / Begin Ch. 3, "Language and Communication"	
9	Discuss Ch. 3 / Time to interview classmates	
14	**Getting-to-Know-Your-Classmate Speeches** / Begin Ch. 4	Ch. 3
16	Ch. 4, "Nonverbal Communication"	Ch. 4
21	Ch. 5, "Listening"	Ch. 5
23	Ch. 5 / Chapter 11, "Preparing and Researching Presentations"	Ch. 11
28	Ch. 11 / Begin Chapter 14 (**Application Paper #1 Due**)	Ch. 14
30	Ch. 14, "Informative Speaking"	

Oct. 5	Ch. 12, "Organizing, Outlining, and Writing Presentations"	Ch. 12
7	Ch. 13, "Delivering Presentations"/ Exam Review / Prepare for Speeches	Ch . 13
12	**Midterm Exam**	
14	**Informative/Visual Aid Speeches**	
19	**Informative/Visual Aid Speeches**	
21	**Informative/Visual Aid Speeches**	
26	Ch. 6, "Developing and Maintaining Relationships"	Ch. 6
28	Conclude Ch. 6	
Nov. 2	Ch. 7, "Managing Conflict in Relationships"	Ch. 7
4	Conclude Ch. 7 (**Application Paper #2 Due**)	
9	Ch. 15, "Persuasive Speaking"	Ch. 15
11	NO CLASS (Veterans Day)	
16	Conclude Ch. 15 / Ch. 8, "Communicating in Groups"	Ch. 8
18	Ch. 8 / Group Activities / Ch. 9, "Leadership and Decision Making in Groups"	Ch. 9
23	Fall Recess — No Class	
25	Fall Recess — No Class (Happy Thanksgiving)	
30	**Persuasive Speeches**	
Dec. 2	**Persuasive Speeches**	
7	**Persuasive Speeches**	
9	Wrap up any course content / Review for the Final Exam / Course Evaluations	

Final Exam for HCOM 100 (Section #___): _____

SOURCE: Personal correspondence with Jason Teven, December 11, 2010. Copyright 2010 by Jason J. Teven. This syllabus and all instructional materials may not be reproduced without written consent from Jason J. Teven. Used with permission.

SAMPLE: HUMAN COMMUNICATION SYLLABUS #2

In the following common syllabus from Blair Thompson at Western Kentucky University, notice the guidelines for the proper use of laptops in the classroom — a pressing issue as more students bring their personal technology to class. This syllabus also provides a particularly comprehensive explanation of the course's plagiarism policy, even pulling material from the student handbook into the syllabus for easy access.

INSTRUCTOR:

OFFICE:

FAX:

PHONE:

EMAIL:

BLACKBOARD:

OFFICE HOURS:

DEPARTMENT OF COMMUNICATION

COMM 145

FUNDAMENTALS OF PUBLIC SPEAKING AND

COMMUNICATION

WESTERN KENTUCKY UNIVERSITY FALL 2010 SYLLABUS

COURSE DESCRIPTION

COMM 145 — Fundamentals of Public Speaking and Communication is designed to increase your understanding of the principles and processes of communicating effectively in a variety of contexts and to facilitate development of your skills in public communication, listening, group communication, and interpersonal communication. This is done through a combination of speaking, listening, writing, and reading assignments. Specifically, you will outline, develop, and deliver extemporaneous speeches incorporating relevant sources. You will learn how to develop and deliver messages that are appropriate and effective for the audience, purpose, and context. When you leave the course, you should be sufficiently armed with a basic understanding of public speaking and with an awareness of other important communication skills so that you can continue to develop effective communication behaviors throughout your life in a variety of contexts. COMM 145 is part of the General Education curriculum and fulfills the Public Speaking requirement (Category A-III).

COURSE OBJECTIVES

Students will be able to

- Design and deliver messages appropriate to various audiences and occasions.
- Communicate a clear thesis and purpose.
- Research, evaluate, and incorporate supporting material.
- Construct and deliver organized presentations with well-developed introductions, main points, conclusions, and transitions.
- Deliver speeches using appropriate and effective vocal and physical behaviors to enhance messages such as vocal variety, articulation, and movement.
- Demonstrate understanding of the communication process.
- Acquire skills to communicate with others, both publicly and interpersonally.
- Understand and identify the basic principles of effective group communication and listening.

Required Text. Seiler, W. J., & Beall, M. L. (2011). *Communication: Making connections* (8th ed.). Boston, MA: Allyn and Bacon.

ATTENDANCE

Penalty for Nonattendance

We learn to communicate by communicating and by observing others; therefore, your attendance is absolutely essential. I expect you to be in class each day. The penalty guidelines are described below:

1. The final semester grade for a three-day-a-week class will be reduced **10 points** (out of the 800-point scale) for each unexcused absence over one.
2. The final semester grade for a two-day-a-week class will be reduced **15 points** (out of the 800-point scale) for each unexcused absence over one.

3. The final semester grade for a weekly class will be reduced **20 points** (out of the 800-point scale) for each unexcused absence over one.

Penalty for Tardiness

Not only are you expected to be in class each day, but you also need to be on time. Tardiness is unprofessional and disruptive. Attendance is defined not only as being present in class, but being present within five minutes of the start of class through the completion of the class session. Unexcused tardiness may be penalized by your not being allowed to make up work done in class prior to your arrival and may lead to the same point deduction as an unexcused absence. If you come to class after the roll has been taken, it is your responsibility to notify me after class that you were present.

Excused Absence Policy

Speeches, homework, and in-class assignments cannot be made up unless I officially excuse your absence, which means you **must provide me with proper documentation**. You are responsible for contacting me regarding any excused absence. You must present written documentation **in advance** of an absence for a university-sponsored event and the day you return to class for any other absence or it will be counted as unexcused. Approved make-up work is due the **first class meeting** of your return. For presentations, the speech order is determined in advance; therefore, if you are traveling for a university-related event, you must swap places with a speaker going on an earlier day.

An excused absence is defined as

1. Illness of the student or serious illness of a member of the student's family
2. The death of a member of the student's immediate family
3. Trips for members of student organizations sponsored by an academic unit, trips for university classes, and trips for participation in intercollegiate academic or athletic events
4. Major religious holidays

RESPONSIBILITIES OF A COMPETENT COMMUNICATOR

In order to build an open, professional classroom atmosphere, everyone should follow certain ground rules. These rules of civility include but are not limited to

1. **Displaying respect** for all members of the classroom community, both your instructor and your fellow students
2. **Paying attention to and participating** in lectures, group activities, presentations, and other exercises
3. **Avoiding unnecessary disruptions** during class such as ringing cell phones, **text messaging**, private conversations, reading newspapers, and doing work for other classes
4. **Avoiding racist, sexist, homophobic, or other negative language** that may unnecessarily exclude or affect members of our campus and classroom community

Cell Phone Policy

Due to recent advances in technology, cell phones, iPods, pagers, etc. will not be allowed out during class time. Any student with a cell phone in hand or on his or her desk during class time will be asked to leave class and will be counted absent for that day. Any student using a cell phone during an exam will receive a zero on that exam and may be subject to other university discipline.

Laptop Policy

Using a laptop to take notes during class can be very effective. However, when students use their laptops to check their e-mail, instant message, and/or play games during class it can be distracting to classmates and hinder the note-taking process. Therefore, students who choose to use a laptop to take notes will be required to sit in the front row of the classroom.

ACADEMIC OFFENSES: PLAGIARISM AND CHEATING

I expect that all of the individual assignments you complete for COMM 145 (and in all of your other courses) are always your own work. However, many students are not sure exactly what "your own work" means, so please read again the information on plagiarism and cheating in your student handbook. Aside from copying others' work **plagiarism includes incorrectly citing sources or presenting someone's information as your own** without crediting the source. To avoid this, you should carefully make notes to keep track of where your information came from. In written form, you must use quotation marks when referring to another's work. In a speech where you are paraphrasing, you can say "According to . . . (give name) . . . ." It does not take much effort to make sure you follow the rules for using another's thoughts.

YOU ARE RESPONSIBLE for telling your audience or reader whether you are

1. directly <u>quoting from a source</u>
2. <u>paraphrasing closely from a source</u>, which means using significant portions of a source's sentences or language
3. <u>using the ideas advanced by a source</u>

Plagiarism Detection

In this course we will be using an electronic plagiarism detection tool, Turnitin. com, to confirm that you have used sources accurately in your speeches and outlines. All assignments are subject to submission for text similarity review to this plagiarism detection tool. Assignments submitted to Turnitin.com will be included as source documents in Turnitin.com's restricted access database solely for the purpose of detecting plagiarism in such documents. I will provide specific instructions in class on how to submit your speech outlines for electronic plagiarism review.

Penalty for Academic Dishonesty

Western Kentucky University and the Department of Communication are committed to the highest standards of ethical conduct and academic excellence. Any student found guilty of plagiarism, fabrication, cheating on an exam, or purchasing papers, speeches, or other assignments will immediately receive a failing grade on the assignment and potentially in the course, and will be reported for disciplinary action.

If you have any questions about whether you may be plagiarizing in your work, please be sure to contact me well in advance of the due date for your assignment.

IF YOU NEED HELP

If you have questions or concerns or find certain materials or assignments difficult, please contact me by e-mail or come by during my office hours. If you are unable to come during my scheduled times, call me to arrange an appointment. If you have a special need that may require assistance or accommodation, please let me know as soon as possible. You need to provide documentation; then, we'll work to make reasonable accommodation. Students with disabilities who require accommodations must contact the Office for Student Disability Services.

ASSIGNMENTS

YOU MUST PRESENT YOUR SPEECH ON THE DAY ASSIGNED. IF YOU MISS CLASS FOR AN UNEXCUSED ABSENCE OR ARE NOT PREPARED TO SPEAK ON YOUR SPEECH DAY AND DO NOT PRESENT AS SCHEDULED, YOU WILL RECEIVE A ZERO FOR THAT SPEECH ASSIGNMENT.

- **Basic Requirements:** This semester there will be three graded speech assignments. You are expected to use topics of your own choice that meet the guidelines for the assignment. Each speech has a time limit that you must meet. This allows all class speakers to complete the assignment on schedule and gives you practice in fitting materials into a given time allotment.
- **Outlines:** Outlines are required for each of the graded speeches. **Late outlines will receive comments from your instructor but will not be assigned points.** The outline should include specific purpose, central idea, a sentence outline of the speech, a list of sources you used in the preparation of the speech, and any other form your instructor may assign.

Speech 1: Introduction Speech (2–3 minutes)

You will do one of two possible types of introduction speech described below, based on teacher preference.

Classmate Interview Speech. The speech serves a number of purposes. It is designed to help you get to know the rest of the class and for them to learn something about you, to practice organizing a speech, and to get you up on your feet and speaking. Each student will introduce someone else in the class. Tell us what makes the person interesting, what her or his future goals are, and so on. Each student will interview another member of the class and organize and present a two- to three-minute speech. Each student must complete an outline. You may use no more than one single-sided index card. The speech must contain an introduction, body, and conclusion. The most effective speeches will center around a theme with two or three main points to support the theme rather than listing random details about the person's life.

"Just Bag It" Speech. This introductory speech gives you the opportunity to start speaking right away and gives your classmates an opportunity to learn a little about you. Select three items, place them in the bag, and be prepared to explain how the three items describe you. For example, you might include a symbol of your place of employment, an item indicating an interest of yours (e.g., a tennis ball if you play tennis), or an item that symbolizes your career interest (e.g., an apple for an education major). In addition to the items you bring, consider using quotations, stories, and examples. You must demonstrate that effort went into the assignment. In other words, someone pulling three textbooks out of a backpack and telling the class which courses they are enrolled in will not receive full credit. This first speech should include the most basic components of any speech — an introduction, main points, and a conclusion. You are required to use extemporaneous delivery, speaking from a brief outline, using no more than one single-sided index card.

Speech 2: Speech of Information and Diversity (4–6 minutes)

This is a four- to six-minute informative speech, which must take a multicultural perspective. You may elect to compare and/or contrast an aspect of two cultural groups or discuss an aspect of one cultural group in detail. Other possible topics include social customs, family traditions, holidays, clothing, food, religious traditions, sports, etc. You must step outside of your own cultural perspective in some way. Focus on presenting information relevant to your audience. You are required to present within the time limit, using a speaking outline of no more than five note cards (one side only). You are to cite no fewer than three different sources and use three or more types of amplification or supporting materials.

Visual aids are required for this speech (PowerPoint, posterboard, video/DVD, etc.).

Speech 3: Problem-Solution Speech (5–6 minutes)

This is a five- to six-minute action-oriented persuasive speech. The purpose of the problem-solution speech is to influence the audience's beliefs or actions. The speech should contain a problem and solutions to the problem, including action steps the audience can take. Possible topics include influencing class-mates to donate blood, start/increase flossing, exercise more or eat healthier, sponsor a child, get involved with a charity, adopt a pet, etc. You are required to present within the time limit, using a speaking outline of no more than five note cards (one side only). You are to cite no fewer than four different sources (only two may be from the Internet) and use three or more types of amplifica-tion or supporting materials. No visual aid is required, but please keep in mind that a visual aid can be a very effective way to persuade your audience to act on your topic.

Communication Theory/Context Paper

Based on the chapters in the textbook, select a communication context (inter-personal, group, team, the workplace or another organization) or communication theory (dialectics, communication privacy management, etc.) you are interested in and write a three- to four-page paper (double-spaced). Explain why you selected this context or theory, why this context represents an important area in which to study/learn about communication, and/or why this theory is important to the study of communication. Include a minimum of three sources cited within the text of your paper (preferably communication journals or books; the text-book does not count as one of your three sources). Discuss what communica-tion scholars have learned about your topic that could be relevant to your own experiences (give examples). Also discuss what you learned about communica-tion from your research (how this will be useful in your life, career, etc.). The paper will be graded on content, organization, and writing. Please include an introduction, clearly organized and supported paragraphs in the body of the paper (please use topic sentences), a conclusion, and source citation along with a bibliography in APA format. You will be presenting your paper informally to the class so that everyone can learn about the theory or concept. Please include relevant and interesting information about your topic from your research, as well as how your topic contributes to the study of communication. The presentations should be three to four minutes long.

CommuniCoach Self-evaluation

Each student will complete an evaluation form using the CommuniCoach system. This evaluation will be done for the problem-solution speech.

Written Work/Homework

In addition to the speeches, you will be graded on several in-class activities and written assignments required by your instructor.

Examinations

Exams and/or quizzes will be used to gauge your understanding of the course material. The exam schedule is located on the tentative daily schedule, but unscheduled quizzes may be given to assess your understanding of the chapter materials. Please come to class having read the chapter we are covering. Exams and quizzes may include various question formats.

GRADING POLICY

Speech One: Introductory/Interview Speech	50 pts.
Speech Two: Speech of Information and Diversity	100 pts.
Speech Three: Problem-Solution Speech	100 pts.
Outlines: 25 pts. each	75 pts.
Communication Theory/Context Paper	100 pts.
Theory/Context Paper Presentation	50 pts.
Participation/activities	100 pts.
In-class Speaking Assignments	
Communication Activities	
End of Chapter Exercises	
Participation in Departmental Research	
CommuniCoach Self-evaluation	25 pts.
Exams (3 exams) test #1 = 50 pts.	
tests #2 & #3 = 75 pts. each	200 pts.
	Total: 800 pts.

FINAL GRADE SCALE

A = 800–720 pts   (90%–100%)
B = 719–640 pts   (80%–89%)
C = 639–560 pts   (70%–79%)
D = 559–480 pts   (60%–69%)
F = Below 479   (Below 60%)

COMM 145: Fundamentals of Public Speaking and Communication — Tentative Weekly Schedule (MWF) FALL 2010

Date	Topic	Reading Assignments
Week 1 August 30–September 3	Introduction to the Course What Is Communication? Communication Process	Ch. 1
Week 2 September 6–10 (September 6 Labor Day: No Class)	Organizing Speeches **Interview classmate or prepare "Just Bag It" Speech** Delivery Dealing with Fear of Public Speaking	Ch. 9 Ch. 10
Week 3 September 13–17	Introduction Speech Informative Speaking Selecting a Topic & Purpose	Ch. 11 Ch. 7
Week 4 September 20–24	Researching Your Topic Description of the Speech of Information and Diversity Visual Aids Conducting Research; Writing a Research Paper Go over topics for theory/context paper	Ch. 7 Ch. 8

Week 5 September 27–October 1	Verbal Communication Nonverbal Communication Review for exam	Ch. 4 Ch. 5
Week 6 October 4–6 October 7–8 Fall Break	**Exam 1** Perception and Listening Self and Identity **Outlines for Speech of Information & Diversity due**	Ch. 2, 6 Ch. 3
Week 7 October 11–15	Interpersonal Communication **Begin Speech of Information & Diversity**	Ch. 13, 14
Week 8 October 18–22	**Finish Speech of Information & Diversity** Review for exam	
Week 9 October 25–29	**Exam 2** Persuasion Analyzing your audience Begin covering persuasive strategies	Ch. 12
Week 10 November 1–5	Understanding Persuasion and Reasoning Continue covering persuasive strategies Developing Persuasive Speeches	Ch. 12
Week 11 November 8–12	Group and Team Communication Workday on Problem-Solution Speeches Review for exam **Outlines for Problem-Solution Speeches due**	Ch 15, 16

Week 12 November 15–19	Exam 3 **Begin Problem-Solution** **Speeches**	
Week 13 November 22–23 **Thanksgiving Break** November 24–26	**Problem-Solution Speeches** (continued)	
Week 14 November 29–December 3	**Finish Problem-Solution** **Speeches** **CommuniCoach evaluation** **due**	
Week 15 December 6–10	**Begin Theory/Context Paper** **Presentations** (Paper due December 9)	
Finals Week December 12–17	**Finish Theory/Context Paper** **Presentations**	

SOURCE: Personal correspondence with Blair Thompson, January 10, 2011. Used with permission.

Professional Development

5

Hiring, Evaluating, and Dismissing Instructors

Growing Pains

The course you coordinate is about to expand, from three sections a year to nearly thirty. This has less to do with your own department's growth and more to do with the School of Business suspending their role in providing the required discipline-specific writing course to their majors. They are doing this in order to protect their "qualified"-to-"unqualified" faculty ratios for accreditation; in the end, they cannot keep employing their large part-time faculty to teach this course and still satisfy their disciplinary accrediting organization. As someone who has successfully provided writing instruction to upper-division communication studies students for years, you submitted an application to get a share of this windfall, thinking that this could become a growth area for part-time instructors in your department — more possible courses for them to teach in what have become increasingly lean budget years. While you would prefer to hire people you know — people who have a history of successful instruction in courses in your department — you decide to give some consideration to the former business school instructors of the course who have been laid off. You review their files, their materials, and their teaching philosophies in hopes of hiring unfamiliar colleagues who will succeed in this now modified assignment.

* * *

It is important to understand from the outset your responsibility in hiring, evaluating, and dismissing instructors associated with your coordinated course. This responsibility involves what we might think of as a global component, in that, as a coordinator, you are selecting and mentoring instructors in order to realize a vision for that course, as well as a more practical or immediate component, in that you must also be familiar with your own particular local (campus, college, or department) employment requirements and customs. While the former requires developing a familiarity with particular instructors, including their strengths and limitations as instructors, the latter requires developing a familiarity with policies, procedures, and the administrative staff that govern hiring and dismissing instructors on your campus.

Knowing the vision or mission of the course and the role it plays in larger department or program efforts will give you, as a course coordinator, a much needed foundation for these employment decisions. From time to time, employment decisions (such as whether to dismiss a particular instructor) can be complex and nuanced, but fortunately, the vast majority of these decisions will be positive and relatively unproblematic. Part of being an effective course coordinator is selecting and supporting those instructors who can help students achieve the learning outcomes for that course in ways that are consistent with the program's and the course's values and commitments. Your program vision will help you articulate the meaning of "good teaching" with respect to this particular course. And, well-designed, this vision will help you determine what to ask of prospective applicants, select who should teach this course, evaluate and communicate appropriate feedback to instructors of the course, and identify who is or is not contributing to the successful operation of the course and to students' learning.

It is also essential that you understand the policies and procedures surrounding hiring, evaluating, and dismissing faculty, as these will vary considerably from one campus or even one department to the next. Whatever your role with respect to hiring, evaluating, and sometimes dismissing instructors who teach this coordinated course, consulting with your supervisor or department chair and relevant contacts in Faculty Affairs, Human Resources, union organizations, the campus attorney's office, and similar offices will help you be fair, consistent, and just in your labor practices. Transparency, clear communication, and scrupulous adherence to law (including as these practices are shaped and defined by campus and union policy) will help sustain your reputation as a good employer, supervisor, or coordinator.

The first step in any effort to navigate hiring and dismissal decisions should be taking stock of your role as course coordinator in the employment decision-making process. This may vary considerably depending on the structure of your program. It may be that you coordinate a course staffed by instructors who were hired by some other administrator (for example, a department chair or a graduate coordinator), and while you are encouraged to offer your thoughts on these instructors' performance, you may not have any direct authority over their status as instructors. Or it may be that your colleagues see you as a direct supervisor to the instructors who teach the course; all decisions with respect to hiring, retention, and dismissal may begin with you. Or it may be that you supervise colleagues who are tenured (or otherwise have security of employment), perhaps even at or above your own rank; here, questions of who ought to continue teaching the course can become quite thorny.

Building from these particular campus-based guidelines, there are general considerations you can use to effectively supervise the instructors who teach this coordinated course.

HIRING INSTRUCTORS

Even if you have inherited instructors selected by a previous coordinator or other colleagues, you may still have some occasion to participate in or organize the hiring process for this course. Hiring, however, may take different forms, depending on the instructors and positions in question. This process may be subtle, like asking the department chair to schedule a particular colleague to teach this course; or it may be formal, from developing position announcements and collecting materials to observing classrooms and preparing annual evaluations.

As with other aspects of your assignment as course coordinator, your sense of program or course vision can help orient and ground you as you make decisions about who should teach the course. Are you looking for people who can teach public speaking or introduction to communication (or critical thinking or some other introductory communication course)? Do you and your colleagues feel there are meaningful distinctions in who can or should teach any one of these courses? What characteristics do you and your colleagues associate with effectiveness in this assignment? Are there any particular skills you and your colleagues will expect, at a minimum, from instructors of this course (familiarity with PowerPoint; past or current participation in nonprofit or advocacy groups; knowledge of particular readings, theorists, or campus programs)? Consulting your program vision early and often will help you make employment decisions you can feel confident about, from crafting a position announcement, to requesting materials that will inform the selection process, to orienting and engaging new instructors in that common vision.

A Note about Unions: Employment decisions will take different forms depending on whether a campus is unionized, the sorts of employees one will hire, and the offices involved in employment decisions. For example, coordinators who work with instructors who are union members must negotiate a series of contractual terms in their evaluation and retention or dismissal; even the question of whether a given part-time faculty member can assume responsibility for an extra section of the introductory communication course can be highly regulated by legal definitions of entitlement. Even where all instructors on a given campus are effectively governed by union contracts, this can become complicated.

For example, Deanna and John are both union members on their campuses and supervise GTAs who belong to a different bargaining unit. Given that there does not seem to be any central repository of information regarding employment decisions on our campuses, we often find ourselves contacting many different offices for information (on topics ranging from what actions are grounds to dismiss a GTA, to what responsibilities GTAs have on furlough days as members of a different bargaining unit, to what actions we should take as their supervisors should they vote to strike) before we isolate the best source. Further, not all coordinators supervise only or primarily GTAs — type of employment is an important factor in the coordinator's decision-making process. For example, coordinators often cannot "hire" or "fire" tenure-track faculty or lecturers who have security of employment in the same way they might make employment decisions about part-time instructors or GTAs.

John's department hires a variety of instructors to contribute to the introductory course teaching staff. These instructors are appointed primarily by the chair, and their assignments are then forwarded to John. While John has some say in the instructors, he is largely not included in the actual hiring — the majority of introductory course instructors are handed to him in a compiled list so that he may assign them to specific sections. On John's campus, NTT (non–tenure-track) faculty have seniority in regard to staffing and, before the department can hire new instructors, it must make sure those individuals who have seniority have received their preferences.

Deanna's department appoints GTAs through a committee selection process and appoints part-time instructors in the light of their "entitlement"—the university's commitment to offering continued employment to instructors based on the amount of courses they have taught routinely in the past (in this way, instructors work toward first one- and then three-year contracts as their entitlements, ranging from two to five courses per semester). Community colleges may also participate in similar processes, for example, by assigning instructors "reemployment preference" after five successful quarters or semesters of teaching. Developing a solid sense of the legalities surrounding your hiring practices, and knowing which resources to consult for questions or concerns, as well as the role you have in these decisions, will free you to make confident personnel decisions from the moment you post the position through the interviewing and training process.

Position Announcements

Position announcements invite not only applicants for a given position, but, crafted in the light of program or course vision, also the *right* applicants for that position. Announcements typically follow a common format, though this can vary somewhat from one program, department, or school to the next. These typically include

- Position title (whether "Graduate Teaching Assistant" or "Lecturer" or "Assistant Professor, Tenure-Track")
- Rank or number (if appropriate)
- Position responsibilities
- Required educational or professional preparation
- Requested materials
- Search chair contact information

They also often include

- Salary range for the position
- Information about the campus community
- A statement about the campus's efforts at nondiscriminatory employment practices

It is possible that, as a course coordinator, you may never need to craft a position announcement; perhaps your course is staffed exclusively by tenured/tenure-track faculty, or it may be that another colleague (for example, the department chair or dean) is responsible for hiring. However, even if you do not write position announcements yourself, you will want to be familiar with the format used by your department. If your department does announce a position related to your course, and you are not the author of that posting, it would be wise to meet with the person or people who will be issuing that call so you feel certain they are accurately representing the program, course, and position.

One reason to familiarize yourself with the way positions are posted is that while position announcements can, whether through what they announce or through the venues they appear in, help to attract instructors who will help realize the program vision, they are also one of your first opportunities to educate prospective instructors on the program's or your own expectations of their performance. See, for example, Deanna's departmental GTA Program position announcement, included on page 110 for reference.

This announcement includes many of the usual elements (e.g., the position title, the start date for the position, the length of time GTAs may remain part of the program, etc.), but perhaps more important are the elements of the announcement that address the qualifications the department expects from applicants and the program requirements once they join. For example, under "qualifications," we note not only that we expect applicants to be M.A. students in the department, but also that "coursework in rhetoric and public speaking is especially desirable." And perhaps more telling of our department efforts to engage and better serve all, but especially underrepresented, students, we note that "applicants must have awareness of and sensitivity to the educational goals of a multicultural population and an interest in teaching students with non-traditional or ethnically diverse backgrounds." In committee, the faculty specifically discuss and rank candidates on these qualifications.

The position announcement Deanna's program uses also introduces teaching expectations to prospective applicants. It notes that, at first, GTAs will teach one section of public speaking each semester, and it helps applicants understand the common day/time configuration for course offerings, office hours, assignments, and participation in the Communication Studies Lab and Resource Center. It also indicates that GTAs will need to take four units of coursework as support for their position, in addition to approximately 50 hours of orientation instruction during the summer prior to appointment. In so doing, it not only indicates something practical and useful to the applicants, but also helps them begin to understand how important it is to this program that they not only teach for the department, but learn to teach well. They introduce the idea that training and professional development are ongoing and in collaboration with the coordinator and their colleagues. In this way, position announcements can also help surface questions for the applicants that will send them to meet with course coordinators and other department or program leaders to discuss the program, their expectations, and their vision.

Other programs and courses may not place as much structure on this process. For example, for other courses in Deanna's program, there may or may not be a formal position announcement (other than a general open request for colleagues to join the part-time faculty pool), and the department chair may or may not seek the input of course coordinators in personnel decisions (depending on the chair, or depending on the instructor or (re)certification issues surrounding a given course). Where John supervises instructors, admission to the graduate program, with few exceptions, is contingent on receiving a teaching assistantship — in this regard, the faculty who serve on the graduate committee select not only incoming graduate students, but also new introductory course instructors. When they send admissions decisions to candidates, they also describe the associated teaching assignment and the obligations this role entails.

SAMPLE: Position Announcement

SAN JOSÉ STATE UNIVERSITY

Announcement of Teaching Associate Positions Available for Students Working Toward the M.A. in Communication Studies

Department of Communication Studies
http://www.sjsu.edu/comm/

TEACHING ASSOCIATE POSITIONS IN COLLEGE TEACHING
Fall 2011

The Department of Communication Studies is seeking applicants for appointment as Teaching Associates (TAs), commencing in the Fall Semester 2011. The Teaching Associate Program is designed to provide training and direct, supervised experience in college teaching for M.A. students in communication studies. Additional Teaching Associate appointments in Forensics are also available.

QUALIFICATIONS: Admission as a classified student to the M.A. program in Communication Studies and a baccalaureate degree with a major in communication studies or a closely related field. Coursework in rhetoric and public speaking is especially desirable. Forensics experience required for Forensics TA appointment. Applications will be evaluated on a competitive basis. Applicants must have awareness of and sensitivity to the educational goals of a multicultural population and an interest in teaching students with nontraditional or ethnically diverse backgrounds.

PROGRAM REQUIREMENTS: Teaching Associates will be assigned to teach one section of COMM 20, Public Speaking. These sections typically meet Monday and Wednesday. TAs are also required to enroll in Comm 285A (Teaching Practicum) for two units of credit in their first semester as a teaching associate; they will enroll in two units of COMM 285B in the second semester as a teaching associate. COMM 285A&B requirements include providing one solo-taught or two team-taught workshops through the Comm Lab each semester. The department provides, and requires teaching associate attendance at, a one-week training workshop (five days × eight hours) in the week prior to the start of Fall semester, as well as 1–2 shorter, late afternoon or evening sessions earlier in the summer.

SALARY: The term salary for Teaching Associates teaching one section is TBD (subject to budget developments). Teaching Associates are also given a tuition fee waiver for up to 6.0 units for teaching one course.

APPLICATION: Your application to our teaching associate program consists of: a cover letter stating teaching experience, qualifications, and objectives; a current CV or resumé; official transcripts of all graduate and undergraduate work; and three letters of recommendation that address teaching qualifications or potential. **Applications, including all materials, must be received on or prior to March 14, 2011, to receive consideration**. We will announce our selections in April 2011. Department faculty will be available at NCA in San Francisco and WSCA in Monterey to meet with prospective candidates.

Please direct all GTA Program Inquiries to the GTA Program Supervisor, Deanna L. Fassett. Please submit all application materials to the Graduate Coordinator by or before March 14th, 2011.

> ## AN EQUAL OPPORTUNITY/AFFIRMATIVE ACTION/TITLE IX EMPLOYER

San José State University as a standing policy does not discriminate against individuals because of their race, color, religion, age, sex, national origin, handicap, or status as Disabled Veteran or Vietnam Era Veterans. This policy applies to all University programs and facilities including, but not limited to, admissions, educational programs, and employment. Such discrimination is prohibited by Title VI and VII of the Civil Rights Acts. Title IX of the Education Amendments, Secs. 503 and 504 of the Vocational Rehabilitation Act of 1973, Age Discrimination Acts of 1974 and 1975, Vietnam Era Veteran's Readjustment Assistance Act of 1974, and other Federal and State statutes and regulations. Inquiries regarding the application of these laws and regulations to the University may be directed to the University's Affirmative Action Coordinator.

Materials for Evaluation

When considering what materials you might ask candidates to supply, remember that these materials will help you to develop portraits of who they are (or might be) as instructors. It is common to ask for

- Cover letter
- Curriculum vitae or resumé
- Evidence of past teaching effectiveness
- Letter(s) of recommendation
- Transcript

You might also consider asking candidates to supply statements of teaching philosophy. Many instructors will understand what this entails, but if you are recruiting from a relatively inexperienced group of applicants, you might frame the statement as the applicant's sense of what "good teaching" is or should be and how she or he hopes to engender that in the classroom. Reviewing a candidate's teaching philosophy will provide invaluable insight into how well she or he is likely to fit within the mission or vision of your particular department, program, and course.

For example, if the vision of your public speaking course entails explicit attention to power, privilege, and inequality, and this is something a candidate explicitly references as a commitment in her or his own approach to situating public speaking concepts in sociopolitical context, this may lead you to give this application additional scrutiny. However, a candidate whose philosophy does not draw connections between the classroom and the community or to advocacy and social justice issues may not be the best choice for teaching that particular course. You might still select this applicant to teach this course, but the teaching philosophy helps inform your (or your selection committee's) reading of the additional materials and of the application overall; it also helps you anticipate any particular orientation or training and development activities you may need to undertake with this instructor so that she or he is fully prepared to assume this academic assignment. As with all employment procedures, discussion of candidates and their materials should be discreet and confidential, consistent with all equal opportunity laws and privacy protections.

Interviews and Teaching Demonstrations

If you have an opportunity to conduct interviews or to request teaching demonstrations, then you are in a position to learn still more about prospective instructors. Many coordinators who must make hiring decisions rely on letters of recommendation and other indirect evidence, in addition to what they can observe directly about instructors during orientation, observations, or assessment or other faculty meetings. However, if you have sufficient resources to interview applicants about their past experiences, their future goals, and how well they feel they fit your particular department, program, or course, that can help you make informed decisions in staffing this coordinated course. Similarly, if you have (or can create) an opportunity to observe the prospective instructor's teaching, then you can ask her or him to prepare a lesson that is consistent with your course content, learning outcomes, and vision. This is similar to how some community colleges hire course coordinators, and it may be that you came to be a course coordinator through an interview process where you demonstrated not only your ability to teach a particular introductory communication course, but also your interest in modeling best practices for teaching that curriculum to other instructors and even your comfort level with supervision (for example, whether you would be comfortable selecting a common course text for all instructors).

Communicating Expectations

Hiring an instructor is typically a happy occasion, full of high hopes and promise. It is, however, still important to clearly communicate the department, program, and course expectations — as well as your own, as course coordinator — to new and newly assigned instructors. In programs where there is little support for course coordination efforts (e.g., community colleges where there are few full-time faculty and a large number of revolving part-time faculty), it may be useful to create a handout or Web site that contains this orienting material. Some of the expectations you might consider discussing with new instructors include

- **The practical demands of the instructional role:** New instructors need to understand where they can find instructional materials and supplies, how to apply for an institutional email account, how to order textbooks, and so forth.
- **A clear sense of the "chain of command":** New instructors should know who their immediate supervisor is, who will evaluate them and when, and to whom they should address their successes, concerns, and emergencies.
- **The course vision:** New instructors should understand the role they play in what your department or program considers successful and meaningful instruction and the achievement of student learning outcomes. You should also share a syllabus template or any required learning outcomes with instructors.

There are many different ways to communicate (and continually discuss and evolve) program and course expectations with new instructors. For coordinators who engage in a more formal hiring process, in addition to sharing expectations in the position announcement, you can also try some or all of the following strategies:

- Invite new instructors to attend or participate in important department events (for example, performances, invited speakers, debate and forensics tournaments, and assessment meetings).
- Recommend readings you and your colleagues find significant or useful.
- Provide clarifying memos and handbooks (that accompany and contextualize a common syllabus, explain which materials the coordinator must review, identify student resources the department relies upon routinely, etc.).
- Require or recommend participation in orientation activities, staff meetings, or support courses where you address and explore the course vision and goals.
- Provide structured feedback through campus evaluation processes (for example, one-on-one discussions following teaching observations or review of annual evaluations).
- Encourage formal and informal mentoring relationships in settings where instructors will interact with their more experienced colleagues, such as in faculty or assessment meetings.

See Chapter 6 for more information on professional development for novice instructors. Even for coordinators who "inherit" or work with instructors they do not screen/hire themselves, many of these options are still possible. For example, if you learn who your new GTAs are from a graduate coordinator, then you can begin by introducing yourself to them via email or post (a formal letter helps create a sense of occasion and can, again, communicate something about your expectations for their efforts as instructors), including or assigning particular readings or exercises and requiring attendance at orientation or other, related activities. If you work with instructors who are part- or full-time lecturers hired by the department chair, then you might consider collaborating with the chair to begin the process of weaving these instructors into the course and department or program visions; you might also invite these instructors to attend meetings with colleagues who are already well versed in the course, provide them with relevant and/or preferred instructional materials, and arrange one-to-one meetings with each to review the evaluation process.

Helping integrate new instructors into program or course vision is essential to the vitality and relevance of that vision; as we explored earlier, visions often emerge through dialogue and consensus. Even the desire for instructors to participate in conversations about program vision is an expectation you should communicate readily from the outset of your working relationship. Identifying for yourself and being transparent with instructors about your own and the course's, program's, department's, and institution's expectations will help form a foundation for how you can evaluate an instructor's success in the classroom.

EVALUATING INSTRUCTORS

Course coordinators are engaged in a constant process of evaluation. We must determine whether a given assignment is meeting course learning outcomes; we must make careful decisions about who will be assigned to teach which sections; we must work with our instructors to better understand their strengths and limitations as teachers, in general, and with this content, in particular; and we must be open to reflection and introspection about our own efforts and actions. It is important to remember, however, that evaluation need not imply harsh or unrelenting criticism. Evaluation, in this sense, is the exercise of judgment — choices and actions that are informed by careful regard and evenhanded attention to both detail and context — and discernment — reflection, sincerity, and a willingness to locate patterns across time and work to render them meaningful. The following section will introduce ways to evaluate instructors, both formatively and summatively, and provide advice on documenting and rewarding instructor performance.

Formative Assessment

It can be very helpful for teachers, at any stage of their careers, to receive and provide both formative and summative feedback. Formative feedback, as we know from reading students' rough drafts and helping them better discern their strengths and limitations, is feedback that helps us gain perspective, build ourselves up, and take actions that inform future outcomes. Providing formative feedback, for example, as a student is engaged in a large research project, thesis, or other public communication, helps that student enter into dialogue with ourselves and others, making possible a stronger, more compelling or effective final effort. Formative feedback for our purposes would consist of communication that does not connote an official or final end result or "grade." In other words, this could be communication (whether face-to-face or otherwise mediated) that gives rise to dialogues with one another about our collective and individual philosophies of teaching. Whether in a staff meeting, over coffee, or in an email post in relation to a common reading, these are moments where we can engage in perception-checking about how we are doing as teachers and what we'd like to be doing differently. Types of formative feedback include observations and discussion.

Observations.   Observations may be a routine part of a coordinator's role, forming a foundation for mentoring conversations at regular intervals throughout the year or semester. Observations may be formal or unannounced — whichever approach a coordinator chooses should be transparent to instructors — and they should always include an opportunity for discussion and debrief of what occurred.

When you observe other colleagues, including part-time faculty and GTAs, you will likely want to first ask for and review their syllabus materials and then, if you are so inclined, suggest that you would like to attend the class unannounced. It is important, where unannounced observations are concerned, to reassure instructors of the purpose and function of these visits: establishing a context for a larger training and development conversation. During observation, you first want to get a feel for what it is like to be a student in this class:

- What is the structure and scope of the lesson?
- What can I expect to learn in this class, and what is its relevance beyond the course?
- What kind of classroom climate exists here?

Second, you want to get a feel for what it is like to be the instructor in this class:

- Where is the burden of responsibility for learning in this class?
- What are the strengths and challenges associated with this particular group of students?
- How does the instructor seem to manage classroom conversation, questions about course content, questions about university policy, and so forth?

It is incumbent on you, as the course coordinator, to reassure instructors that these observations are not meant to "catch" instructors; since any day in any classroom will be imperfect, and since your purpose is to help instructors become more effective at what they do, it should be not only permissible but ideal for you to see a less than perfect day. We recommend that you approach this differently only when you are concerned about what is happening in a particular instructor's classroom (for example, if you have received a complaint from a student or students, if the instructor reports that something is happening in the class that is concerning to her or him, or if you feel uncomfortable about something you have observed in the instructor's interactions with you, colleagues, or students); in such cases, we recommend scheduling the observation in advance, asking to review the instructor's lesson plan, and initiating a conversation with your supervisor about the questions or concerns you have. Of course, observations may play a role in summative feedback as well — which we address below. For example, a coordinator is likely to rely on observations to inform an annual evaluation or to better understand and document troubling circumstances in a given instructor's classroom.

John, for instance, conducts observations of each of his new instructors during the first semester of instruction. After his observation, he writes a two- to three-page letter that describes what he witnessed in order to provide a sense of what occurred (and for the instructor to reexperience her or his practices in the classroom), an assessment that is more constructive than evaluative, and a series of recommendations based on the observation. The letter is a good source of documentation for both the program and the instructor, and it helps both develop and improve.

Discussions.   By discussions as a means or method of evaluation, we mean all the many sorts of pedagogical conversations coordinators might have with their colleagues. This is perhaps easiest to illustrate with GTAs: The GTA supervisor may, in addition to directly observing the instructor in the classroom or during office hours and reviewing instructor evaluations, interact with her or him in a teaching support course or staff meetings, in one another's offices, in other classes that may have little to do with communication education, in assessment or faculty meetings, over Facebook and other social media sites, and so on. With part-time or full-time faculty, many of these avenues still remain, though these instructors are less likely to participate in more formal coursework related to their assignment. Any of these occasions can invite a conversation between coordinator and instructor that makes possible dialogue and feedback. Sometimes these conversations are spontaneous, bubbling up in the hallway or in the context of another meeting; but sometimes they are also purposeful, as when an instructor seeks a coordinator's input or a coordinator reaches out to an instructor because she or he has overheard something exciting or troubling with respect to this class.

In other words, while there are, no doubt, formal evaluation criteria that come to play in summative evaluations (such as annual evaluations), the course coordinator still has a broad array of information from which she or he may discern how a particular instructor or course is functioning. As course coordinators, we have answered questions and engaged in troubleshooting with instructors in all these settings. These are conversations that help us spot where an instructor is talented and where she or he might be struggling; we can make referrals to appropriate colleagues or resources, and we can involve the department chair, dean, or other offices on campus as necessary.

SGID (Small Group Instructional Diagnosis). It is also possible to use additional formal instruments to develop insight into what is happening across multiple sections of a coordinated course (or even within one particular section of that course). For example, some programs in our discipline, including our own, use a mid-semester instrument called the SGID: Small Group Instructional Diagnosis (Redmond & Clark, 1982). The protocol is relatively simple and easy to implement with relatively novice instructors. In effect, an instructor would arrange for a colleague to attend his or her class, arrange students into small groups, and ask them a series of three questions (What do you like about this course? What about this course needs improvement? And what recommendations do you have for how to accomplish those improvements?). For each of these steps, the person facilitating the SGID emphasizes consensus; if the SGID facilitator reports comments on which students have reached agreement, then an instructor can respond to that feedback, making adjustments to her or his teaching as appropriate, with a greater degree of confidence that the majority of students share this particular perspective (and no vocal minority dominates). The facilitator may also note dissenting views, indicating how many (often in terms of percentage or number of students) feel this way.

Over time we have come to nuance this process a bit so that it better serves our needs as a group. For example, John's instructors have adapted the SGID questions to better meet their needs: What do you like about this course; What can the instructor do to improve the course; What can the students do to improve the course? In Deanna's program, instead of asking students what they like about a given course, we ask what is working about that course, acknowledging that we might not "like" some experiences that are, in actuality, effective or meaningful. Further, SJSU instructors now ask a fourth question similar to SIUC's process: What can you do, as a student, to help implement the changes you recommend? While students often share as part of their recommendations suggestions for their own behavior in the class (e.g., complete assigned reading), asking this fourth question helps students understand that they are collaborators in this classroom experience and that their actions (or inactions) help to create that experience as successful or unsuccessful, meaningful or irrelevant. These formative forms of assessment can help inform and contextualize what coordinators can learn from summative assessment.

Summative Assessment

In contrast to formative feedback, summative feedback is more finite, may feel more official, and is often the end result of an evaluative process (resulting in, for example, a grade, promotion, or other endorsement or lack thereof). Summative feedback typically occurs as part of routine institutional processes, including end-of-the-semester student evaluations of teaching and annual evaluations.

End-of-the-Semester Student Evaluations.   Perhaps the most common summative evaluations instructors and students think of are student evaluations of teaching. While practices vary from school to school, most instructors administer these instruments to students toward the end of the semester. They can include a quantitative survey component, where students complete a series of Likert-type scales about their experiences in the class. For example, Deanna's campus instrument, the SOTE (Student Opinion of Teaching Effectiveness), asks students to rate instructors on qualities like whether the instructor was responsive to students' questions and comments, showed strong interest in teaching the class, and provided meaningful feedback on students' work. John's campus instrument, the ICE (Instructor/Course Evaluation) includes some 20 questions about the instructor and another series on the course. Many student evaluations also include a qualitative component, where students can provide written feedback to instructors about their strengths and areas for improvement. If you are able to access this data for the instructors who teach the courses you supervise, you can not only develop a keen sense of where the entire cohort of instructors is strong and where it is struggling, but you can also arrange for meetings with individual instructors to discuss and troubleshoot any items where they appear to be below norm range for the department, college, or university.

Each semester, we use students' teaching evaluations to inform related ongoing conversations surrounding assessment, training, and development as instructors; in this way, the summative exercise of student evaluations is useful formatively as well. Particularly, we review all GTA evaluations for each semester in which they remain part of our programs; we treat these as assessment data in that we look for patterns in students' perceptions of what they feel their instructors do well and where they feel their instructors could improve. (From time to time, in her capacity as a course coordinator, Deanna has also reviewed students' teaching evaluations for part-time faculty, following a similar process.)

A persistent challenge for SJSU GTAs is their performance on an item that asks students to rate whether their instructor helped them analyze complex or abstract ideas. These GTAs routinely score well on enthusiasm for teaching, responsiveness to students' diversity, and demonstrating the relevance of course content; but this item has continued to give us trouble. As a community, we are then able to raise this item as a question in two contexts: (1) in assessment meetings, as part of conversations about whether our public speaking course is sufficiently challenging and whether we communicate it as challenging (as opposed to "easy" or something "everyone does all the time") to our students, and (2) in training and development meetings, as part of conversations about how we talk with students about the rigor and complexity of communication. GTAs, in their effort to create supportive, community-oriented classrooms, often minimize the rigor of the assignments they ask their students to undertake (observing, for example, "See, was that so bad?" or "Now we'll do a fun activity . . . "); these discussions help GTAs clarify the role of the course as fundamental and challenging even as it is highly applicable and social.

Adjunct faculty on John's campus are encouraged to request end-of-the-semester evaluations, but these, like many pedagogical assessments, are the property of the instructors. If instructors wish to continue teaching in the department, they may submit these as evidence of teaching excellence, but they are not required to include them. Full-time instructors/lecturers, like the tenured and tenure-track professors, are required to do annual evaluations and often include the ICE reports as part of their evaluation paperwork.

Annual Evaluations.   The practice of annual evaluations can vary considerably from one program to the next and one coordinator's experience to the next. For example, for a course that employs tenure-track faculty and long-term lecturers, the annual evaluation process will likely follow that department's review, tenure, and promotion calendar (in which case, the course coordinator may serve in an advisory capacity to that review, but may not have a formal role in the evaluation process). Or in a program where GTAs are appointed for a given period of time (e.g., three years), then the assumption is that a GTA will continue in this role unless there is a documented problem (in which case, there may not be a formal annual review). It is possible that a coordinator may complete this evaluation herself or himself, or it may be that she or he completes it in consultation with a department chair or department personnel committee. In general, though, annual evaluations serve as an important means of communication between the institution, department, and instructor. They include attention to what the instructor is already doing well (as evidenced by teaching evaluations and other sources of information, such as an instructor's annual summary of achievements) as well as any areas the instructor needs to attend to, including specific performance expectations for improvement.

Documenting Evaluation

It can sometimes be challenging to know what sorts of employment and evaluation documentation to keep and for how long. When it comes to questions about archiving documentation, it is wise to consult with the department chair, dean's office, or another authoritative source (e.g., the campus attorney). As a coordinator, you function as a site of institutional or program memory, for both the program and the people who participate in it. For example, you might need to refer to your observation notes in a meeting with your department chair about whether to dismiss an instructor; or you might need to write a letter of recommendation on behalf of a part-time faculty member you worked with five or more years ago. Your efforts at documentation — and organizing these documents — may save you and others considerable frustration. Depending on the needs of your department, you may consider maintaining records of the following:

- The ongoing assessment of the course and any communication you may have had with the governing bodies who approve/review it
- Employment documents
- Teaching evaluations

- Communication from students about the course
- Family or health leave information
- Archived examinations and assignments
- Observation and meeting notes
- Memos to indicate acknowledgment, awareness, and/or approval of particular actions (for example, admitting someone to the GTA program, sharing a list of employed instructors to the campus parking office for employee permits, or approval of a family leave)
- Documents tracking emergent issues (i.e., keeping notes for all meetings and communication with respect to a particular situation)
- Routine notes (such as what you and instructors discussed at the most recent staff meeting or your observation notes)

Especially in the case of instructors about whom you are concerned, documentation takes on a new, more complex dimension. For better or worse, we often devote more attention to creating documentation when someone (whether course coordinator, instructor, student, or campus office) raises a concern about a given classroom or instructor. Cases of particular interest to course coordinators and other supervisors and administrators include student concerns or complaints; allegations of unfair treatment, discrimination, and sexual harassment; and safety issues (e.g., rooms with insufficient lighting or other hazards).

Generally speaking, keeping documentation on file is unproblematic until the moment you need to share those documents with someone else. While most documentation you create as a course coordinator will remain confidential, it is important to discern which documents you should share, when, and with whom; often a department chair or other supervisor can help you navigate these concerns. For example, in the last 15 years, we have worked with instructors who have needed health leaves; who were accused of, were victims of, or witnessed sexual harassment in the classroom; who negotiated both responsible and unreasonable grade challenges; who needed to document and prepare charges of academic dishonesty; who have attempted suicide; who have been physically threatened by students or colleagues; who have experienced campus violence in their classroom; who have been addicted; and who have had some trouble getting the hang of different aspects of teaching (like classroom management). In each case, it is helpful to have a trusted colleague or mentor (ideally, though not necessarily, your supervisor or department chair) who can help you determine when to invoke which campus processes. For example, in the above cases, we found it helpful to consult our department chairs, deans, the Bursar's Office, the university attorney, Human Resources, the Office of Student Conduct and Ethical Development, the campus ombuds, the director of counseling services, and the University Police Department. As you can imagine, some of these issues warranted careful attention to detail, and we were relieved to be able to share from our own notes about each specific case, especially where versions of events appeared to conflict with one another.

Awards and Recognition

As guardians of institutional memory, course coordinators not only document policy changes, instructors' participation in the course or program, or the negative and challenging aspects of higher education instruction (as when we must dismiss an instructor); they also help to celebrate the accomplishments of the community and individual members within it. This can take the form of offering awards at the end of each year, recognizing outstanding instruction — for example, an "outstanding GTA" award — or a convocation speech or professional development seminar that celebrates all graduating GTAs and their contributions to the course and program. It is all too easy to remember to document those moments that seem troubling to us, but in order for a community of teacher-scholars to recognize their strengths and continue to grow from them, these moments of ceremony and appreciation are essential. One method of evaluation to which we course coordinators should return regularly is expressing our appreciation for our colleagues. To this end, we might consider eliciting feedback from course instructors about how to celebrate what is working and how to honor instructors who demonstrate excellence and/or considerable growth. If you do not have awards for instruction in your department, we recommend creating them. Awards can be of minimal cost to a program, yet they can provide a much-needed boost to morale for hard-working, collegial instructors.

DISMISSING INSTRUCTORS

At some point in your experience as a coordinator, it will likely be necessary to dismiss an instructor who does not meet school, program, or course expectations. This can be an uncomfortable process, but it is an important one to undertake, in part so that students' learning is not compromised, and in part so that qualified or promising instructors have an opportunity to show they can effectively teach students this subject matter. It is also likely that at some point you will be called upon to advocate for the rehiring of effective, trusted instructors.

That said, it is unlikely you have exclusive latitude to hire or dismiss instructors associated with the course or courses you coordinate. Most course coordinators have, at a minimum, the accountability of discussing these issues with a colleague, often the department chair or graduate coordinator. Further, the process by which someone becomes an instructor of a given course can vary considerably from program to program. For example, with courses staffed by GTAs, instructors may be assigned to teach by virtue of their admission to the graduate program. Or the process could be more complex, as when instructors from among the existing faculty are appointed by the department chair, while prospective GTAs must apply to teach through a rigorous screening process separate from graduate admission.

In cases where it is becoming clear that an instructor is not meeting course, program, or department expectations, it is important to involve other decision makers as soon as possible. For example, when a graduate coordinator admits students to a graduate program and also selects GTAs, it is important that she or he knows what is happening with a struggling instructor, as it may affect other aspects of departmental decision making. Similarly, where the department chair is involved in employment decisions, it is important to keep her or him current on what is happening with this instructor or section. In either event, these other parties are likely to need formal documentation of your concerns about this particular instructor, including any evidence you can bring to bear on your evaluation. While evaluation of adjuncts and part-time faculty may be beyond your complete control, you can provide documentation of problems to the department chair for use in annual reviews. In one specific example, John had to document repeated concerns about an adjunct instructor; these reports, combined with other disturbing patterns elsewhere, were grounds for not re-appointing this teacher for the next year. Importantly, this kind of effort helps protect the integrity of your program and enables you to have greater control over the sections under your supervision.

Documenting Personnel Decisions

It is important to be accurate in documenting reasons for rehiring or dismissing instructors, as this can have long-term consequences for their future employment. For example, if a department or program dismisses a problematic instructor using lack of funding as rationale (instead of, as would be more appropriate in this case, student complaints, poor teaching evaluations, and lack of compliance with stated general education learning objectives), then the instructor does not learn all she or he can to improve and the program risks having to rehire this instructor at a later date (especially if decision makers cannot clearly distinguish between this problematic instructor and another, effective instructor). This is true of rehiring as well. Instructors have a right to know what the course coordinator, as a representative of the department or program, believes to be their strengths and limitations. As a course coordinator, you mentor effectively when you help instructors grow and strengthen their skills from one term to the next.

Dismissal in a Tough Economic Climate

There can be considerable and varying degrees of anxiety associated with the processes of rehiring and dismissal—not least because, due to insufficient funding, a department or program might not be able to ask even effective and long-standing instructors to return from one semester to the next. GTAs often enjoy a degree of mentoring and stability other instructors do not. Their rehiring is, as a result, typically less fraught with tension (except when they fail to meet the minimum expectations of their position); most of the time, GTAs can and are encouraged to learn from their mistakes. On Deanna's campus, for example, GTAs are technically appointed semester by semester in their first year, and then receive a one-year appointment in their second year; the department assumes, however, that they will remain in the two-year program unless their performance (as a student or as an instructor) suffers or they graduate. Part-time faculty, however, especially where they do not serve by annual or multiyear contracts, may not receive the same degree of employment security.

The question of whom to rehire and whom to dismiss can be complex where budget resources are limited. In turbulent economic circumstances, when there are far more qualified and interested instructors than available sections of a given course (or, more to the point, funding to create and staff additional sections), a course coordinator may be called upon to rank prospective instructor assignments. Certainly if an instructor is meeting or exceeding program and course expectations, it would be wise to rehire her or him. But in cases where many instructors meet or exceed expectations, it can be difficult to rank and make selections from among them. Here it can help to constitute an evaluation or personnel committee of three to five people who each have a stake in the successful operation of the course. Through careful review of materials and deliberation, it may be possible to create a consistent and transparent ranking system that facilitates rehiring decisions. The process is still more complex in programs that employ past graduates as part-time instructors. It can be difficult to make even the best, soundest decisions when you know and care about the people whose livelihood is at stake.

This helps demonstrate the ways in which our own permeable boundaries, as coordinators, are a mixed blessing. As much as it is delightful to hear about our former students' and colleagues' successes, as when they have babies or find jobs, it is difficult and frustrating to learn of their troubles when times are hard, such as losing health benefits or having to move back in with parents or other family members. While the vast majority of course coordinators are not trained counselors or therapists, these colleagues with whom we have worked so closely have come to depend on us and our guidance, and it is important that we try to support them as best we can. Provide what support and encouragement you can during lean years (including, for example, offering moral support, providing direction and counsel regarding possible career directions, facilitating networking, and sharing what you know about unemployment, furloughs and layoffs, COBRA, and so forth).

CONCLUSION

Employment decisions surrounding hiring, evaluating, and dismissing instructors are a significant part of how you, as a leader, realize the vision of this coordinated course. In navigating employment decisions, it is important to be reflective, to consider the role these decisions play in your own and others' lives. Being professional in this instance involves respect, candor, transparency, and a willingness to mentor others to greater awareness of their strengths and limitations. It may also help for you to reflect on the strengths and limitations you bring to this aspect of your leadership role. Where you succeed, take stock — learn what you can from what you have enabled others to do; where you struggle, exercise unflinching introspection and compassion into where and how you have made mistakes — again, learn what you can.

REFERENCE

Clark, J., & Redmond, M. (1982). *Small group instructional diagnoses final report*. Seattle Department of Biology Education, University of Washington (ED 217 945).

RECOMMENDED READINGS

Foster, T. J., & Foster, M. S. (1993). Instructor evaluation in the basic course. In L. W. Hugenberg, P. L. Gray, & D. M. Trank (Eds.), *Teaching and directing the basic communications course* (pp. 185–199). Dubuque, IA: Kendall/Hunt Publishing.

A comprehensive overview of how to build a transparent, consistent, and effective assessment program for instructors associated with an introductory communication course. This reading is especially helpful for programs that need help creating an evaluative process for faculty that extends beyond seniority to quality of instruction.

McDonald, K., & Mongeau, P. (2007). Hiring a new colleague: The search committee's perspective. *Spectra, 43*(9), 10–11.

This is a brief, practical article that helps those who are unfamiliar with interview processes consider what might be most helpful for surfacing insights about a prospective instructor's "fit" for a program, such as creating conditions to interact with students.

6

Training and Development Opportunities for Less Experienced Instructors

Teaching People to Teach

At the end of what feels like an endless orientation week, you delight in reading the GTAs' evaluations — their sense of what was useful to them, as well as what they'd like to cover more in staff meetings throughout the year. "Microteaching" figures prominently in these evaluations; nearly every GTA appreciates the opportunity to plan and teach a lesson for her or his colleagues, the opportunity to learn what it feels like to make mistakes before classes begin in earnest, and the delight of playing both student and teacher and engaging each lesson through both roles. Each orientation, staffed by a willing group of volunteer former and current GTAs, affords opportunities to discuss teaching and learning, to try out different teaching styles, to troubleshoot scary situations (like responding to a grade challenge or helping a troubled student), and to acquire practical skills.

* * *

This chapter will address the components of a comprehensive training and development program for less experienced or relatively inexperienced instructors. "Inexperienced" instructors, in this instance, are those who may be new to teaching in general or new to this particular teaching context. On most campuses, the largest faction of instructors that constitutes this group are GTAs, though this group may also include, for example, an adjunct faculty member who first starts teaching after earning the M.A. or Ph.D. These are teachers who need to learn not only discipline-specific pedagogy, but also, generally, how to teach. In order to cultivate effective professional growth in this group of instructors, coordinators must organize, enrich, and adapt what will become a vast repository of wisdom with respect to teaching, to teaching in communication studies, and to teaching this particular coordinated course.

Training and professional development, as a process, describes a community's efforts to grow and learn from one another. To put a new spin on an old proverb, it takes a village to run a comprehensive, multisection communication course, and for the course to succeed, you must help members of this teaching community share their insights and experiences with one another and with you. In the case of the coordinated course, this will likely entail sharing and learning how best to teach certain perhaps difficult aspects of the course, how to respond to particular challenges in the classroom (for example, academic dishonesty or classroom management), how to be more effective and time-efficient as teachers, and the like. These are the activities that, as a community, we believe (because we have read about them in published scholarship and/or because they have emerged from our own experiences in the classroom) will help us become stronger, more effective teachers.

There are many different methods for training and development of less experienced instructors, and the particular combination of activities you pursue as a course coordinator will emerge from the vision and mission of the course. In taking this charge seriously, you serve not only your particular course or program, but also the discipline of communication studies. It is important to note that pulling together training and development materials (from resources instructors will find useful, to activities that help teachers and students learn communication concepts and skills, to understandings of campus and student culture *in situ*) has relevance not only for the novice instructor but for the experienced teacher. While accomplished educators will usually be able to step into foundational courses for which they are qualified, but perhaps unfamiliar with, they will still need to explore the collective wisdom of the people who have taught the course (see Chapter 7 for training and development opportunities for more experienced instructors).

This chapter will first address the objectives of training and development and then discuss the components of a comprehensive training and development program, including new instructor orientation and post-orientation support.

TRAINING AND DEVELOPMENT OBJECTIVES

What are we really teaching, when we work to help others learn to teach? As Doris Lessing (1999/1962) argues, "Ideally, what should be said to every child, repeatedly, throughout his or her school life is something like this: 'You are in the process of being indoctrinated. We have not yet evolved a system of education that is not a system of indoctrination'" (p. xxi). This needn't feel as hostile as it may sound — Lessing's words can serve as a reminder to educators that we must reflect on, and at times challenge, our most deeply held assumptions and the effects they have on our students and ourselves. While we typically would not describe our efforts as indoctrination, most of us would acknowledge that we work to encourage some actions and beliefs and discourage others. Course coordinators would do well to understand what our role is in education or indoctrination, reflecting on what does and does not serve us, our communities, and our discipline. Where graduate teaching associates and other relatively inexperienced colleagues are concerned, we must acknowledge and respect the experiences they bring with them to their roles, and also remember that we contribute to their development as educators in ways we might not fully realize. We play our part in their development, encouraging them to embrace some behaviors, attitudes, and understandings and reject others.

Our own interest in social justice–oriented pedagogy led us both to approach the question of training and development in a critical, appraising way. For many years, we blustered at the notion of "training," feeling uncomfortable with the idea that what we might be engaged in is, as Lessing suggests, indoctrination. Instead we embraced the notion of "professional development," a descriptor that felt more accurate to us (and more in keeping with our feelings about what it is that we do, which is to develop professional educators). Recently, a respected friend and colleague, Geri Merrigan, who is the chair of the Communication Studies Department at San Francisco State University, has challenged us on the issue of terms associated with professional development. Geri, astute organizational communication scholar that she is, reminded us that "professional development" is sometimes code for the sort of policing and boundary-keeping we found off-putting in the term "training."

In this chapter, we work to weave these two terms together. We still use the term "professional development" as a means of reminding ourselves that what we are working toward as a community is a professional commitment to teaching and learning. We also find it helpful to remember that "training" occurs with new instructors, and that the form and function of these sessions follow from our, and our colleagues', beliefs about what constitutes effective instruction. Instead of feeling frightened at the prospect of indoctrinating others, we invoke this term as a reminder to reflect as carefully as we can on the assumptions we bring to the process of teaching people to be teachers. Inevitably, some of these assumptions will be helpful and some less so (and some perhaps even downright harmful) but, through reflection and dialogue with colleagues both novice and experienced, we can grow as a community. Below, we offer advice on incorporating teaching philosophy and program vision into training and development goals, and provide some guiding questions that can help you tailor training exercises to your needs. These suggestions should help you reflect constructively on your training and development goals, needs, and practices.

Philosophy and Vision in Training

A coordinator's teaching philosophy is likely to inform not only the vision of the course she or he coordinates, but also the approaches she or he takes to preparing and supporting instructors of the course. Above all else, the coordinator's efforts must be consistent with the vision of the course and program.

If, for example, it is part of the vision of the course to uphold a commitment to social justice in the classroom, emphasizing interrogation of inequality and dialogue toward social change, then instructors should experience this as part of their own preparation to teach the course. Orientation sessions may emphasize how to engage in difficult conversations surrounding thorny subjects, to teach particular lessons on concepts like hegemony or muted group theory, and to explore their own experiences of power and privilege as teachers and learners. Or if it is part of the vision of the course to establish and reinforce effective workforce communication, then training and development sessions should prepare instructors toward this end. These sessions might familiarize instructors with local employers' expectations and with PowerPoint and other communication tools, while encouraging them to reflect on their past and current experiences in industry.

Both programs may also include sessions on lesson planning, classroom management, or grading. However, each program will likely approach these topics according to their particular goals, values, and commitments. Ideally, the coordinator participates fully in these exercises, working toward her or his growth and exploration too.

For an example of the links between vision, coordinator philosophy, and GTA training, consider the training and development activities we organize each year for our colleagues. Every summer, we each help to develop an orientation for GTAs who teach public speaking that emerges from the vision we have articulated for the public speaking course. Both our communities encourage and celebrate collaboration, careful reflection, and dialogue (among students, between students and instructors, and among instructors); while not all instructors enter and extend this vision in exactly the same way, as a collective, they model these values for their new colleagues. Deanna's orientation is staffed by current and former GTAs, and together they adapt from one year to the next so that the sessions feel relevant, purposeful, and appropriately challenging. John revises his orientation yearly with input from the faculty and his assistant director (an advanced doctoral student) toward creating thematic, practical, and critically reflexive conversations about the work instructors will be doing in their public speaking classrooms. In each, the colleagues who run sessions are often available to GTAs as mentors (both formally and informally), and they routinely attend large chunks of the orientation for their own benefit. In this way, the community can come together to make sure our new instructors are well (if, necessarily, incompletely) prepared for the challenges of their role.

In recent years, as we have moved from one station to another along the tenure track, we have also developed an intense interest in helping teachers enjoy vitality and longevity in their careers. This has led us to work with interested colleagues to select readings from Parker Palmer's (1998) *The Courage to Teach* and other pedagogically oriented texts, to develop lessons surrounding paradoxes that teachers — especially less experienced ones — experience. These lessons might discuss the tension between being friendly with and being a friend to students, or they might model mundane time-management skills. In this way, what functions as training and development work within our program is an imperfect and evolving, but nonetheless meaningful, amalgam of program vision and goals, the experience and wisdom of ourselves and other experienced faculty, and the needs and interests of the novice instructors themselves.

Guiding Questions for Training Exercises

There are several important considerations for focusing training objectives into training and development exercises for less experienced instructors.

- **Who are these instructors?** Audience analysis, an important component of all communication, is useful here; exploring what you do and do not know about these people, their strengths and limitations, will help structure anything from orientation sessions to assigned readings to selections within a mentoring program. For example, it may be useful to create sessions specifically for instructors on how to navigate the tension between being students and being teachers, or, depending on who staffs this course, it may be useful to create sessions specifically for International Teaching Assistants (ITAs). These sessions may range from the intensely practical (e.g., how to grade) to the more theoretical (e.g., why we grade and how that process is both helpful and harmful).

- **Who are the students the course serves?** Training and development exercises may emerge from what instructors perceive to be students' strengths and limitations. For example, when SJSU Communication Studies GTAs felt as though their public speaking students were overly focused on the practical, "how-to" of public speaking at the expense of exploring the ideas students were advancing through their speeches, a small subset of the community developed a workshop on thematizing speeches in the public speaking classroom (Haiker, 2009). These more advanced GTAs helped their colleagues learn how to facilitate conversations on clusters of socially significant topics, such that speech rounds became more coherent, credible, and engaging. While these sessions emerged initially from GTAs' frustrations, part-time faculty who were relatively new to teaching public speaking also found them helpful—especially the reminder to engage the content of students' communication and not just its form. Training and development exercises may also be tailored to the students the course serves by helping new instructors learn how to respond to the needs of students with disabilities, students who are English language learners, or international students.

- **What do assessment reports and committees say about the effectiveness of the course?** Training and development exercises may emerge from the needs of assessment or other oversight groups. For example, if the instructors of a course routinely struggle at achieving a particular learning outcome, then a workshop concentrating on that particular issue, whether on ethics or social significance or patterns of grammatical error, may help.

- **What do teaching evaluations say about the effectiveness of the instructors and the course?** Patterns in instructors' evaluations may also reveal a need for a particular kind of training and development exercise. For example, as a coordinator, you may discern a pattern across end-of-the-semester evaluations that suggests that students do not perceive instructors' grading to be fair. Developing a session for instructors that helps them develop consistent and transparent grading practices will be of service not only to the instructors, but to the students as well.

- **What resources do you have?** Resources may mean money, but could also include less tangible, put perhaps equally helpful, resources like time and energy. Shaping the coordinated course so that all participants understand their responsibility in its effective functioning can help galvanize the efforts of motivated and capable people toward not only training and development activities, but also other important initiatives in your program.

- **What are your strengths as a coordinator?** Here it is useful to assess your strengths — where you excel and what you enjoy — as a leader, as a teacher, as a colleague, as a learner, and in other aspects of your life. Are you creative? Are you a meticulous planner? Do you have expertise in a particular teaching method or with some distinct area of the field? In drawing on these strengths as you plan training and development activities, you not only develop congruence between this role and other aspects of your life you cherish, but you influence the tenor and tone of the program or course, and you model how others might share their best with one another in kind.

By addressing these questions, successful training and development efforts develop in the same way as effective teaching: in relation to a context, through reflection and collaboration, and as a process.

There are many different components of training and development that are appropriate for less experienced instructors. Some of these are formal and some may be more ad hoc. While it is not necessary to adapt each and every component for a successful coordinated course, it is likely that you will want to use the answers to the guiding questions above to tailor many of these components to the needs of your particular course, instructors, students, and institution. The next sections will discuss components and techniques of new instructor development and training, dividing them into orientation and post-orientation support. These two classes of support are not hard and fast, and you should feel free to try modifying advice in the orientation section toward training later in the semester, or vice-versa, to reflect the needs of your program.

NEW INSTRUCTOR ORIENTATION

Orientations, especially for new or less experienced instructors, are crucial. While many universities run orientations that serve all campus instructors or all GTAs, it is absolutely essential that, as coordinator, you also develop an orientation that provides discipline-specific instruction with this course (Jones, 1991; Ronkowski, 1998; Wulff, Nyquist, & Abbott, 1991). Though your instructors do need to understand their role as university employees (and relevant associated policies, for example, regarding sexual harassment, accommodations of students with disabilities, and so forth), they also need to be able to access a collective repository of information about this particular course and how best to teach it. This helps them benefit from the wisdom (and occasional lack thereof) of their predecessors, so that they — and you — are not attempting to reinvent the wheel each fall. In addition, preparing a departmental orientation will make it possible to better address instructors' developmental growth.

Developmental approaches to training take into consideration how instructors, as learners, grow and change over time and with experience. In their work that explores GTAs' training and development from a developmental perspective, Jody Nyquist and Jo Sprague articulate three different roles GTAs assume and explore in their efforts to become professional faculty members: The *senior learner*, the *colleague-in-training*, and the *junior colleague* (Nyquist & Sprague, 1998; Sprague & Nyquist, 1991).

- The senior learner spans the gap between student and teacher, struggling with the tensions of that role, worrying about credibility and authority.
- The colleague-in-training is characterized by her or his efforts to master teaching methods and disciplinary concepts.
- The junior colleague is concerned with students' learning and how she or he may best facilitate that learning.

To illustrate, the senior learner wonders "Will students like me?"; the colleague-in-training wonders "How do I lecture?"; and the junior colleague wonders "Are students getting it?" (Nyquist & Sprague, 1998, p. 67). Awareness of these stages can help shape training and professional development exercises. For example, structured mentoring activities that pair them with more experienced instructors may be helpful to senior learners; colleagues-in-training may benefit by additional attention to and guided practice in different teaching methods; and sessions on assignment and examination design as meaningful assessment may also be useful. For the coordinator who supervises new GTAs each year, knowing that most will likely be senior learners can shape the direction and approach of the orientation.

Orientations will vary in tenor, size, and scope, according to your campus and department cultures and resources. For example, in Deanna's department, GTAs meet for approximately 50 hours of departmental training prior to the start of the semester (2.5 hours in June, 2.5 hours in July, and then 40 to 45 hours the week before classes begin). Part-time and full-time faculty are welcome — though not required — to attend orientation, and some return to do so each summer. In contrast, in John's department, GTAs attend a five-day orientation week where they participate in university orientation, department graduate student orientation, and GTA orientation. Often, course coordinators take what they can get at first, later chipping away at any structural or institutional constraints that interfere with course or program vision. Given that course coordination is usually only a portion of one's academic assignment, it is important to remember that orientation need not consist of the course coordinator running every single session, for 10 or 25 or 50 hours. If your goal is to introduce instructors to (or keep them engaged in) the vast reservoir of knowledge associated with this course, then more experienced instructors (as well as alumni of the program, knowledgeable colleagues, and so forth) can play a role in offering different sessions on different topics.

Deanna's departmental GTA orientation is an evolution and adaptation of the University of Washington model (Wulff, Nyquist, and Abbott, 1991); her colleague Jo Sprague brought this approach with her in the early 1990s. Their approach is structured in the light of Nyquist and Sprague's developmental work with GTAs and includes sessions on syllabus design and teaching methods, as well as discussion of both theoretical and practical readings, and mentoring conversations surrounding the tensions new teachers may experience as they prepare to enter the classroom. Southern Illinois University, where orientation was first instituted by Jan Hoffman in the early to mid-1990s, uses a similar model. What SJSU and SIUC Communication Studies GTAs experience these days is an extension of these earlier efforts — over the years, each program has flexed and fluxed to engage more profound diversity of students, instructors, and ideas.

Deanna's June orientation consists of introductions and discussion of GTAs' expectations and fears of their role. She asks them to reflect on their most meaningful teachers and the most lasting lessons in order to create their own teaching philosophies (i.e., what they feel "good" teaching is or should be). In her July orientation, she builds on this assignment; they discuss the commonalities and divergences in their teaching philosophies, and then she asks the GTAs to proceed down the hall to their "first" public speaking class. One of their more experienced public speaking instructors then, in character, takes them inside the first 45 minutes of the first day of class. They debrief this experience, and then discuss the instructor's lesson plan, including attention to lesson planning format and effective phrasing of student learning objectives. They learn that they will be teaching a lesson ("microteaching" — or, as they sometimes tease one another, "microtorture") during orientation week in August.

The orientation week in August consists of these microteachings and their attendant debrief discussions, as well as meetings with key department figures, activities that help familiarize them with campus resources from an instructor's perspective, and readings and discussions that help encourage reflective thinking and informed action.

John's orientation is a week-long intensive workshop that introduces both the specifics of their teaching assignment (syllabi, polices, survival skills, etc.) as well their role as new graduate students. Sessions emphasize two key components of the SIUC support program: mentoring and critical reflection. First, large portions of the orientation are centered around advanced students who serve as mentors to the new GTAs. From providing experiences, advice, and sample syllabi and assignments, the mentors are the front line of support for new instructors. New GTAs are assigned to mentors from a pool of available teachers who, selected by John, represent the best teaching practices in the department. Second, sessions explore critical reflection — a commitment to not just contemplating what to teach or how to teach it, but also why instructors make the choices they make and to what end these choices develop. It is important for new teachers to ask these complicated questions throughout their first semester of teaching in order to enhance their overall experience and prepare themselves for entering the profession.

Below, we discuss some of the most significant elements of new instructor orientation — lesson planning, microteaching, simulation activities, grading, and shared texts — in more detail. These are a culmination of the practices we both use in training and development, though our programs diverge in whether and how to implement each of these in a given year. We also offer our own orientation schedules for reference at the end of the section, on pages 139–148.

Lesson Planning

A session on lesson planning is an undeniably important aspect of any orientation work that involves new teachers. While orientation sessions help instructors understand the strengths and limitations of their teaching, learn the skill sets demanded by course content, and cultivate troubleshooting skills, a key component of success in the classroom involves knowing how to develop unit, weekly, and daily lesson plans for meeting course learning outcomes. Such a session can be preparatory to microteaching, so that new teachers have had some instruction in lesson planning before trying to teach for the first time. We usually have three objectives in mind when teaching lesson planning:

1. By the end of the session, new teachers should be able to identify a learning objective or outcome and how that is distinct from any particular goals they might have as a teacher. In other words, they should be able to distinguish between "I want to get through Chapter Three" and "Students will be able to identify at least three strategies for attracting and retaining an audience's attention."
2. By the end of the session, new teachers should be able to articulate the importance of modeling — naming the parts of the lesson plan and how they mirror different aspects of a well-crafted public speech. For example, an effective "intro" for a lesson usually establishes and maintains rapport, draws the learners' attention, offers a structural preview of how the lesson will proceed, and grounds all parts of the lesson in relevance or value for the learner (not only in terms of upcoming course assignments, but also beyond the classroom).
3. By the end of the session, new teachers should be able to, at a minimum, understand that there is much more to successful teaching than asking students, "So, what did you think of the reading?" This is to say that new teachers, at least at first, need to develop more material for their lessons than they think they'll need (knowing that, if they run out of time, they can reprioritize activities, lectures, etc.).

The GTAs we supervise practice this skill for as long as they remain in the program. Deanna, in fact, collects lesson plans for every class period for the first semester they teach (as part of a portfolio of materials they submit for Comm 285A, the first half of a two-part, four-unit practicum sequence), and she asks to see lesson plans when she meets with GTAs individually to troubleshoot issues they may be having in the classroom. John requires samples of lesson plans in the portfolios new GTAs turn in as part of their support course, SPCM 539. In both programs, portfolios contain not only lesson plans, but assignments, activities, and a reflective journal — each with critical commentary on each item (e.g., assignment, lesson, exam) as to what the instructor (and her or his students) learned from the experience.

While lesson planning might seem exclusive to sessions for novice instructors, there is some value to offering sessions on this skill to more experienced instructors. With time, instructors may have to guard against the tendency to prepare for their classes by bringing a couple of questions on the reading to class. Whenever an instructor indicates that she or he is struggling with managing class time or achieving learning outcomes, we recommend reflecting carefully on the lesson planning process. For example, if an instructor needs help managing class time, it may help to indicate specific clock times on the lesson plan (e.g., 9:30–9:45 a.m.) rather than ranges of time (e.g., 15 minutes). Or if students commonly challenge the value of class assignments or appear disengaged from important stages in the development of particular projects (like major speeches), then we would encourage an instructor to review her or his syllabus for when, how, and how often he or she underscores with students the relevance of class work for not only upcoming assignments, but also beyond the classroom.

Microteaching

Microteaching can form an important core experience within a department orientation. Microteaching may take many different forms, depending on whose account of it you read. As Deanna implements it, microteaching involves participants engaging in classroom instruction; each instructor takes her turn serving as teacher, while the remaining participants model typical student behaviors. Because she typically supervises 15 GTAs at any given time, she has had a lot of success with asking each GTA to assume responsibility for developing a lesson plan for a single day in the semester. The GTA chooses a particular day in the course calendar for which she or he prepares a lesson plan (often for a 75-minute class period); during orientation, she or he will teach this lesson as though it is that day of the course, using any strategies she or he feels will be helpful for the time of day the class meets and at the time of the semester the lesson will occur. The GTA begins at the start of class and continues "in character" until it is time for the next person to have a turn; this may last 15 minutes or more, depending on what else is occurring in orientation that day. She typically asks other GTAs and audience members to subtly model the behaviors instructors commonly see in students at that time of day or time of semester or with that particular course content. This experience provides instructors a valuable opportunity to feel what teaching is like prior to meeting with their students for the first time. In effect, the GTA is in a position to make these first, early errors in a relatively "safe" space, with people who are role-playing students. We debrief these experiences together, identifying strengths for each instructor as well as questions and common patterns of limitation for the group of instructors who taught that day. Deanna also asks new GTAs to meet with their mentors that day for lunch so they can discuss the experience one-on-one.

While it is not always possible, in large programs, to invite all instructors to practice teaching in this way, it might be more feasible than you would first think. For example, while there is certainly some value to the coordinator witnessing all microteachings, it may be that assistant coordinators or other trusted colleagues could play a role in the evaluation process. Further, while you may rely on microteaching as a significant indicator of whether a GTA should be assigned a section (at SJSU, GTAs must "pass" orientation), the experience has much value as formative assessment alone. While microteaching is perhaps most immediately relevant for the instructor who has little experience teaching, it can also be meaningful for instructors who would like to strengthen their teaching skills in light of feedback from their peers, as well as for instructors who may have experience teaching in general, but little experience teaching in communication studies courses particularly.

Microteachings have been invaluable for Deanna's work as a coordinator, as they have helped not only assess individual instructors' strengths and limitations (on anything from credibility and organization to time and classroom management), but also identify topics and exercises for staff meetings based on their collective strengths and limitations. Deanna is also able to provide feedback on their first lesson plans, which helps them as they begin to plan the next 30 class periods (and they have experienced quite a few class periods and instructional approaches in the scope of their orientation). Later, these experiences inform a continued conversation about teaching that extends into unannounced observations in instructors' classrooms.

Simulation Activities

It is important to provide new teachers with structured practice opportunities during orientation and periodically throughout the school year. In addition to microteaching, which can be useful in helping new teachers cultivate lesson planning, immediacy, and other plannable skills, it is wise to engage new teachers in sessions and activities where they can confront the threatening and unfamiliar in structured and guided ways. Reading, discussing, and role playing scenarios from case studies can be helpful in surfacing challenging issues with new teachers before they become issues in their own classrooms. Please note, with these sorts of activities, that it is less important for new teachers to acquire specific solutions to classroom problems (given that classroom situations can vary considerably depending on any number of contextual factors), and more important that they learn a troubleshooting or problem-solving process that takes them to the appropriate resources in your preferred sequence: their colleagues, their mentors, their supervisors, the relevant offices on campus, and so forth.

You will find it helpful if you and your instructors begin to reflect on common classroom difficulties (and interesting or challenging variants of these). For example, as a coordinator, you might find it helpful to maintain a journal or notebook of memorable situations, issues, readings, and other items you can use to help others learn how best to teach this course. Some of this can be archived in your email program (as GTAs or other relatively inexperienced instructors email for advice). For example, in preparing for orientation, we find it helpful to review the sorts of troubles GTAs or other part-time faculty have experienced in the past year or two. We also might ask new GTAs, as they submit a portfolio of the materials they developed during their first semester teaching, to develop case studies that evoke challenges they faced that semester. Case studies for an orientation typically include grade challenges, blurry boundaries between professional and personal relationships, and students' life challenges that affect their learning. Another way to activate this careful thinking about teaching and learning is to ask instructors to maintain teaching journals, where they can reflect, however briefly, on what is and is not working in their classrooms and why they feel that is the case.

Forum theatre, from Boal's (1985) *Theatre of the Oppressed*, has worked very well with GTAs and part-time instructors in both our programs. Strategically placed in the last half of our orientation week, when new instructors have acquired a whole host of anxiety-provoking thoughts about the classroom and what can happen there, these sessions move beyond role playing of critical incidents in the classroom to a substantive engagement in perspective-taking surrounding teaching and learning. Boal's contention is that theatre is rehearsal for revolution. He draws a distinction between acting or role playing as passive consumption, as processes with limited value for change and growth, and forum theatre as an active process of engagement. All participants are "spect-actors," involved in the transpiring event. To this end, people must move ways of thinking and seeing through their bodies; they must attempt to empathize with perspectives they might not readily take; and they must consider a multiplicity of different possible outcomes of a given situation.

In Deanna's forum theatre orientation exercises, instructors work together to brainstorm different scenarios that illuminate or exemplify a particular concern they have at this stage in their development. They first stage this scenario, and then, performance by performance, they begin to envision how it might be otherwise. For example, in a staged grade challenge between a student and a professor, all instructors would first witness the scenario as scripted. Then, after that first (or sometimes second, if the scenario is complex) viewing, people may choose to step into one role or another to see if they might take the scenario in a different direction, to a different outcome. While instructors often worry whether they have the "right" answer, that is less important at this stage; what is more important is that all the instructors in the room have now experienced an array of different possible strategies for how to address that situation. Some of these approaches will work better for some than others, but experiencing the variety, and assuming the different perspectives involved, is instructive and applicable long after orientation. John uses this approach as well; however, he has also included image theatre, asking new GTAs to create bodily images that capture their previous experiences in university-required courses and juxtapose those with images of what they hope those experiences could become. Here, we can talk about how to move from the emotional/physical experience to what kind of pedagogy might enable such responses.

In debriefing, we discuss the nuances of the scenarios — how it felt, what surprised them, what they learned, what they feel they still need to learn — paying particular attention to any particular resources they should draw on (e.g., consulting their mentor, supervisor, or department chair, calling counseling or the university police, etc.) should they face something similar. This will encourage them and you to seek out and introduce material that can help them envision possibilities in their classrooms.

Grading

One of the most pressing concerns for new GTAs (and new instructors or instructors who are returning to teaching after an absence or to a content or type of assignment with which they are unfamiliar) is grading and how to avoid grading challenges. Sometimes these fears stem from concerns that, even though they are instructors, they are still students, and perhaps unable to judge the quality of student work. Sometimes these fears stem from the challenges they fear they will face to what feels like their very fragile authority. Discussions and activities surrounding grading are useful to the course coordinator: They afford opportunities not only to discuss authority and boundary management with less experienced instructors, but also to discuss the purpose and value of grading (and any preferred rubrics or guidelines for this process) and our common and divergent expectations with respect to the quality of student work. From a coordination standpoint, such sessions invite calibration: between coordinator and instructors and among instructors, in light of university, department, program, and course expectations.

As an example, Deanna has developed, in dialogue with current and previous instructors, three different grading-related sessions:

- **Practice Feedback and Debrief:** For this session, Deanna asks GTAs to view and provide feedback to two different student speeches (recorded digitally from actual classes and screened with speakers' permission). They are to write a letter to each student indicating the strengths and limitations of her or his speech. When everyone gathers during orientation to discuss this process, they concentrate on how burdensome this felt to GTAs, where they enjoyed the process and where they struggled, and how they might approach these activities in such a way as to enjoy (and continue to enjoy) them.
- **Reading and Discussion on the Purpose and Value of Grading:** So that they might feel more confident about their roles as instructors (especially with regard to a grade challenge) and engaged in discussions about assessment, Deanna asks GTAs to read a brief article by educator Alfie Kohn (1994) entitled "Grading: The Issue Is Not How but Why." This article helps surface some of the limitations and challenges associated with grading, helping to contextualize this institutional practice. This is often where instructors begin to discuss assessment as a process.
- **Practice Grading and Comparison of Expectations:** In this session, GTAs view one to three student speeches against the assignment criteria and grading rubric. They provide feedback to these students as they might during the course of their public speaking class. As a group, instructors discuss questions that emerge from using the grading rubric (e.g., the student could be a better extemporaneous speaker — should one take points from

the delivery portion of the grade, or also from the introduction and other portions of the assignment where delivery adversely affected the speech?), as well as the grades that instructors assigned these students.

There are, no doubt, many more possible sessions that could address the benefits and challenges associated with grading. A course coordinator can adapt any or all (or none) of these to fit the particular challenges and demands of the course she or he supervises. This topic may also, sometimes in conjunction with particular readings, give rise to discussions well beyond orientation.

Shared Materials

Less experienced instructors need help in realistically anticipating the sorts of experiences they can expect in the classroom. Be on the lookout for materials that will help your instructors do their jobs more effectively (i.e., "smarter, not harder"). You have probably already had the experience of supportive reading materials as a GTA; books like Svinicki and McKeachie's (2011) *Teaching Tips*, Hendrix's (2000) *The Teaching Assistant's Guide to the Basic Course*, and Curzan and Damour's (2006) *First Day to Final Grade* are all helpful to the beginning teacher. While they do not raise larger philosophical issues (like why we grade), they do offer teachers quick "sound bites" of advice (about, for example, plagiarism and cheating, test design, or structuring a lecture) that may see them through until they can meet with you or attend their next staff meeting. There is also a series of listservs, like Stanford University's Tomorrow's Professor, that can spark useful discussions among colleagues.

Well-chosen common readings can help produce meaningful conversations about teaching and learning. For example, Parker Palmer's (1998) *The Courage to Teach: Exploring the Inner Landscape of a Teacher's Life* invites teachers to consider the effects of their profession on their lives, on how they might live long and happy lives, because of and not despite their careers. Paulo Freire's (2003) *Pedagogy of the Oppressed* helps to bring up questions of privilege and social justice and may encourage teachers toward a more cautious and collaborative stance toward empowerment and sociocultural change. These readings need not engender a similar mind-set regarding teaching — again, these instructors will not and should not all become the same teacher — but they are likely to encourage people to feel engaged in teaching, to feel as though they have agency (though tempered by social-structural circumstances), and to encourage a respect for having a teaching philosophy that is intentional (and therefore more readily shared with students).

Of course, the usefulness of readings is not limited to orientation; if your resources permit, consider maintaining resource libraries for the instructors you supervise to consult any time they need extra support. Often, textbook publishers are more than happy to send along examination copies of textbooks and instructors' resource manuals; taken together in a browsing library, these can help GTAs and other less experienced instructors explore many possible lesson plans for a given subject or concept. If possible, you should try to share through purchases or donations from retiring colleagues, copies of the books about teaching you enjoy reading, books about the discipline, and relevant journals (if they are not otherwise available electronically). This gives less experienced instructors one more place they can turn as they navigate the joys and challenges of their assignment. Several other readings on teaching and learning are listed in the Recommended Readings section at the end of this chapter.

Below, we've included a sample orientation schedule from each of our programs, as a reference and example of some of the ways in which the orientation week can be structured.

SAMPLE: GTA ORIENTATION SCHEDULE #1

GTA Orientation, Department of Communication Studies

San José State University

16–20 August, 2010

Monday, 16 August

9:00	Welcomes and Overview of the Week, Deanna Fassett, GTA Supervisor, and Stephanie Coopman, Department Chair, HGH 225
10:00	Discussion: Rawlins's "Teaching as a Mode of Friendship," Teresa Teng, GTA Alum
11:00	SJSU Resources, Krista Nilsen and Mary Anne Sunseri, Returning GTAs
12:00	Lunch
1:00	Introduction to Supplemental Resources, Mary Anne Sunseri, Returning GTA
2:30	*First Year GTAs*: Multimedia Resources in Comm 20, Dana Morella, GTA Alum
	Returning GTAs/Mentors: On Mentoring, Krista Nilsen, Returning GTA
3:30	Microteaching Lesson Plan Peer Feedback, Krista Nilsen, Returning GTA
4:30	Office Assignments, Krista Nilsen and Mary Anne Sunseri, Returning GTAs

Tuesday, 17 August

9:00	Announcements, questions, etc.
9:30	On Assessment, Deanna Fassett, GTA Supervisor
10:30	Microteaching: 1. Developing Your Purpose and Topic, Laurina Lanham
	2. Adapting to Your Audience, Stephanie Anderson
	3. Delivering Your Speech, Taylor Braun
	4. Organizing and Outlining Your Speech, Sarah McGaffey
12:30	Lunch
1:30	Responding to Students' Work, Part I, Carol Perez, GTA Alum
	Read: Alfie Kohn chapter, "Grading: The Issue Is Not How but Why"
2:30	Case Studies in the Comm 20 Classroom, Teresa Teng, GTA Alum
4:00	Discussion: Freire's *Pedagogy of the Oppressed*, Julia Salvador, GTA Alum

Wednesday, 18 August

9:00	Announcements, questions, etc. (*Greensheets are due at this time*)
9:30	Conflict in the Classroom, Larissa Favelas and Ambica Gill, GTA Alums
11:00	Microteaching: 5. Researching Your Topic, Matt Mathias
	6. Using Language Effectively, Rob Gutierrez
	7. Integrating Presentation Media, Randy Marchman
	8. Understanding Argument, Karl Haase
1:00	Lunch
2:00	Engaging Critical Communication Pedagogy (Forum Theatre Workshop), Amy Kilgard, SFSU, and Keith Nainby, CSU Stanislaus

Thursday, 19 August

9:00	Announcements, questions, etc.
9:30	Entering the Professional Community, Shelley Giacalone, GTA Alum, Gavilan College

11:00	Responding to Students' Work, Part II, Minna Holopainen, GTA Alum
12:30	Lunch and HR
2:00	Discussion: "Pedagogy of the Distressed," Julia Salvador, GTA Alum
3:30	Managing Expectations, Michelle Zajac, GTA Alum

Friday, 20 August

9:00	Time to get Tower Cards, Parking Permits, etc., etc.
10:00	Introduction to D2L, Minna Holopainen, GTA Alum, IS 134
11:00	Communication Studies Lab & Resource Center, Shannon Doyle, GTA Alum, Clark 240
12:00	Returning GTAs' Orientation to the Office, Krista Nilsen and Mary Anne Sunseri, Returning GTAs
1:00	Lunch and Resource Presentation, Courtesy of Cengage Publishing
2:30	A sense of closure, what to expect at the faculty meeting . . . and anticipation of COMM 285A, Deanna Fassett, GTA Supervisor

Sunday, 22 August

4:00	Welcome Back Party, Beth and Steve Von Till's House

Monday, 23 August

8:00	Faculty Meeting, Clark 240
10:30	College of Social Sciences Fall Faculty Meeting (followed by lunch), WSQ 207

SAMPLE: GTA ORIENTATION SCHEDULE #2

2010 Graduate Student (Re)Orientation
Department of Speech Communication,
Southern Illinois University at Carbondale
[Schedule subject to minor revisions]
16–20 August, 2010

Monday, August 16: Welcome!

Time	Location	Activity	Presenter(s)	Participants
9:00–9:30	Comm. 2005	Welcoming & continental breakfast	N. Stucky, R. Pelias, J. Warren, and C. Saindon	ALL new graduate students and mentors
9:30–10:30	Kleinau Theater (Comm. 2014)	Mentoring	J. Warren	Mentors
9:30–10:30	Comm. 2010	Payroll forms; building tour; Carbondale information	B. Prell and C. Saindon	New graduate students
10:30–11:15	Kleinau Theater	Mentor program	J. Warren and C. Saindon	New graduate students and mentors
11:15–12:00	Trolley pick-up outside Comm. Building	Campus tour	SCO	All new graduate students and mentors

12:00–1:00	Alumni Lounge (Rec. Center)	Picnic lunch (Lunch provided)	SCO	Grads, faculty, and staff
1:30–2:00	Kleinau Theater	SPCM 101 Syllabus — what's required and what can be added	J. Warren and C. Saindon	ALL new GTAs
2:00–2:45	Kleinau Theater	First Time Teaching	J. Warren	First-time teachers only
2:00–2:45	Comm 2010	First Time Teaching at SIUC	C. Saindon	Experienced teachers new to SIUC

Tuesday, August 17: Strategic Planning

Time	Location	Activity	Presenter(s)	Participants
9:00–10	Comm 2005	Policies, Procedures, and Expectations of GTAs	J. Warren	All new GTAs
10:15–12	Kleinau Theater	Surviving the First Week	C. Saindon and graduate student mentors*	All new GTAs
12–12:50	Comm tba	Pizza lunch and SCO info. (Lunch provided)	SCO	All new GTAs

*Graduate teaching mentors offer hands-on strategies for negotiating your first week of lectures, activities, and grading responsibilities.

| 1:00–4:30 | Lawson 141 | University GTA Workshop: SIUC Policies on Sexual Harassment and Academic Dishonesty | Graduate Dean and staff | All new GTAs** |

**All new graduate teaching and research assistants are required to attend.

Wednesday, August 18: Departmental Culture and Curriculum

Time	Location	Activity	Presenter(s)	Participants
9:00–9:45	Kleinau Theater	Introduction to office staff and Department procedures	N. Stucky, L. Sims, J. Warren, and B. Prell	All graduate students
10:00–10:30	Kleinau Theater	Masters Program	R. Pelias	All MA and MS students
10:30–11:00	Kleinau Theater	First Year Ph.D. Program	R. Pelias	First year Ph.D. students
11:00–11:30	Kleinau Theater	Continuing Ph.D. Program	R. Pelias	Continuing Ph.D. students

11:30–12:30	Kleinau Theater	Introduction to faculty	N. Stucky and faculty	All graduate students and faculty
12:30–1:30	Student Center food courts	Lunch together (Lunch not provided)		All graduate students and faculty
1:30–2:30	Faculty offices	Advisement and course sign-up*	Faculty	New graduate students only
2:30–???	Comm. Lobby	Group registration, ID, Parking**	C. Saindon	New graduate students**
2:30–3:30	Faculty offices	Advisement and course sign-up*	Faculty	Returning graduate students only

*Registration forms and materials should be turned in at Woody Hall after advisement.
**Optional group meeting to go through class registration, parking permits, and student IDs.

NO LATER THAN 3:45, ALL GRADUATE TEACHING ASSISTANTS MUST LEAVE FALL SCHEDULES WITH DR. WARREN BEFORE DEPARTING

Thursday, August 19: The Reflective Teacher-Scholar

Time	Location	Activity	Presenter(s)	Participants
9:00–9:30	Comm 2010	Civic Engagement and Our Role as Public Intellectuals	J. Warren	All SPCM 101 GTAs

9:30–10:15	Kleinau Theater	New Textbook, Speaker's Forum, and Distribution of Teaching Assignments	J. Warren and C. Saindon	All SPCM 101 GTAs
10:15–10:45, 10:50–11:20, 11:25–11:55	Kleinau Theater and Green Room, Comm 2012, and Comm 2005	Critical Discussion Groups (small-group discussion of provided readings)	Graduate student facilitators	All GTAs
12:00–1:30	Comm 2012	Kleinau Theater lunch (Lunch provided)	Perf. Studies faculty	All interested in the 2010– 2011 Kleinau Season*
1:30–2:30	Comm 2012	Center for Academic Success	C. Saindon	CAS teachers only
1:30–2:30	Comm 2005	Saluki Advantage	J. Warren	SA teachers only**

*Optional — only for those interested in participating in the Kleinau season or finding out more information about Kleinau productions. Others can go for lunch in groups or on your own.
**If you are teaching both a Center for Academic Success and a Saluki Advantage section, go to the CAS discussion.

Friday, August 20: Putting Theory into Practice

Time	Location	Activity	Presenter(s)	Participants
9:00–10:00	Kleinau Theater	Answering Questions from Multiple Perspectives	J. Warren, C. Saindon, N. Stucky, et al.	All GTAs
10:15–11:15	Kleinau Theater	SPCM 101, Saluki First Year, and the Early Alert System	J. Warren and Saluki First-Year representatives	All GTAs
11:30–12:30	Kleinau Theater	Managing Life in Graduate School: A View from the Trenches	C. Saindon and Graduate student panel	ALL new graduate students
12:30–2:00	Kleinau Theater	SCO meeting followed by lunch (on your own)	SCO Officers	All graduate students
2:30–4:00	Individual offices	One-on-one consultation to review syllabi, teaching strategies, etc.*	J. Warren and C. Saindon and mentors	All GTAs who are interested

*This time is set aside to help GTAs (new and returning) with individual concerns about teaching. You may want to make an appointment, but it is not absolutely necessary.

<u>BE SURE TO FILL OUT</u> AN EVALUATION FORM FOR THIS ORIENTATION. YOUR FEEDBACK ON THE ORIENTATION CONFERENCE IS VITAL IN PLANNING FUTURE CONFERENCES.

Saturday, August 21: Department Picnic

Time	Location	Activity	Presenter(s)	Participants
5:30–9:00	Daughton/ Stucky Residence	Department Picnic (Potluck; drinks provided)	The Speech Commu- nication Department Community	All graduate students, faculty, staff, family, and friends invited

BEYOND ORIENTATION

The need for support, training, and development doesn't disappear after orientation. In fact, training is just as important and presents new challenges *after* new teachers jump into the "deep end" — the classroom. Here we discuss several means for supporting instructors struggling to learn to teach while teaching — support courses, staff meetings, and electronic resources. And please note that some of the techniques addressed above, such as simulation activities and shared materials, can be extremely useful after orientation as well.

Support Courses

One option for mentoring less experienced instructors who are still earning graduate degrees (i.e., M.A. or Ph.D. students) is to develop and require their enrollment in a course that helps them reflect frequently and intentionally on what it means to teach their particular subject to their particular students. These courses may include reading assignments, role-play and other exercises, written work, and/or the development and collection of teaching portfolios (which may include lesson plans, graded student work, PowerPoint presentations, and so forth).

Deanna's support courses are Comm 285A and Comm 285B; John's support course is SPCM 539 (you can find syllabi for these at the end of the chapter, on pages 151–171). Deanna's courses each carry two units and John's three; GTAs must take them in their first year in the program (these units, in total, constitute the equivalent of an elective graduate seminar). Conversationally, Deanna refers to these sessions as "staff meetings," and while her second year GTAs do not receive units, they must participate as long as they remain in the program.

GTAs meet every other week for two hours. However, more experienced faculty teaching the public speaking course submit their syllabi to the course coordinators for review and approval, attend the first faculty meeting of the semester, teach their courses, and then meet at the end of each semester for an assessment meeting. This meeting gives both GTAs and more experienced faculty an opportunity to discuss new developments and challenges in the course.

Staff Meetings

In Deanna's department, staff meetings and a support course are one and the same, but not having a support course built into your program doesn't mean you can't take advantage of staff meetings. While at Bowling Green State University, John held regular staff meetings several times a semester; since some of his instructors were from another college on campus, the staff meetings provided one of the rare times the full instructional staff could meet together. These staff meetings were regularly scheduled occasions for instructors teaching the course to discuss their successes and difficulties in meeting particular learning outcomes, commiserate about workload and other challenges (in this sense, they serve a community-building/sustaining function), and connect with the coordinator (eliminating the need for a series of one-on-one meetings). These can occur at whatever interval best serves the course, instructors, and program.

Perhaps one of the most important concerns you can give space for in staff meetings or other gatherings of less experienced instructors is, to put it broadly, boundary and role management. The same challenges you may have faced on becoming a graduate teaching assistant — seeking balance between your professional life and your personal life, creating time for both work (your own as a student and for grading your students' work) and play, amassing resources you can rely on when you're struggling — will continue to challenge you as a course coordinator. This is an area of common ground between you and your less experienced colleagues. One of the aspects of course coordination, particularly if you work closely with graduate teaching assistants, that is most difficult is also one that is most rewarding: In mentoring them, in helping them grow as colleagues and teachers, you must often work to locate the permeable boundaries that help you see where you end, where your investment or worry ends, and they — their own resources — begin.

Fortunately, training and professional development opportunities are ongoing and adaptive — they can have formal structure, or they can emerge as needed. When Deanna needed to have surgery the week before orientation a few years ago, she was lucky enough to have many current and former GTAs to help her. Even so, she felt overwhelmed by the volume of questions they had about their new roles; she wanted to answer all of them, but was concerned about her health. Deanna reflected on her own experiences as a mentor when she was a GTA; she had never been a mentee in a mentoring program, but she recalled the pleasure she took from being there for other, less experienced instructors. Deanna met with one of the second-year GTAs who helped create a structured but simple mentoring program, whereby new GTAs learned in July who their mentors would be and the role they would play in the coming year. Mentors became the first-line response to all new GTA questions; Deanna would field questions that the more experienced GTAs could not answer or did not feel it was appropriate for them to answer. Mentors and mentees also observed in each others' classes, performed each others' SGIDs, and went to potluck gatherings once or twice a semester. This is an illustration of how a meaningful professional development idea emerged organically, inexpensively, and collaboratively.

Electronic Resources

Depending on the size of your program, you may find it helpful to link all of your instructors electronically, using either a campus-based (e.g., course management software program) or free, publicly available listserv (such as Google groups or Yahoo! groups). In this way, you are able to communicate with all instructors at once, pass along additional reading materials, answer questions so that others might follow along, and so forth. Moreover, because all instructors are linked to one another in this way, more experienced instructors are better able to mentor less experienced instructors; you may go to your email and see not only the original question, but the five or more helpful replies. Wikis are similarly useful in that you can maintain all resources having to do with the course in a central repository (in a sense, this is like having a Web page for your instructors, but one where they can each play a role in developing and organizing the site). Instructors can, for example, post and review particularly effective lesson plans, in-class engagement activities, and sample syllabi.

A SPECIAL NOTE ON TRAINING ADJUNCTS

While the greater part of this chapter centers on GTA training, much of it is also appropriate for smaller campuses that hire adjuncts and part-time faculty. When possible, discussion boards, staff meetings, orientation programs, and such can greatly enhance the instruction experience of these teachers. However, it is often true that adjuncts can come with a considerable amount of experience and therefore do not need the same kind of assistance. For instance, all the part-time faculty and adjuncts John has supervised over the years have come to their role with extensive experience. From professional and instructional contexts, the majority of the adjuncts really only required specific direction on what the department required for the course (i.e., policies and assignments). For this reason, we recommend assessing the experience the new adjunct instructor brings to the position and evaluating the degree to which she or he requires training as a new teacher.

CONCLUSION

Training and professional development opportunities are an important aspect of any coordinated course, particularly for less experienced faculty who are learning to teach even as they are learning (and learning to teach) their discipline. These opportunities are even more powerful where they invigorate and reinforce course and program vision. It is easy to assume that training and professional development activities are formal, planned well in advance, and highly structured, but training and professional development can occur in a number of unexpected places as well: in office hours, over coffee, or at the end-of-the-year celebration dinner. It is through these opportunities, both planned and emergent, that you, as a course coordinator, help less experienced instructors understand their role and responsibility in achieving and adapting the course or program vision. These efforts serve not only the individual instructors or their students, but also the course itself, as these instructors come to educate one another to more effective instruction, participate eagerly and meaningfully in assessment meetings, and represent the program well to a variety of groups on and off campus.

SAMPLE: SUPPORT COURSE SYLLABI #1 & #2

San José State University
Department of Communication Studies
COMM 285A, Teaching Associate Practicum I, Fall 2009

Instructor:	Dr. Deanna L. Fassett
Office hours:	Mondays, 2–4 PM, Drop-In (Comm 200R only); Wednesdays, 2–4 PM, Drop-In (Graduate Program only); and Tuesdays, 10 AM–12 PM (by appointment only). For people with scheduling conflicts, it may be possible to arrange an appointment for another day/time.
Mandatory Furlough Days:	Due to mandatory furlough of CSU employees, I am not permitted to engage in university business (including, for example, teaching classes or holding office hours, responding to email, or grading student work) on the following days: 9/21, 9/22, 9/23, 9/24, 10/19, 10/30, 11/25, 12/11, and 12/18.
Class days/time:	Tuesdays, biweekly, 1–3 PM (please see attached calendar)
Classroom:	Marie Carr Conference Room, HGH 215
Prerequisites:	Graduate Standing; Appointment as a Graduate Teaching Associate

Framing Thoughts

Ideally, what should be said to every child, repeatedly, throughout his or her school life is something like this: "You are in the process of being indoctrinated. We have not yet evolved a system of education that is not a system of indoctrination. We are sorry, but it is the best we can do. What you are being taught here is an amalgam of current prejudice and the choices of this particular culture. The slightest look at history will show how impermanent these must be. You are being taught by people who have been able to accommodate themselves to a regime of thought laid down by their predecessors. It is a self-perpetuating system. Those of you who are more robust and individual than others will be encouraged to leave and find ways of educating yourself — educating your own judgment. Those that stay must remember, always and all the time, that they are being moulded and patterned to fit into the narrow and particular needs of this particular society." — DORIS LESSING, *THE GOLDEN NOTEBOOK*

There is the fallacy that the great object of education is to produce the college professor, that is, the individual who adopts an agnostic attitude toward every important social issue, who can balance the pros against the cons with the skill of a juggler, who sees all sides of every question and never commits himself [or herself] to any, who delays action until all the facts are in, who knows that all the facts will never come in, who consequently holds his [or her] judgment in a state of indefinite suspension, and who before the approach of middle age sees his [or her] powers of action atrophy and his [or her] social sympathies decay. — GEORGE COUNTS, *DARE THE SCHOOL BUILD A NEW SOCIAL ORDER?*

Catalog Description

Instruction and supervised experience in teaching university-level courses in communication studies. Topics include curriculum design, instructional objectives and activities, and evaluation.

In COMM 285, as a "reflective practicum," we will combine practical experience with scholarly reflection. Our purpose is to reflect on the philosophy and practice of teaching and to use our immediate experience as teachers (however novice) to inform our discussions and make them relevant and useful. Through structured readings and assignments, we will work toward a more nuanced understanding of the roles and responsibilities of educators, while improving our teaching practice.

By department policy, teaching associates are required to take 2.0 units of COMM 285A in their first semester; in their second semester, teaching associates are required to take 2.0 units of COMM 285B. TAs, including those in their second year, are always required to attend staff meetings, as arranged by the TA supervisor. As you progress through the four-semester TA program, your role and your responsibilities will evolve. Your accumulated experience is integral to the ongoing development of COMM 285/staff meetings and to our community of teacher-scholars.

Required Texts

Hendrix, K. G. (2000). *The teaching assistant's guide to the basic course.* Belmont, CA: Wadsworth/Thompson Learning.

Palmer, P. J. (1998). *The courage to teach: Exploring the inner landscape of a teacher's life*. San Francisco, CA: Jossey-Bass.

Assignments and Grading Policy

In order to complete the 2.0 units in COMM 285A, each TA will meet the following requirements:

1. Active participation at 285A meetings: Tuesdays, 1–3 PM, as scheduled.
2. Develop a COMM 20 portfolio, and complete all assigned readings.
3. At least once, facilitate discussion of assigned reading from Palmer's *The Courage to Teach*.
4. Present one solo-taught workshop (or two team-taught workshops) for the Communication Studies Lab and Resource Center.
5. Collect all assessment data, pursuant to your contract with the department (i.e., GE assessment data, SGID reports) and submit to relevant parties by their respective deadlines.
6. Arrange to observe your peer mentor (and to have your peer mentor observe you) by or before October 1; please apprise Dr. Fassett of your

arrangements once you know them so that she may participate in the debriefing, as appropriate.

7. Arrange to meet with Dr. Fassett within one week of her observation in your classroom.

8. Review in a timely fashion all materials related to your instructional assignment (e.g., emails, listserv communication, mailbox flyers, etc.), and communicate with respective offices as appropriate.

COMM 285A Portfolio Assignment

This portfolio is a record of your work in COMM 20 and the reflection and self-evaluation that attend such work. The portfolio will include your assignments, lecture notes, exams, and evaluations used in your classrooms. Each item will be accompanied by a narrative description of your goals for the assignment, a rationale for its design and sequence in the semester, an assessment of its overall effectiveness for your students, and a plan for adjusting or enhancing it for future use. The portfolio will culminate in either a reflective essay that surveys your experience teaching COMM 20 and the various strengths, weaknesses, dilemmas, and delights you encountered as a teacher, or a case study that illuminates a classroom challenge you faced in your first semester of teaching. The portfolio will be turned in for feedback at two points during the semester.

Materials That Must Be Included in the Final Portfolio

1. Syllabi materials: greensheet, including calendar and grade monitoring form, student waivers, any additional course policies or text you have added (including rationale)

2. Engagements and other assignments: include a copy or written record of <u>each one</u>

3. Complete lesson plans for every class period

4. Instructor's critical response to <u>four</u> items of student work: two speech evaluations and two paper (outline or self-evaluation) evaluations. For each type of work, one must illustrate student work evaluated as high quality and one must illustrate work evaluated as relatively low quality.

5. Frames and commentaries for engagements

6. A brief reflective essay that synthesizes and celebrates your experiences teaching COMM 20 (and identifies areas for future growth) <u>OR</u> a case study of approximately one page, single-spaced, that illuminates an issue relevant to our own ongoing professional development as university educators

7. Additional materials of your choice that you believe are reflective of your teaching but not appropriately collected elsewhere in the portfolio

<u>Engagements and Other Assignments</u>. The "description" of these items should be the actual handout you would give students, or a reasonable facsimile in the event that instructions are given orally. It should include a clear and explicit description of procedures as well as criteria for evaluation when relevant. If you debrief or discuss afterwards, you should include the list of discussion questions or a recap of the students' talk.

<u>Lesson Plans and Lecture Notes</u>. These should not look exactly like a chapter summary, but rather, include the examples you use, any questions you pose to students, and a description of discussion issues. In other words, follow the model we used this summer. Notes with handwritten comments and examples are perfectly fine. I am interested in how you organize and present material, as well as how examples and discussion might emerge in your classroom. A complete lesson plan includes objectives, a sense of where the lesson fits in relation to prior/subsequent lessons, necessary materials, a time frame of what will happen when, a sense of how you'd know whether students had met the objectives, and a brief (i.e., three to four sentences) assessment of the lesson.

<u>Frame and Commentary</u>. There should be a frame preceding and a commentary accompanying each engagement/other assignment. While they may be of varying lengths depending on the assignment, keep in mind that a frame must include more than "I did this the second week of class," and a commentary needs to be more reflective than "It went well." Understand that <u>the primary material I am evaluating is the quality of your critical reflection</u>. This means that you want

to focus your time/energy on framing your work in terms of course goals and objectives (i.e., what you wish to achieve or have your students understand/ experience and why this assignment/lecture/etc. will aid you in achieving that objective). Commentaries should provide sophisticated, candid insight into how students experienced the assignment/activity, the degree to which it met your learning objectives, and any suggestions you have for enhancing the educational experience in the future.

Evaluations. Since I am focusing on the quality and tenor of your critical conversations with students, select an evaluation of student work (speeches and written assignments such as self-evaluations or outlines) that truly demonstrates your sensitive/critical voice in action. For both the written and oral genres, include one response to a highly evaluated piece of work and one that was problematic enough to merit a low evaluation. This means only four samples total. You must seek your students' permission to use their work in this way. Remember: no student names are allowed or you breach the contract you established with them.

Tips on Content and Format for COMM 285A Portfolios

1. Decide who you wish your primary audience to be (TA supervisor, potential employer, self) and target the portfolio to that audience (note: this will affect the style and formality of the discourse). I will then assume that role as your reader. Be internally consistent with whatever format and level of formality you choose.
2. Use TABS to separate/identify sections of the portfolio and make a cleaner presentation overall.
3. Syllabus, calendar, and grade monitoring form should be the first entries in the portfolio. If you have varied from the standardized materials or added items of your own, then include these with an explanatory frame.
4. Clearly label every page if you use separate pages for portions of an assignment (e.g., Frame for Engagement 1, Engagement 1, Commentary on Engagement 1). Make sure that the title of the engagement or probe is on the frame and commentary page, or as section headings for easier reference. In other words, don't assume your reader knows

what purpose an item is serving simply because of where it's placed.

5. Make sure to remove all student names or other identifying markers before including their work. Include a blank copy of the student waiver immediately after syllabi materials.

6. Give attention to the "look" of the portfolio. This public document should be professional, neat, complete, carefully and logically organized, and very reader-friendly. At some point you may wish to use this to document your work to an employer or other outside reader.

7. You may organize your portfolio either chronologically (by sequence in the semester) or generically (by genre, e.g., speeches, engagements, etc.).

8. If you are doing your portfolio on computer, would you consider submitting it on disk at the end of the semester? These documents promise to be marvelous teaching tools for incoming and experienced teachers if they can become part of our ongoing collection of resources.

How Am I Evaluating Your Portfolios?

These portfolios comprise the major project of 285A. As outlined above, you will turn them in twice before the end of the semester. Each time they will receive ungraded, but focused and specific feedback. <u>I expect such feedback to be considered and incorporated (or at least addressed) into the portfolio</u>. While each time you turn it in I will be focusing on the "new" sections, I will be reading these pages through the lens of my previous comments/responses. I advise you to incorporate suggestions (including making changes to the document) as we go along — but I expect all requested changes to be made/incorporated by the final collection of the portfolio. At that time I will read/respond to it as a complete document. My feedback will be based on the following considerations:

1. Are you drawing connections from the course textbook to your classroom with a level of forethought, detail, and insight?

2. Are you thinking about the decisions that you're making in the classroom at both a micro (class period) and macro (course and curriculum) level?

3. Is the course unfolding with a coherent logic — one that is in keeping with the department objectives for COMM 20 and reflective of your own developing instructional philosophy?

4. Does the portfolio follow the specifications I've made, such as the "frame-item-commentary" sequence? Is it careful and professional in its presentation?

5. What is the tenor and tone of your conversations with students as indicated in your written responses, handouts, lesson plans, and lecture notes?

6. Are your reflections substantive, candid, and relevant rather than cursory and incidental? In short, to what degree does this portfolio document your careful reflection on and assessment of your work in COMM 20?

COMM 285A: Teaching Associate Practicum I, Fall 2009, Class Schedule

Week	Description	Assignments
1. 8/25	The First Day!	Hendrix, chs. 1, 2, and 4 (recommended)
3. 9/8	Becoming a Teacher	Palmer, intro & ch. 1
5. 9/22	No Staff Meeting — Mandatory Furlough Day	Finish reading Hendrix, remaining chapters
7. 10/6	Meaning vs. Coverage	Palmer, ch. 2; portfolio collection 1
9. 10/20	Relationships & Authority	Palmer, ch. 3
11. 11/3	Knowing in Community	Palmer, ch. 4; portfolio collection 2
13. 11/17	Teaching in Community	Palmer, ch. 5
15. 12/1	Learning in Community	Palmer, ch. 6
Finals 12/14 by 4 PM		Final Portfolios Due!

San José State University
Department of Communication Studies
COMM 285B, Teaching Associate Practicum II, Spring 2010

Instructor:	Dr. Deanna L. Fassett
Office hours:	Wednesdays, 11 AM–2 PM (drop-in), and Tuesdays, 10 AM–12 PM (by appointment only). For people with scheduling conflicts, it may be possible to arrange an appointment for another day/time.
Mandatory Furlough Days:	Due to mandatory furlough of CSU employees, I am not permitted to engage in university business (including, for example, teaching classes or holding office hours, responding to email, or reading student work) on the following days: January 29, February 15 and 26, March 2 and 16, April 5 and 26, and May 6 and 17.
Class days/time:	Tuesdays, biweekly, 2–4 PM
Classroom:	Marie Carr Conference Room, HGH 215
Prerequisites:	Comm 285A; Graduate Standing; Appointment as a Graduate Teaching Associate

Catalog Description

Instruction and supervised experience in teaching university level courses in communication studies. In addition to advanced discussion of topics from COMM 285A, topics will include theories of teaching and learning, identity, culture, and power.

In COMM 285B, as a "reflective practicum," we will combine practical experience with scholarly reflection. Our purpose is to reflect on the philosophy and practice of teaching and to use our immediate experience as teachers (however novice) to inform our discussions and make them relevant and useful. Through structured readings and assignments, we will work toward a more nuanced understanding of the roles and responsibilities of educators, while improving our teaching practice.

By department policy, teaching associates are required to take 2.0 units of COMM 285A in their first semester as TAs; in their second semester, teaching associates are required to take 2.0 units of COMM 285B. TAs, including those in their second year, are always required to attend staff meetings, as arranged by the TA supervisor. As you progress through the four-semester TA program, your role and your responsibilities will evolve. Your accumulated experience is integral to the ongoing development of COMM 285/staff meetings and to our community of teacher-scholars.

Required Texts

There is no single required text for Comm 285B. However, we will take up readings as they are appropriate and useful. These may include selections from journals like *Communication Education*, *Basic Communication Course Annual*, and *Communication Teacher*, samples of conference papers, and other materials given the group's research interests at the intersections of communication and instruction.

Assignments and Grading Policy

In order to complete the 2.0 units in COMM 285B, each TA will meet the following requirements:

1. Active participation at 285B meetings: Tuesdays, 1–3 PM, as scheduled
2. Present one solo-taught workshop (or two team-taught workshops) for the Communication Studies Lab and Resource Center
3. Develop and document a line of investigation regarding communication and instruction and complete all assigned readings
4. Collect all assessment data, pursuant to your contract with the department (i.e., GE assessment data, SGID reports) and submit to relevant parties by their respective deadlines
5. Arrange to observe a colleague (and to have your colleague observe you) before <u>March 9</u>; please apprise Dr. Fassett of your arrangements once you know them so that she may participate in the debriefing, as appropriate

6. Arrange to meet with Dr. Fassett within one week of her observation in your classroom.
7. Review in a timely fashion all materials (e.g., emails, listserv communication, mailbox flyers, etc.), and communicate with respective offices as appropriate.

COMM 285B Scholarship of Teaching and Learning Assignment
You will prepare, in stages, a project that may take any one of the following forms:

1. A draft of a research investigation paper (approximately 15–20 pages), suitable for publication or presentation at conference. You should address a communication question or phenomenon that stems from your own experiences as a GTA, locate and read any relevant research on that topic, and engage in data collection as is appropriate to your question/interest. Your work may engage the intersections of communication instruction at the university level through any paradigmatic perspective, theoretical orientation, or methodological procedure. You may choose to work as individuals, in pairs or small groups, or as a larger research team. We will discuss the research process, including HS-IRB review, in stages, at each staff meeting. Please consider submitting this work to the WSCA annual conference (deadline 9/1 of each year).
2. A fully developed orientation session (including visual aids, handouts, lesson plan, appropriate readings, and any other necessary materials) on some topic related to communication and instruction, including the GTA (or part-time faculty member) life. As with option one, you will propose your idea, identify suitable readings, indicate specific deliverables, and arrange to "publish" or share your work.
3. A plan of continued reading and journaling on your experiences in the classroom. This document may take whatever form you wish (e.g., blog, notebook), so long as it consists of at least two entries per week and I am able to review it at intervals. Your first entry should review your strengths and limitations as an educator, as well as your goals for both this semester and the future. Subsequent entries should

identify and address questions you have about teaching and learning, insights from your experiences in the classroom, reflections on readings, and so forth.

4. Perhaps you have something you'd like to propose. If this is the case, let's discuss what you have in mind. As with the other options, I will expect you to develop a plan that includes relevant readings or other experiences, writings, and appropriate deadlines.

Meeting Schedule: COMM 285B: Teaching Associate Practicum II, Spring 2010

You will negotiate your own project parameters; please use this space to indicate your own individual tasks and deadlines. Each staff meeting will follow a similar structure, i.e., initial announcements and updates (15 min.), discussion of emergent issues (60–90 min.), and discussion of ongoing professional development projects (30–60 min.).

Week	Description	Assignments
January 26	The Scholarship of Teaching and Learning Engaging in Meaningful Assessment	
February 9	Discussion of GTA Program and Teaching as SoTL	Read Comm 210R and Comm 244R reports.
February 23	Discussion of Project Ideas	Submit project proposals — include concise description of what you'd like to do and all deadlines. Allow for at least one occasion where I provide feedback while your work is still in progress.
March 9	Teaching Observation Discussion	

March 23		OPEN: We can use this time to revisit key themes from Palmer; address other common reading relevant to our discussions; give space for GTAs to present what they're learning from their projects or road-test their case studies, orientation materials, and other outcomes; etc.
April 6		Also OPEN: See above.
April 20	Begin discussion of 2010 Orientation	
May 4	Project Discussion	Be prepared to share your project and what you've learned (are learning) from it.
Finals		Final Versions of Projects Due. Be sure to allow yourself time to complete Comm 20 assessment tasks.

SAMPLE: SUPPORT COURSE SYLLABUS #3

Speech Communication 539
Teaching Speech Communication at the University Level
Fall 2010
Wednesday (4:30–7:00 PM)
1022 Communication Building

To live life fully is to live it as if it is an act of criticism. (Bonnie Marranca)

Professor

Name: John T. Warren, Ph.D.
Office hours: M/W: 10–noon; 1:30–3 & by appointment

Texts

> Hendrix, Katherine Grace. *The Teaching Assistant's Guide to the Basic Course*. Belmont, CA: Wadsworth, 2000. Print.

> Nathan, Rebekah. *My Freshman Year: What a Professor Learned by Becoming a Student*. New York: Penguin, 2005. Print.

**and a packet of readings to be made available to you during class (see reading list included in this syllabus)

> Education as the practice of freedom — as opposed to education as the practice of domination — denies that [wo]man is abstract, isolated, independent, and unattached to the world; it also denies that the world exists as a reality apart from people. — Paulo Freire

> While nominally a skills-training curriculum, vocationalism thus creates a whole authority-dependent personality. It is a social psychology for a dominated character. — Ira Shor

> My intent is to help construct a pedagogy of possibility, one that works for the reconstruction of social imagination of human freedom. — Roger I. Simon

> Democracy [. . .] is primarily a mode of associated living, of conjoint communicated experience. The extension in space of the number of individuals who participate in an interest so that each has to refer his [/her] action to that of others, and to consider the action of others to give point and direction to his [/her] own, is equivalent to the breaking down of those barriers of class, race, and national territory which kept [wo/] men from perceiving the full import of their activity. — John Dewey

> In a word, learning has been decontextualized. We break ideas down into tiny pieces that bear no relation to the whole. We give students a brick of

information, followed by another brick until they are graduated, at which point we assume they have a house. What they have is a pile of bricks, and they don't have it very long. — ALFIE KOHN

Course Description

This course deals with real-life issues. While we all enter this conversation with a variety of experiences related to teaching and learning (from being a student to teaching for years), we can all learn more about our craft. This class takes seriously the premise that our pedagogy matters and that, when we talk and learn together, we can always improve on the foundations we already have. While this course is tied to the SPCM 101 program, it is nonetheless a graduate seminar and as such I take our work and our efforts here to be of the utmost importance — I am honored to talk about pedagogy with you this fall.

The course is designed for university teachers of speech communication. It offers research, theory, issues, methods, and practical applications within the field of communication studies. The course builds on personal experience and research, investigating both the everyday doings in the classroom as well as critical and innovative pedagogy.

I view communication pedagogy at the crossroads of communication and education — that is, I see both the historical and theoretical threads in these fields as central. The work we will read this semester, the concepts and practical applications of this course we will examine, as well as the nature of our conversations, will inevitably circle around the cross-section of these two disciplines. Even in our own field, we have a diverse set of approaches to the study of instruction; communication education (or the teaching of speech/communication), instructional communication (or the study of communication in instructional contexts), and communication pedagogy (or the study of communication as the vehicle of educational practice) are complex areas of study, each with its own histories and ideologies. There are other courses in this program that approach this complex matrix of questions and tangles (i.e., SPCM 533 and SPCM 537). Our work here, rather, is to gather bits and pieces of information from each that help best meet our needs for teaching speech communication here at SIUC. This is an exciting course. I look forward to our conversations and the opportunity to share our collective successes and struggles together.

Course Goals

- To reflect on teaching with specific attention to current practice
- To explore pedagogy in/through our own experiences as well as in/through critical and reflective texts on pedagogy
- To practice our pedagogy in a workshop-like environment
- To enhance analytical writing and talk about pedagogy

Structure

All social situations involve rules that work to define the situation. As in any social situation, we will develop many rules during the semester to support our work. And, as in any social situation, some rules have already been established:

1. **Attendance/Participation:** Every member of the class is expected to complete all assigned readings for the assigned day and to demonstrate having done so by participating in discussions of the readings. Everyone (myself included) is expected to come to each and every class. Should an emergency arise, please let me know in advance. Also, everyone (myself included) should be to class on time. Patterns of tardiness and absence will be noted and will affect final grades. As a graduate course, I assume the following: everyone will be at every class, on time, and well prepared for class discussion.

2. **Written Engagements:** I will be asking the class to engage their own pedagogical philosophies, the course readings, and the class discussions throughout the semester. The writings will vary from reflective pieces to small analyses. The goal is for a processual engagement with the course content as we move through the course. Assignments for written engagements will be made the class before they are due. You can expect between four and eight during the semester. The general writing format (unless specified otherwise) includes:

   - one to two pages in length
   - typed, single-spaced, etc.

- no cover pages
- is well-thought-out and proofread
- uses proper citation (APA, CMS, or MLA)
- email me before class the day it is due
- **always** use active voice and practice good writing skills

I will review each and return it as soon as I can. I do not put numbers or grades on these; they are marked instead with qualitative feedback that is to assist you in developing argument, writing, and pedagogical perspective. Occasionally, a rewrite might be requested; such requests could vary in meaning (i.e., they could mean you missed the point, the writing was below my expectations, or the ideas can be further developed). Also, note that you can rewrite any writing through the semester. I can certainly meet with you any time if you need more specific feedback on where you stand in these assignments — my goal is not to hide my assessment here, but to provide you with generative feedback that challenges you. The final "grade" for these writings is produced after the writings have been completed and I can see the progression in your work.

3. **Discussion Facilitation:** Each student will lead discussion on a reading during the semester. Early in the semester, each student will sign up for a reading/date. Each facilitation should include a **one-page handout** (any format) that (1) captures the central arguments of the reading; (2) poses central questions or interrogations of the claims and ideas in the essay/text. Additionally, each facilitation should begin with a **brief** opening (about five minutes) in which the discussion leader directs the class toward the point or issue she or he wishes us to engage (these can be summary points, questions, or performances). The final component for the assignment is to direct and sustain the conversation in the reading.

4. **Teaching Observations:** During the semester, you will have two observations of your teaching. One will be conducted by myself, set up early in the semester and conducted sometime before the Thanksgiving holiday; the second will be by a peer, either your departmental

mentor or a colleague in the class. Each observation will need (1) a written report and (2) a face-to-face conference on the class session. The observations are less evaluative and more generative, so do not feel this is an additional level of oversight. Rather, these are meant to be productive spaces for dialogue on your pedagogy.

5. **Final Teaching Portfolio Project:** The major work you will produce in this class is a teaching portfolio: a collection of your exams, engagements, lecture notes, activities, written assignments, handouts, and other teaching materials. It should be organized into teaching "units" with a clear indication of the learning objectives for each unit, what activities facilitate the objectives, and what means you have to assess the students' learning. I will provide further information about how to organize your portfolio, but basically every activity (from lectures, to assignments, to exams) should be included in the portfolio. Your final portfolio should also include a log of your classroom visits and the write-ups they produce. In the past, successful portfolios have included these additional items: a journal of your semester (or series of reflective writings), copies of essays written in the course of SPCM 539, and brief written commentaries on the assignments, exams, and lectures you gave to students over the course of the semester.

Grading

Written Engagements	30%
Discussion Facilitation	20%
Teaching Observations	10%
Teaching Portfolio	40%

At midterm, I will provide feedback to each of you regarding your progress in the class thus far.

Schedule

This schedule is subject to change. The dates and assignments are attempts to determine where the class will be on a given date, but since we have not yet had the course, it is impossible to determine if we will in fact follow this schedule completely.

August	25	**Syllabus and Welcome** Gajjala et al. Simpson Kanter
	30	**Getting Started** Hendrix 1–3, 5
September	8	**Teacher Persona** Hendrix 4 Kozol
	15	**Public Speaking Pedagogy** Lucas
	22	**Pedagogical Documentation: Portfolios and Vitas** Seldin 1–3 Hendrix 10
	29	**Evaluations: Teacher** SGID Handout Curzan & Damour
October	6	**Evaluations: Students** Hendrix 6–9
	13	**Evaluations: A Critical Perspective** Kohn "preface" & "Lures"
	20	**Problem Posing** Shor
	27	**Ethics** Anderson
November	3	**Toward a Critical Communication Pedagogy** Fassett and Warren
	10	**Culture, Power, and SPCM 101** Fotsch Sedaris

	17	NCA
	24	No class: Thanksgiving Holiday
December	1	**My Freshman Year** Nathan
	8	**Discussion of Final Portfolios** Due: Portfolios
	15	**Final Exam meeting**

Readings

Gajjala, Radhika, Natalia Rybas, and Yahui Zhang. "Producing Digitally Mediated Environments as Sites of Critical Feminist Pedagogy." *SAGE Handbook of Communication and Instruction*. Ed. Deanna L. Fassett and John T. Warren. Thousand Oaks: SAGE, 2010. Print.

Simpson, Jennifer S. " 'What Do They Think of Us?': The Pedagogical Practices of Cross-Cultural Communication, Misrecognition, and Hope." *Journal of International and Intercultural Communication* 1 (2008): 181–202. Print.

Kanter, Jodi. " 'Incident': Performing as a Moral Act Two Decades Later." *Text and Performance Quarterly* 26 (2006): 405–13. Print.

Kozol, Jonathan. "Why Are We Here? What Is the Job That We Are Being Asked to Do?" *On Being a Teacher*. Oxford: OneWorld, 1981. 3–9. Print.

Lucas, Stephen E. *"Teaching Public Speaking." Teaching Communication: Theory, Research, and Methods*. 2nd ed. Ed. Anita Vangelisti, John A. Daly, and Gustav W. Freidrich. Mahwah, NJ: LEA, 1999. 75–84. Print.

Seldin, Peter. Chapters 1–3. *The Teaching Portfolio: A Practical Guide to Improved Performance and Promotion/Tenure Decisions*. 2nd ed. Boston: Anker, 1997. 1–14. Print.

Curzan, Anne, and Lisa Damour. "Feedback from Students." *First Day to Final Grade: A Graduate Student's Guide to Teaching*. 2nd ed. Ann Arbor: U of Michigan P, 2006. 166–74. Print.

Kohn, Alfie. Preface. *Punished by Rewards: The Trouble with Gold Stars, Incentive Plans, A's, Praise, and Other Bribes*. Boston: Houghton Mifflin, 1993. xi–xiv. Print.

Kohn, Alfie. "Lures for Learning: Why Behaviorism Doesn't Work in the Classroom." *Punished by Rewards: The Trouble with Gold Stars, Incentive Plans, A's, Praise, and Other Bribes*. Boston: Houghton Mifflin, 1993. 142–59. Print.

Shor, Ira. "Problem-Posing: Situated and Multicultural Learning." *Empowering Education: Critical Teaching for Social Change*. Chicago: U of Chicago P, 1992. 31–54. Print.

Anderson, Kenneth E. "Ethical Issues in Teaching." *Teaching Communication: Theory, Research, and Methods*. 2nd ed. Ed. Anita Vangelisti, John A. Daly, and Gustav W. Freidrich. Mahwah, NJ: LEA, 1999. 519–530. Print.

Fassett, Deanna, and John T. Warren. "Pedagogy of Relevance: A Critical Communication Pedagogy Agenda for the 'Basic' Course." *Basic Communication Course Annual* 20 (2008): 1–34. Print.

Fotsch, Paul. "Race and Resistance in the Communication Classroom." *Basic Communication Course Annual* 20 (2008): 197–230. Print.

Sedaris, David. "Go Carolina." *Me Talk Pretty One Day*. Boston: Back Bay Books, 2000. 3–15. Print.

REFERENCES

Boal, A. (1985). *Theatre of the oppressed*. New York, NY: Theatre Communications Group.

Counts, G. S. (1932). *Dare the school build a new social order?* Carbondale, IL: Southern Illinois University Press.

Curzan, A., & Damour, L. (2006). *First day to final grade: A graduate student's guide to teaching* (2nd ed.). Ann Arbor, MI: University of Michigan Press.

Freire, P. (2003). *Pedagogy of the oppressed: 30th anniversary edition*. New York: Continuum.

Haiker, H. (2009). Thematizing public speaking: Toward meaningful exploration of social significance. Paper presented at the Western States Communication Association Annual Conference, Mesa, AZ.

Hendrix, K. G. (2000). *The teaching assistant's guide to the basic course*. Belmont, CA: Wadsworth/Thompson Learning.

Hendrix, K. G., Hebbani, A., & Johnson, O. (2007). The "other" TA: An exploratory investigation of graduate teaching assistants of color (GTACs). *International and Intercultural Annual, 30*, 51–82.

Jones, C. N. (1991). Campus-wide and departmental orientations: The best of both worlds? In J. D. Nyquist, R. D. Abbott, D. H. Wulff, & J. Sprague (Eds.), *Preparing the professoriate of tomorrow to teach: Selected readings in TA training* (pp. 135–141). Dubuque, IA: Kendall/Hunt.

Kohn, A. (1994). Grading: The issue is not how but why. *Educational Leadership, 52,* 38–41.

Lessing, D. (1999/1962). *The golden notebook.* New York, NY: HarperPerennial.

Nyquist, J. D., & Sprague, J. (1998). Thinking developmentally about TAs. In M. Marincovich, J. Prostko, & F. Stout (Eds.), *The professional development of graduate teaching assistants* (pp. 61–88). Bolton, MA: Anker.

Palmer, P. J. (1998). *The courage to teach: Exploring the inner landscape of a teacher's life.* San Francisco, CA: Jossey-Bass.

Ronkowski, S. (1998). The disciplinary/departmental context of TA training. In M. Marincovich, J. Prostko, & F. Stout (Eds.), *The professional development of graduate teaching assistants.* Bolton, MA: Anker.

Sprague, J., & Nyquist, J. D. (1991). A developmental perspective on the TA role. In J. D. Nyquist, R. D. Abbott, D. H. Wulff, & J. Sprague (Eds.), *Preparing the professoriate of tomorrow to teach: Selected readings in TA training* (pp. 295–312). Dubuque, IA: Kendall/Hunt.

Svinicki, M., & McKeachie, W. J. (2011). *Teaching tips: Strategies, research and theory for college and university teachers* (13th ed.). Belmont, CA: Wadsworth, Cengage Learning.

Wulff, D. H., Nyquist, J. D., & Abbott, R. D. (1991). Developing a TA program that reflects the culture of the institution: TA training at the University of Washington. In J. D. Nyquist, R. D. Abbott, D. H. Wulff, & J. Sprague (Eds.), *Preparing the professoriate of tomorrow to teach: Selected readings in TA training* (pp. 113–122). Dubuque, IA: Kendall/Hunt Publishing.

RECOMMENDED READINGS

There are a few excellent collections that will be of use to the course coordinator who works with less experienced instructors, including:

Marincovich, M., Prostko, J., & Stout, F. (Eds.). (1998). *The professional development of graduate teaching assistants.* Bolton, MA: Anker.

Nyquist, J. D., Abbott, R. D., Wulff, D. H., & Sprague, J. (Eds.). (1991). *Preparing the professoriate of tomorrow to teach: Selected readings in TA training.* Dubuque, IA: Kendall/Hunt Publishing.

Prieto, L. R., & Meyers, S. A. (Eds.). (2001). *The teaching assistant handbook: How to prepare TAs for their responsibilities.* Stillwater, OK: New Forums Press.

While somewhat dated in places, these collections help the new coordinator explore the history of graduate student instructors in communication courses. Further, these readings address developmental mentoring of novice instructors, including training and development activities.

For coordinators who work with International Teaching Assistants (ITAs), the following sources are helpful for their specific attention to the role of culture in the classroom and specific communication skills ITAs can use in order to be perceived as clear and credible in the classroom:

Ross, C., & Dunphy, J. (Eds.). (2007). *Strategies for teaching assistant and international teaching assistant development: Beyond microteaching.* San Francisco, CA: Jossey-Bass.

Sarkisian, E. (2006). *Teaching American students: A guide for international faculty and teaching assistants in colleges and universities* (3rd ed.). Cambridge, MA: Derek Bok Center for Teaching and Learning.

Finally, there are a number of excellent articles regarding GTA training and development in our discipline in *Communication Education* and *Basic Communication Course Annual.* That said, you can find articles on issues of relevance to GTA supervisors in other journals in our discipline (for example, Hendrix et al.'s [2007] excellent piece on the experiences of GTAs of color) and beyond. When you sign up for the Basic Course Directors listserv at the National Communication Association annual conference, consider also subscribing to Tomorrow's Professor (a listserv published by Stanford University on topical classroom issues facing college professors — many of these postings are engaging fodder for staff meeting or online discussions of teaching and learning) and the *Chronicle of Higher Education.*

7

Professional Development Opportunities for (and with) More Experienced Instructors

Teaching Teachers

Each semester, you hold an assessment meeting for all the instructors who teach the introductory human communication course. You're eager to hold this gathering, as it's an opportunity for you to check in with the instructors of the course and for them to spend time with each other. Often what starts as a discussion of where students do and don't achieve a particular learning outcome turns into an interesting blend of rapport building, sharing best teaching practices, and comparing experiences with different campus resources. However, scheduling this meeting can be a hassle. The GTAs, whom you supervise, routinely attend and actively participate. The part-time faculty often attend, when they're not teaching at other schools or working at other jobs; most seem to enjoy connecting with their colleagues, the people they pass in the hallways and on the freeways. However, the instructors with more job security — the people who are on multiyear contracts or tenure-track appointments — can sometimes be less sanguine. A handful of them contact you before each meeting, explaining that they have other professional commitments that prevent them from attending and observing that they have attended other, similar meetings for some years. You know you can go to the chair about this — he will remind all instructors that their attendance is required at this meeting or they risk forfeiting a sick day — but are there other, better ways to encourage all your colleagues to participate? And is there a message about training and development activities in this reluctance on the part of the most experienced faculty?

* * *

As we have discussed at length elsewhere in this text, course coordination assignments and responsibilities vary from one department and one campus to the next. While course coordinators are often GTA supervisors, there are still other coordinators who supervise a blend of GTAs, part-time and full-time faculty, and still others who do not work with GTAs at all. Course coordination is a form of supervision irrespective of the instructors involved, but how the coordinator names and practices that supervision may vary depending on whether she or he is working with novice or more experienced instructors. More experienced instructors, for our purposes here, are colleagues who have been teaching long enough that they feel relatively confident and comfortable in their teaching assignment. These instructors may be recent graduates of an M.A. or Ph.D. program (where they had experience as GTAs), or they may be well established enough that they feel secure in their position as a member of a particular program or department, whether as "adjunct freeway flyers" who teach across an array of campuses, or as tenured/tenure-track faculty members. Experience in general, and experience teaching this particular course in particular, are key in determining who is a "more experienced" instructor; tenured/tenure-track faculty, lecturers, and even (though to a lesser degree) GTAs may all be more experienced instructors.

Where course coordinators must supervise more experienced instructors, they face a somewhat different series of challenges than when they work with novice instructors. For example, novice and veteran instructors differ not only in the volume of questions they ask about teaching, but also in the kinds of questions they ask. They may also vary in their willingness to seek help for teaching challenges as they occur. In addition, more experienced instructors are often closer to course coordinators as colleagues, challenging us to be more transparent and earnest in our role.

Take, for example, the perceived relevance of assessment meetings. While GTAs and other less experienced instructors will often participate in training and professional development activities because they feel these activities will help them grow as instructors, more experienced instructors may need help locating the intrinsic value of these activities when they are already accomplished in this profession. Indicating that a meeting is mandatory is usually not enough to ensure instructors' attendance and sincere participation. It can be tempting to justify an assessment meeting in terms of institutional demands — in other words, all instructors must attend the meeting because it is necessary for continued GE certification or accreditation. This might secure a fair number of participants, but it risks rendering assessment conversations as hoops through which instructors must jump — a costly move in terms of fostering a constructive understanding of assessment in your department. You know the importance of the interactions you hope to foster, and clarifying this with your colleagues will help the more experienced instructors understand the relevance of their role in contributing to the collective wisdom and spirit of inquiry regarding this course or in mentoring their less experienced colleagues. In effect, you're looking to teach the teachers — people who may have many more years' experience than yourself; and in order to do so, you will need to make the exercise meaningful and relevant to them.

Coordinators must understand professional development for more experienced instructors as distinct from other seemingly similar endeavors, since these more experienced colleagues are sources of training and development knowledge themselves. They perform an important modeling and mentoring function with their colleagues, helping them create and join a program to which they want to belong. They are also an important resource to a new course coordinator in that they can share valuable institutional memory (about the course in particular, about the personalities involved in course recertification, about campus resources, and so on). It is important to remember, however, that more experienced instructors still struggle with their role; they, too, need training and professional development opportunities — ones that take seriously the contributions they make and the challenges they face — and training objectives and activities must take on additional dimensions to allow this to happen. This chapter will touch on the ways coordinators can incorporate experienced instructors' expertise into their course's training and development program, identify specific training goals for experienced instructors, and explain techniques that can benefit this group of knowledgeable teachers.

DRAWING ON INSTRUCTOR EXPERIENCE

Professional development opportunities for more experienced instructors must take seriously those instructors' existing strengths as educators — that is to say, a large part of incorporating experienced instructors into a training and development program should actually be drawing on their existing experience for the benefit of those around them. While it would be unwise to assume that even the least experienced instructor/GTA is a blank slate — she or he has often experienced more than 15 years of structured education as a student and often teaches others in a variety of contexts even if she or he doesn't assume the title of teacher — instructors who have been teaching for some time have a wealth of experience they can share with their colleagues. These are instructors who know what has and has not worked for them over the semesters and over the years, and sharing these insights with their colleagues can help improve and nuance instruction across the course. To return to a metaphor from the previous chapter, if it takes a village to run a comprehensive, multisection communication course, then, as a coordinator, part of your responsibility is to challenge and organize all the members of this village to see themselves as such.

Inviting effective and experienced instructors to play a role in designing, promoting, and sustaining professional development opportunities will help them feel involved and respected. This can provide satisfaction that part-time faculty may not otherwise feel in departments that don't invite them to participate in curriculum development or other governance work with tenured/tenure-track faculty. Over the years, we have both enjoyed working with a variety of part- and full-time colleagues in the development and organization of the GTA summer orientation. Sometimes as many as 20 colleagues participate by offering sessions for orientation, on topics ranging from how to grade speeches, to how to help students select socially significant speech topics, to how to practice self-care, even and especially during the most hectic parts of the semester. We consult with prospective presenters, working together to make sure the orientation session fits both the interests of the presenter and the needs of the GTAs. Over time, this has helped to create a department and program culture where instructors are concerned with their colleagues' success.

From a continuity standpoint, this process can also help shore up the vision of the course and program over time: The vast majority of our public speaking instructors are our own current or former GTAs (further, the vast majority of community college instructors in our regions are former GTAs and alumni of our programs). Driven by memories of what they loved about and struggled with teaching as GTAs, our part-time colleagues often assume mentoring roles beyond the orientation, in the hallways and in office hours, at assessment meetings and holiday dinners. Less experienced instructors are not the only ones who benefit, though; orientations, assessment meetings, and department functions become occasions for more experienced instructors to connect with one another on a campus where people often pass by one another on their way to other campuses or commitments.

More experienced instructors can be valuable collaborators toward quality instruction and strength of vision for your program. Their perspectives help inform assessment conversations, illuminating what is and is not working with the course. Their contributions can show less experienced instructors that good teaching, as a process of learning and growth, is fluid and creative, a matter of evolution and reflection. More experienced instructors can help their colleagues, whether more or less experienced, learn from their past mistakes, showing that even the best teachers are rarely perfect and that it is how we learn from our experiences in and out of the classroom that matters.

"Best practices" sessions, where instructors share particularly effective lessons and assignments, are a great way to involve more experienced faculty in the professional development of their colleagues. Other professional development activities for more experienced instructors where they can share their expertise with their colleagues include discussions of current readings in the discipline or in pedagogy and roundtable-style discussions of classroom struggles (for example, on responding to academic dishonesty, accessing campus resources, or adjusting assignments to better accomplish particular learning outcomes).

The expertise of more experienced instructors associated with your course raises an important consideration for you as a course coordinator: To what extent should you invite, expect, or require experienced instructors' participation in professional development opportunities?

In order to best take advantage of your colleagues' expertise, there are a series of questions you should consider.

- **What unique struggles or exigencies affect the participation of your program's more experienced faculty in professional development activities?** For example, at SJSU, where many of the public speaking instructors are lecturers whose campus employment is highly structured by a union-negotiated contract, it is important to be judicious in requiring attendance, reserving this for assessment meetings and other essential instructor functions. It can be a challenge to draw faculty to professional development activities, and it is important to avoid placing undue or exploitive demands on their time. That said, it would be a mistake for our program to assume that part-time faculty would not attend professional development activities simply because they already have a lot of responsibilities. Here it will serve you to adopt an invitational approach to professional development opportunities, distinguishing the optional from the required and always working to establish the value of those opportunities for the instructors.

- **What are your needs as a course coordinator?** For example, do you need to open a conversation about how to respond to any concerns other groups have raised about this coordinated course? Or has there been a global, national, or local emergency your instructors must prepare themselves to address? More experienced instructors, who have navigated any number of academic storms in their collective experience, are resources for you in terms of reaching out to all of the instructors of this coordinated course. Especially where you are interested in an exchange of ideas or a means of modeling, for less experienced instructors, a number of options for navigating what might be a complex or difficult situation, a larger gathering of instructors — one that includes more experienced faculty — is essential.
- **What are the strengths associated with this group of instructors?** Across a group of more experienced faculty, you are likely to find individuals who are early adopters of classroom technology, who can lead sessions with other faculty on how to effectively implement these new tools. Or you may find someone who is adept at developing games and simulations for your particular course (or who develops highly regarded case studies, or whom students report to be an excellent writing instructor); she or he can then share insights into this experience, along with an activity or two, with the entire group. Community colleges are riches of various professional and applied strengths that can directly connect the work of a course with the larger community. How can you build from that experience in order to enhance all your sections, all your courses?
- **What are the needs associated with this group of instructors?** Perhaps instructors need guidance in implementing a new course text with their students or options and resources for addressing increasing numbers of academic dishonesty cases. In any event, more experienced instructors will continue to learn more about their profession throughout the course of their careers; working with them to anticipate and meet their needs as professionals will help you identify important areas for discussion and additional training.

While more experienced instructors are an important resource that course coordinators should not overlook in the mentoring and growth of newer instructors, coordinators should remember that even the most experienced instructors also benefit from continued professional development discussions and activities.

TRAINING AND DEVELOPMENT OBJECTIVES

Beyond enriching the training program for all instructors involved, more experienced instructors still need training and professional development tailored to their own needs and knowledge. Unlike new instructors, who are likely to need some guidance on the basics of teaching (from how to design a syllabus, to how to grade speeches or essays, to how to structure a discussion or small-group activity), more experienced instructors need help keeping current about new developments in teaching, in general, and about their discipline, in particular. Further, more experienced instructors, especially if they are spread across multiple days of the week, multiple departments, or multiple campuses, may need help in staying connected with their colleagues and with the vital center of the department or program.

New Developments in Teaching

While there are some teaching skills that will remain valuable and central — e.g., methods such as lecture, small- and large-group discussion, and so forth — structural changes and intellectual developments have given rise and will continue to give rise to new aspects of teaching and learning. More experienced instructors, particularly those who teach across a number of different campuses in a given semester, may struggle to develop awareness and mastery of new developments in effective pedagogy, especially if few or none of these programs offer meaningful professional development opportunities.

In just the last 10 years, we have witnessed increased attention to and interest in better understanding and meeting the needs of particular student populations (for example, students with disabilities, English Language Learner [ELL] students, returning veterans, and so on). Perhaps more startling have been the sudden and swift developments associated with technology in and for the classroom. These technologies do more than simplify or automate different aspects of an instructor's workload; they also help instructors share digital, editable materials with their students — of key importance to students who use screen readers and other assistive technology. This explosion of technology has included interest in and attention to the accessibility of course management systems like Blackboard and Desire2Learn, popular social networking sites like Facebook and LinkedIn, widely available media repositories like YouTube, plagiarism detection services like Turnitin.com, and even the development of tablet PCs, clickers, and other hardware. As part of SJSU's commitment to accessibility and access for students with disabilities, during the 2009–2010 academic year instructors in Deanna's department attended sessions on navigating a new learning management system; developing accessible Word documents, PowerPoint presentations, and .pdf files and forms; and exploring the campus's new Web site builder program. With few exceptions, all faculty, from GTAs to tenured full professors, attended these professional development activities. For faculty who attended all the workshops, the department provided, in conjunction with the campus Center for Faculty Development, certificates in accessible instructional material design. Recognition of these efforts was essential, as instructors learned more than techniques or shortcuts; they also engaged in discussions about their values and expectations, including their understandings of and stereotypes surrounding disability, access, and inclusion.

Professional development exercises can feel organic and meaningful where they emerge from instructors' concerns for continued growth and education, from developments in the discipline or instructional technology, or from current campus events, initiatives, and concerns. For example, an articulation meeting, where instructors from several different campuses meet to discuss how courses transfer from one institution to another, can precede a larger conversation about the role of introductory communication courses in supporting students' growth as writers. In one such session, Deanna facilitated a discussion of best practices in responding to students' writing, introducing, as appropriate, information that would help these instructors respond to English Language Learners specifically. Immediately following the events of September 11th, 2001, Deanna's colleagues (of all ranks and appointments, including GTAs) gathered to discuss how best to support students during this tragic and deeply unsettling time. This conversation was not without conflict, as the community challenged each others' positions regarding the role of values and objectivity in the classroom; but the conversation gave everyone space to learn where their needs and interests as individuals and program goals intersect. Particularly where instructors identify needs a coordinator can help address — often this is a matter of creating a conversational space, but sometimes it also includes sharing insights from research — professional development can be purposeful and its benefits can be lasting in terms of renewing and sustaining a course, department, or program community.

Community colleges are often the most inventive sites for service learning and innovative pedagogies that connect the college to industry and community programs. Such efforts can create a sense of relevance for both students and teachers, while directly affecting the community the college serves. Many community college instructors are working professionals above and beyond their role as instructors, and still others participate in nonprofit organizations and community groups; building connections between foundational communication courses and the community can help fulfill the mission of the course, the department or program, and the college. During John's work at Bowling Green State, several of the instructors he worked with entered the workforce as community college instructors and then shared their experiences with others at Bowling Green, bringing new and innovative techniques and activities. One instructor in particular used a service learning assignment to connect his introduction to communication course to local public service. Students worked to provide a public service (for example, repairing a school), and, with approval from the college, then connected the service project to what they were learning in their classroom. Further, this instructor assigned students to speak with other students and community members about what they were learning and why they were dedicating a portion of their class time to service. It was a project that directly connected the students in the course with their college campus and, as a result, aided in learning across multiple lines of inquiry.

New Developments in the Discipline

At most schools, the lion's share of coordinated courses in communication studies are introductory courses. Often these address public speaking or a mixture of communication theories (regarding, for example, interpersonal, small-group, or intercultural communication) and public speaking, and so they do not require the specialized expertise a doctoral seminar might. That said, even the most seemingly staid foundational course changes along with developments in the field. More experienced instructors, particularly if they are part-time faculty who are years away from their graduate coursework and who may not receive support for conference participation, may struggle to stay abreast of disciplinary developments.

In recent years, there has been increased interest in contextualizing the study of communication, situating it with respect to modern civic engagement, social protest, and examinations of culture, power, and community. Textbooks now reflect greater diversity in paradigmatic approaches to the study of communication; they also reflect a greater diversity in what constitutes communication research, developing insights into heretofore lesser explored areas of the discipline (for example, communication in blended families, LGBTQ relationships and families, ally communication, multiracial identity and communication, non-Western approaches to rhetoric, etc.). Often these sorts of adjustments to the introductory course emerge from students' concerns and lived experience; for example, at San Francisco State University, where students tend to be profoundly diverse and activist oriented, it makes sense for the course to adopt a social justice- or critical theory–oriented approach to communication studies. It is also common for course coordinators to bring their own areas of disciplinary expertise, introducing new developments in communication studies, to the introductory course. It is important, however, to introduce more experienced instructors to new disciplinary developments in such a way as to respect their expertise and welcome them into a conversation they may or may not wish to readily join.

Deanna has found this a difficult line to walk with more experienced instructors. Where GTAs will often eagerly embrace introductory course concepts that are consistent with the curricula they experience in their graduate seminars, long-term part-time or tenured faculty — perhaps less actively engaged in the continued development of the discipline — may be less sanguine. As a coordinator of an upper-division writing course, Deanna found herself struggling with her charge to share current models of writing in the communication studies discipline with all students. As an instructor of that same course, she had considerable success in asking students to engage in autoethnographic writing (i.e., a relatively new approach in our discipline where writers explore how they are both products and producers of culture in ways that are both evocative and scholarly), but while many of her former students knew this form of writing, many of her colleagues did not (or harbored misunderstandings of it as a research method). As coordinator, she developed the final project assignment so that it would give students a choice between autoethnography, media criticism, literature review, case study analysis, and handbook/manual design. Many instructors wanted to immediately remove the unfamiliar elements of this list, and, through assessment meetings and one-on-one discussions, they discussed the advantages and limitations of these kinds of writing for the course learning objectives. Deanna also offered instructors a collection of examples of all the different forms of writing so they could make informed decisions about whether to share all these options with their students. Where instructors do not enthusiastically embrace a particular professional development opportunity, it is important to underscore the relevance and value of the exercise, not just for the instructors, but for their students' learning as well.

Where the majority of instructors of a coordinated course are well-established full-time or tenured faculty, continued disciplinary professional development may involve developing a reading or other discussion group (where they can read and discuss, for example, emerging research). These sessions are similar to the sorts of conversations GTAs routinely experience during orientations, staff training meetings, or graduate seminars — the very sorts of sessions more experienced faculty seldom experience once they are no longer students. While GTAs would, no doubt, benefit by such conversations, it might be important to hold gatherings of people of similar rank or experience; depending on the topic, instructors may need to build a sense of trust in order to be candid in their responses. To this end, it is also important to clarify whether a session is required or recommended, the learning objectives or outcomes of the session, and the role of attendance and participation in subsequent employment decisions (if there is one). While many faculty would dearly enjoy having a large gathering to discuss a new book or published article, it is important for part-time and other instructors who do not have security of employment to know that their participation is invited, not expected (unless it is).

TRAINING AND DEVELOPMENT ACTIVITIES

In order to facilitate exchange and learning between experienced and novice instructors, and to share new developments in teaching and in the discipline, you may want to call upon one or a combination of techniques, including mentoring, workshops and meetings, discussion groups and social gatherings, and electronic resources. Because experienced instructors are often part-time or adjunct faculty who teach sections of the course across a number of different campuses, these colleagues may be teaching considerably different preparations of the same course (adjusting for particular academic calendar/day/time configurations, different course learning outcomes, or different course texts and assignments) in different campus cultures. No matter what professional development techniques you choose, once everyone is together, make sure to build in sufficient time for instructors to recalibrate, recalling this particular course's vision and goals.

Mentoring Less Experienced Faculty

Above, we discussed drawing on the knowledge and skills of experienced teachers to help less experienced instructors grow. But teaching and mentoring less experienced peers is also a way to help more experienced instructors continue to grow and develop as educators. This can occur as part of GTA orientation or assessment meetings, but it can also emerge from a mentoring program (whether structured or informal). Just as we develop a more nuanced mastery of concepts and skills from teaching them to others, working to help others become more effective instructors is likely to heighten the more experienced instructor's awareness of different pedagogical issues and questions. She or he may also develop empathy for the coordinator's role in cultivating continuity across the multiple sections and multiple teaching styles and personalities associated with this course.

Mentoring relationships will often emerge organically, as instructors seek advice from one another in this particular assignment, though this will vary from one campus culture to the next. Course coordinators can help facilitate these relationships in structured and unstructured ways. For example, a coordinator can partner two differentially experienced instructors based on their interests, the particular student populations they serve, or even when they teach. We have been very thankful and appreciative of experienced instructors who have been willing to invite instructors who are new to a given teaching assignment (or teaching method) to sit in on the class, review course materials, and share success stories. Or a course coordinator may assign (or recommend assigning) offices or desks in such a way as to encourage mentoring; for example, in the two GTA "bullpen" offices at SJSU, first- and second-year GTAs mix with carefully selected and willing part-time faculty from several different previous years' cohorts.

At community colleges, pairing experienced instructors with less experienced teachers can help professionals as they transition or return to the classroom. This is especially true if the mentor is someone who has a similar background and can help the new teacher profitably explore her or his experiences in industry in the service of teaching. Because of their diverse backgrounds and experiences, community college instructors have important lessons to share, and by connecting teachers in such mentoring relationships, you can help enhance instruction across many classrooms.

Workshops and Faculty Meetings

Gatherings of faculty are excellent opportunities not only to gain insight into instructors' experiences of the course — about what is and is not working — but also to foster dialogue about those experiences in such a way as to strengthen instruction in the course. Assessment meetings often give rise to important professional development topics, as instructors will already be considering where they feel they are succeeding and where they feel they are struggling.

For example, instructors of any experience level may raise alarm about an increase in instances of plagiarism in the introductory communication course; in addition to an immediate discussion, time permitting, of what instructors have attempted in an effort to respond to and reduce these instances, a course coordinator can then consult campus and departmental resources regarding academic honesty. She or he can return to a future meeting with information about the campus conduct office, strategies for how to design assignments so that they are more difficult to plagiarize, and/or technological resources for plagiarism detection.

These sessions are likely to feel more relevant and meaningful to the instructors where workshop topics emerge from their own direct experiences with or concerns about the course. And while instructors might not always take advantage of this process, course coordinators may consider inviting instructors to review and make additions to the agenda in advance of a particular meeting in order to surface any discussion topics coordinators and other participants should address.

Workshops will also emerge in relation to different campus developments and opportunities, such as the acquisition of a new learning management system, the selection of a new common course text, or the arrival of a guest speaker. Where the instructors of the coordinated course are drawn in many different directions, it will help to schedule these professional development activities so that they occur in conjunction with other, required campus events (for example, faculty meetings, awards receptions, welcome convocations, and so forth). These should be appropriately rich, layered sessions, addressing multiple learning outcomes at once so that instructors feel not only that they were able to give careful consideration to the issue(s) at hand, but also that the session was efficient and well-planned. For example, if instructors must all learn to develop accessible instructional materials, then it might be wise to schedule a brief workshop on this topic for immediately before or after a faculty meeting they are otherwise required to attend. Further, while the session itself may focus on, for example, the use of the document map navigation function in Microsoft Word to create headings that help students locate key information in a document, it would be wise to also consider the ways in which the document map function can help the instructors in other aspects of their teaching and writing (to, for example, navigate through a large document like a thesis, book manuscript, or grant application), as well as how this particular skill complements the course or program vision.

It may be very difficult to discuss grading with more experienced instructors, as they may already have long-established practices and expectations associated with this aspect of teaching. To this end, it may be more useful for the coordinator to surface calibration discussions — occasions where instructors can discuss their grading expectations in light of shared sample student work. In these conversations, instructors can affirm what matters to them about teaching (about what they believe they and their students can and should do), as well as evaluate how different assignments assess different course learning outcomes; and they can do so in ways that help individual instructors better discern where they stand with respect to the grading practices of their peers. (For example, are they spending significantly longer than others preparing feedback? Are they routinely assigning A grades where students meet, but do not exceed, assignment parameters? Or are they returning student work much earlier or later than their peers?) A coordinator can then follow up with individual instructors privately, arrange mentoring relationships with more experienced colleagues, or recommend helpful readings and other resources.

Because more experienced instructors may struggle to retain and practice the lessons of the professional development workshop (for example, if they teach on multiple campuses, they may use multiple learning management systems), course coordinators should consider drawing on all the attention and interest strategies they encourage their instructors to use and teach. Charts, acronyms, FAQ (frequently asked questions) pages, simple and elegant PowerPoint presentations, and other efforts help instructors retain "take-away" points. And while it may seem like a small gesture, instructors appreciate refreshments, whether lunch or coffee and tea; when possible, this can help strengthen morale and encourage both attendance at the session and lingering conversations immediately before and after.

Discussion Groups and Social Gatherings

Professional development opportunities need not always feel structured and directly linked to the course instructors teach. For example, instructors may enjoy gathering informally to discuss readings in the discipline (as in a reading group) or share their own writing projects (as in a writing group). These discussions may not intentionally address specific issues from the coordinated course, but when the participants all teach the same course, they are likely to surface. Depending on the readings (or the writings), these conversations may also help keep instructors engaged in both the discipline, in general, and the department culture, in particular. Similarly, questions and issues related to the coordinated course are likely to emerge in all manner of department functions; these conversations can inform more structured mentoring or professional development opportunities for instructors.

Electronic Resources: Listservs and Wikis

It can be immensely useful to link all instructors for a coordinated course along a single listserv or group (for example, Yahoo! groups or Google groups, though other options may include social networking sites like Facebook). Not only does this help the coordinator avoid sending separate emails to what may be a large group of faculty, but it facilitates discussion across instructors about common questions and concerns. It is then possible for the coordinator or an instructor of the course to review archived messages over the course of a few weeks or a much longer period of time. With a large group of faculty, it can be challenging to help them develop a sense of group identity or connection to the program or course; listservs can help a coordinator easily check in with a group of instructors or share invitations to department functions like graduations or picnics.

Wikis serve a similar archival function as listservs; with minimal structure, a wiki can facilitate the development of a repository of lesson plans, exercises, activities, test questions, and other instructional materials. Wikis also make possible group collaboration on a given document or presentation; a coordinator may invite instructors to extend and revise an assessment report, a significant assignment's instructions, or a policy for inclusion on a common syllabus.

Where instructors may struggle to connect with one another face-to-face, these electronic resources can facilitate virtual meetings.

CONCLUSION

Professional development opportunities for more experienced instructors may take a variety of forms, depending on the particular group of faculty you supervise. Irrespective of their particular levels of preparedness and skill as instructors, it is important for coordinators and more experienced instructors to understand their role in both mentoring and modeling. Instructors of all different experience levels have meaningful insights to share with one another, but more experienced instructors have the responsibility to model effective teaching and collegiality for their less experienced colleagues. Coordinators can encourage more experienced faculty to share their insights and contribute to the repository of wisdom regarding their particular courses through professional development opportunities. To the extent resources permit, coordinators can strengthen these efforts by recognizing and/or awarding experienced faculty for their efforts. It is important for course coordinators to advocate for the value of these contributions in evaluation and retention meetings. These teachers teach not only their students, but also their colleagues and the coordinator.

RECOMMENDED READINGS

Buell, C. (2004). Models of mentoring in communication. *Communication Education, 53*, 56–73.

While many of us have the experience of formally and informally serving as mentors in academic contexts, Buell's work helps the course coordinator better understand the communication behaviors associated with mentoring (grouping them loosely under the models cloning, nurturing, friendship, and apprenticeship) and make informed choices not only about her or his interactions with novice and more experienced instructors, but also in developing structured mentoring programs.

Hall, D. E. (2002). *The academic self: An owner's manual.* Columbus, OH: Ohio State University.

Well worth reading by any college professor or aspiring professor, Hall's work helps academics better understand the stresses and strains on their professionalism, including burnout, and helps them approach their academic assignments, however configured, reflectively and proactively.

Madsen, D. J., & Mermer, D. L. (1993). A part-time instructor's perspective. In L. W. Hugenberg, P. L. Gray, & D. M. Trank (Eds.), *Teaching and directing the basic communications course* (pp. 103–107). Dubuque, IA: Kendall/Hunt Publishing.

A succinct writing that addresses the specific communication challenges and opportunities between a course coordinator or director and part-time faculty members. Madsen and Mermer help coordinators specifically consider organizational culture, leadership style, and communicator style as appropriate to their programs.

Palmer, P. J. (1998). *The courage to teach: Exploring the inner landscape of a teacher's life.* San Francisco, CA: Jossey-Bass.

Perhaps one of the most foundational texts in teaching as a vocation, Palmer's work helps instructors (and course coordinators) reflect compassionately and thoroughly on their successes and struggles, joys, and fears in the classroom. It is a simple but deep exploration of how the academic life can be painful and fragmentary and how we can work, individually and together, to live whole and undivided lives.

CHAPTER

8

Directing the Course toward Meaningful Teaching and Learning: Aligning Pedagogy and Vision

Revising Expectations

You've had to shift your expectations a bit, but you're finding out that's not such a bad thing after all. After nearly a year of searching, you landed a job as a course director at a large communication program in the Midwest. Unlike the place you went to school, where GTAs are the instructors of record in the introductory course, here you teach three separate large lectures of introduction to human communication and a variety of part-time instructors staff smaller "break-out" sections. While you were really looking for a position as an intercultural communication specialist — where you could focus on teaching and writing without any large service commitments at first — you have found that there are many aspects of the course that are interesting and challenging to you. You have already shaped the syllabus and assignments for the course so that, as the semester develops, from perception to interpersonal communication, the students confront questions of power and privilege, and you're beginning to wonder whether there are other ways to bring your research interests to your students. You know from your own experience as a student that some of the most powerful learning experiences you had were in dialogue — and sometimes extended conflict — with other students, in small groups and not in lecture halls. Perhaps students might benefit by a shift in course delivery, from large lectures to independent sections? In casual conversation with your colleagues, however, you find they're not as enthusiastic about the idea; they fear a lack of continuity across the different classes. You realize that making the shift won't be easy, but it is a change you're interested in exploring, and it could be a significant contribution to how students learn communication on your campus.

* * *

In Chapter 2, we discussed the importance of program vision — of reading an existing program culture and working with colleagues to shape (or reshape) that vision according to common values and common goals. Because what we regard as common continuously evolves (both as instructors and students join and leave a given program and as instructors challenge and refine their understandings of not only communication studies, but also instruction), exploring program vision remains an essential responsibility of the course coordinator. Program vision, as it evolves over time, will influence pedagogy, from instructors' teaching philosophies to their day-to-day implementation in classrooms and office hours. As coordinators work with instructors, they often encourage innovations that are in line with the common goals and values of the community, which may range from service learning to honors courses to particular technological enhancements. In what follows, we will explore ways to better align vision and pedagogy and thus make a better environment for teaching, learning, and professional growth.

In particular, we will discuss how pedagogy emerges and diverges from, and contributes to, existing course/program vision in significant ways, resulting in immediate and meaningful best practices in course coordination and instruction. First, we will discuss strategies for making significant structural changes to help bring course organization into alignment with vision. Next, we offer guidance on refining and shaping a program or course that is already in good shape in terms of the coherence of pedagogy and vision. And finally, we address responding to outside factors that alter program or course structure and affect learning. Undergirding this coverage is our overarching belief in course coordinators as visionaries — as professionals who are capable of meaningful change, excellent instruction (of both students and teachers), and continued growth and evolution along with the courses they supervise and communities to which they belong.

IMPLEMENTING EXTENSIVE CHANGE

Sometimes it is important for a course coordinator to implement extensive change in order to meaningfully align the vision and practice of a program in support of students and instructors. Extensive change will often need to occur in situations where there has been an absence or lapse in coordination efforts (for example, because of significant staffing changes or because a program has yet to engage in coordination and assessment efforts). When you assume a role as a course coordinator, and periodically during your tenure as a coordinator, you should take stock of the effectiveness of the program. In evaluating the relative strengths and limitations of the program, take into account its reputation on campus and the feedback you receive from administrators, instructors, students, and community members. These factors will help you discern what sorts of changes need to occur in a given program and whether these are minimal or extensive. Guiding your sense of program change should be your assessment of whether and how the program is achieving course learning outcomes and your own and your colleagues' feelings of satisfaction with the course and its role on campus.

Take, for example, the experience of a colleague who inherited a program with a long-neglected vision at a large university in the Midwest. The introductory course had had transient leadership for the preceding five years; before this colleague arrived, several different directors had kept the course alive but, in doing so, had left it largely stagnant. The format was a large lecture course with small breakout sections staffed by approximately 40 GTAs. This teaching staff came not only from different departments on the campus, but also from different colleges. When this coordinator started, the logic surrounding the course was to provide the same experience to each student, regardless of instructor or section. As a coordinator, this meant emphasizing with the instructional staff what they should cover in their lab sections.

This emphasis on coverage and control ran counter to this coordinator's beliefs and values: that the purpose of student teaching is to apprentice to teaching as a vocation that is valuable not only as a means to better learn communication, but also in its own right, and that undergraduate students best learn communication by engaging in it with their peers in guided practice with an instructor. Thus, his preference as a teacher and administrator of this kind of course was that small class sizes are ideal. So, with these values in mind, he set out to change the way the course was structured. It took several years to implement these changes, but in the end they helped result in a more coherent, satisfying, and effective program.

In any case like this one, in which a coordinator wants to effect significant changes in his or her course or program, there are several measures that can facilitate this process. In particular, we recommend considering the role of imagination in the redesign process, keeping course vision/mission central to all revisions, pursuing incremental changes with the guidance and support of colleagues, remembering the viability of compromise, and mitigating conflict.

Respect Tradition, but Imagine What Is Possible

Changes in the operations of an introductory course are most valuable when they are informed by a coordinator's desire to improve students' and instructors' learning. As a discipline, we often ground introductory courses with tradition and the lessons we have learned as a field; at the same time, we often, willingly and unwillingly, grapple with innovation and growth. Both forces — stability and change — are, of course, essential to the continued vitality of the course and the people who make it possible. A coordinator should respect tradition but also be unafraid to ask questions such as "What could the curriculum look like? What's possible?" and not only "How do I maintain the current vision of the course?" Decisions about textbooks, learning outcomes, and training programs should not be exclusively defined by how these have looked in the past.

In recent years, it has become increasingly important for some programs to focus on civic engagement and service learning as part of achieving the service missions of their colleges and universities. As a result, introductory communication courses are emerging to address this challenge; revisions to these courses range from the small (including course texts that incorporate discussions of advocacy or community involvement, or modifying an assignment so that it challenges students to share their communication studies knowledge and skills with members of their communities) to the significant (course and unit configurations that include a formal service learning component).

Similarly, programs with a significant investment in access and inclusion of students from a large geographic region both enjoy and grapple with technological innovations in the design of the introductory communication course. For example, programs may adopt major changes by developing online versions of the course or adding online components to all classes (reducing the number of times students must travel to campus for meetings).

On the one hand, communication courses must respond to what is and has historically been our field (i.e., what we agree as members of a discipline constitutes foundational and essential skills associated with public speaking or other aspects of introductory courses). But on the other hand, current developments in theory (for example, how a program embraces or rejects changes in disciplinary approaches to the content of introductory courses) and pedagogy (for example, new synchronous online communication technologies) may aid us in developing adaptations and renovations that are consistent with our values and goals.

Change Is Most Effective When It Supports the Mission of the Course

Change is most effective when it supports the mission of the course and program; clearly articulating the connection between these is key to making lasting changes happen. Here it is important to remember that changes should not, ideally, emerge from sudden new fashions and fads or capricious likes and dislikes on the part of the coordinator, but rather from the collective will and commitment of the people tasked with the successful operation of the course. In many organizations, it is tempting for someone who is new to a leadership assignment to immediately change many different aspects of the course, especially those associated with qualities she or he did not embrace in her or his predecessor. These can include changing the course text or assignments, ruling in (or out) online instruction in public speaking or other oral communication intensive courses, and immediately embracing new developments or technologies (involving, for example, new software or equipment licenses or new campus initiatives that foreground emergent causes or questions). Take care, when considering changes, that what you propose is consistent with your program or course's visions, and work diligently to ensure that your colleagues perceive it that way as well.

Change Is Incremental and Begins Close to Home

Change is incremental, developing slowly and gathering momentum, beginning in our own offices and departments or programs. It is helpful to remember, as a coordinator, that effective change begins close to home by garnering support in tiers, starting with those closest to the course, from students and instructors, to colleagues and department chairs, to deans, provosts, and other offices on campus.

Returning to the example of our colleague who inherited a program that required extensive change, his first effort was to build consensus within his own unit on campus. Securing shared commitment from his colleagues meant helping them to see that: (1) the current structure of the course was at odds with the values and goals of the department's undergraduate mission, and (2) they could fix this problem and strengthen the course. He needed the faculty to agree that teaching a class called "interpersonal communication" to 900+ students at a time was antithetical to the very content of the course and, further, betrayed the faculty's commitment to critical and engaged pedagogy. This took some work. The coordinator met individually with faculty members, addressed their central concerns in faculty meetings, and asked for input from the graduate student teaching staff. At first, his colleagues did not believe the course was problematic; they would often tell him, "If it isn't broken, don't fix it." He needed his colleagues to understand that the course was, in fact, broken — not broken within every department around the country or in our field, but broken at this university, at this time.

Once his colleagues began to agree that the course did not match their espoused values as a community, he moved on to his second major premise: This was a problem they could fix. In an era of diminishing budgets, he found that the largest response from faculty, once they believed he was right about the need for a structural change, was that it would be impossible to locate the administrative support for the shift, noting both the economic and cultural roadblocks that they saw in its path. The problem was "too big" to solve at this time and, while this coordinator was right, it would be impossible to change it. This coordinator needed the faculty, department chair, school director, and graduate students to believe that they could change the course. He began to demonstrate on paper the one-time adjustment to room reservations, the almost negligible alterations to graduate student loads, and the modest amount of additional funds they would need. In fact, when he presented this to the director of the school, the coordinator said, "Really, we aren't asking for much here at all." In the end, the biggest obstacle was not financial; it was cultural. Colleagues had only ever known this course as a large lecture and always assumed it would remain so. Further, many took the contact hours between students and professor to be a point of pride; it took some time to help these colleagues understand that the quality of these hours, at a faculty-to-student ratio of 1 to 900, was at issue.

Importantly, before this coordinator had any contact with university officials, he made sure that his office neighbor was supportive of the changes he was advocating. Not only did he want each member of his department to be in favor of this change; he also wanted them to be knowledgeable about it, so that they, too, could be voices of change on campus (whether with respect to this course, or in regard to their own projects and communities). Because this coordinator had already earned the support of his colleagues, he was able to speak with more authority in meetings with higher levels of university administration; this change was no longer a question of whether they should effect the change, but rather a matter of how to make the change occur.

Compromise While Maintaining Long-Term Vision

Compromise in order to make possible a more long-term or long-range vision possible is essential; this amounts to choosing one's battles carefully, giving in order to receive. Often we think of compromise as having to accept something distasteful or disappointing (whether permanently or for a short time) in favor of a more satisfying end result. In our colleague's efforts to revise the configuration of the introductory course at his school, this meant asking instructors to screen prerecorded communication lessons in their classes until he could help administrators understand that instructors could achieve continuity across multiple sections through other means. Compromise may also mean implementing a change in stages, even when we desperately want to advance to the final form of the revision. For example, as a course coordinator, you may want to develop a comprehensive assessment plan, but you may have to first cultivate positive instructors' attitudes (and minimize negative attitudes or confront stereotypes they have) before you can learn what they currently do to assess students' learning, and then work together toward a common rubric for a given assignment and other steps in the process. Programs of any size may have to make some concessions to preserve their support from the institution; for example, if you are experiencing pressure to offer online-only oral communication courses and you and your colleagues do not wish to do so, there may be some value to considering hybrid course configurations or "pilot" sections of online courses. This helps you gather data about the effectiveness of the approach administrators are asking you to take while also making it possible for you to network with colleagues facing other, similar pressures.

As a coordinator, you will find it useful to keep in mind that the vision you and your colleagues hope to achieve is incremental, something you can accomplish in stages. This will help you choose your battles and bolster your morale.

Dealing with Conflict

Especially for coordinators who do not have a lot of experience with structural change in a long-established institution, navigating curricular revision can be complex and fraught with misunderstandings of change itself. While it is possible for an institution, department, or program to move quickly, more often change is incremental, recursive, and difficult to discern when you are in the middle of it. Remembering that this is an inherently communicative process can be key for course coordinators, beginning with how you speak with your colleagues about your proposed changes. Recognizing how slow the process can be at times can help you be more realistic about what you feel you should be able to accomplish and when. It may not be a simple process to change people's cultural expectations surrounding a coordinated course; however, where these changes emerge from program vision and shrewd understanding of the process, they will be worth your effort.

It is important to focus on how your proposed changes will benefit students and instructors. Whether your changes are large or small, it is important that others do not perceive them as your "pet project." Clarifying how each change emerges from your program's collective efforts to better achieve the learning outcomes associated with the course will help not only to educate other leaders and decision makers on your campus about the meaningful learning that occurs in your program, but also to strengthen the vision (and sense of community investment in the vision) of your program.

Perhaps an example might help illuminate this. Recently, a friend of ours interviewed for a position as basic course director of a multisection course in a very diverse and changing department in which the previous course director was still on faculty. Our friend was asked to present a vision of the course to the department that would revitalize it and connect it more coherently to the department's mission. However, the mission of the department was (1) not easy to discern given the diversity of viewpoints represented by the faculty, and (2) a clear refutation of the previous director, who, according to some, had let the course lay dormant for too long. Our friend had to meet the interpersonal obligations of both parties — those who sought change and those who valued the course's past. To do this, our friend chose not to side with either, but to present a measured response. His vision of the course would be to build from the past but conduct a needs assessment based on current student and faculty desires, while also researching new trends and movements in the course nationally. Rather than impose a vision, he would build one with the department. Such a solution does not give too much power to any one group (and keeps the coordinator in control of the vision and the course), but does empower those he works with to contribute and "buy in" to the process of updating the course. Keeping the mission of the program intact while still advancing change can be hard, but the balance can produce a stronger presence for the program and can enhance the coordinator's reputation as a fair and responsive leader.

ADDING CREATIVELY TO AN ESTABLISHED AND EFFECTIVE PROGRAM

Though some programs will require change, there are many that are already functioning well; that said, even well-run programs can benefit from creative revisions. As you might imagine, there are many changes a course coordinator might make to strengthen a given program that do not require a major overhaul. These may include a change to the course text or other common readings; revised or reinvigorated training and professional development sessions and discussions; or modest cocurricular programs (such as adding or enhancing a communication center or speakers' competition or series). As you consider the role you can play as a course coordinator in an established and coherent program, you may find it helpful to consider how you can build on the successes of this inherited program; through small creative gestures — your own and others' — you can achieve lasting and meaningful improvements to the course.

Build on the Successes of the Program You Inherit

A successful program remains so not because it is always already crafted to meet the learning needs of students, but because it is responsive and adaptive over time. As a course coordinator, you aid in this process by assuming responsibility for evaluating the program's strengths and limitations and making sound recommendations for how to further strengthen the program. Many of the same questions you would use to assess the coherence of the vision of your program, such as "What do others (instructors, students, administrators, or community members) think of this program?" or "Where is there energy and excitement in this program?" can help you evaluate the health of the program at different points in your stewardship of it.

One way to think about building on to the successes of the program you inherit is to consider how you came to be its coordinator: What makes you a good coordinator (in your own mind, but also in your colleagues')? What can you bring to this program that will help strengthen it? For example, when one of our colleagues, Kristen Treinen, began to supervise the introductory course at Minnesota State University-Mankato, she took stock of her research interests and expertise to make meaningful changes to the program, adding elements to instructor training and development that included careful consideration of critical race theory and diversity as appropriate to the needs and challenges of that particular student and instructor population. However, another way to think about building on the successes of the program you inherit is to ask similar questions of your colleagues: How might the work of other people involved in this course be extended to make meaningful contributions to this program?

When John assumed the role of director of the introductory course at Southern Illinois University, his first goal was simple: Don't screw it up. John's immediate predecessor in this assignment was Dr. Jonny Gray, associate professor of rhetoric and performance studies, who had directed the program for close to a decade. In this role, Jonny instituted a number of innovative ideas into the program, including a Speaker's Forum. While it has evolved over the years, the basic premise of the forum is to showcase civil dialogue on a topic. From "going green" to binge drinking on campus, the forum has, for years, been an amazing opportunity for students in the introductory course to apply speaking skills toward a very public event on campus that would feature competitively selected speeches on a topic that would challenge the campus to think more deeply on a pressing topic.

For instance, in the fall of 2010, the Forum committee selected the following topic: "Do we eat ethically?" This theme provided the SIUC community an opportunity to explore a variety of questions about topics including factory farming, meat eating and vegetarian diets, genetic engineering of food, food allergies, growth hormones in animals, ideology and the food pyramid, and world and local hunger. The intent was to showcase a variety of ethical questions that arise when we engage in the mundane act of eating. Themes like these challenge students to explore questions of local concern (e.g., factory farming is a significant issue in southern Illinois), as well as consider how these local questions are matters of global significance (e.g., factory farming means that our own local decisions affect food production worldwide as we now eat less and less food grown in our own geographic regions).

When he inherited the director position at SIUC, John wanted to maintain the reputation of the Speaker's Forum, which has become a signature part of the larger departmental identity. However, his interest was in how to create, other than the expected connection to public speaking, a heuristic connection between the introductory course and the Speaker's Forum.

John encouraged instructors to explore meaningful connections between the introductory course and the theme associated with the Speaker's Forum. Each semester, the instructor could, if she or he was willing or interested, use the Forum theme as a context to study public speaking, thus framing the assignments and other aspects of the course with the topic of the Forum and creating a clearer connection between the event and the class. In the end, John's hope was to make trying out for the Forum a logical next step for the course and for students, creating rewards for them in terms of credit for the course if they participated. Through this shift, as a course coordinator, he was able to create a sense of "buy in" for the Forum for both students and instructional staff, and he was able to create a (social, political, ethical, and/or cultural) context for this public speaking course. Thus, the Forum theme could help instructors move their students from classroom speeches to engagement in the metaphorical town square. This wasn't a seismic change in the program; instead, it was a natural progression, building on the program's existing strengths.

Course Coordinators Can and Should Be Creative

Course coordinators can and should be appropriately creative. Creativity need not consist of a wholly original idea, but instead can be a carefully crafted and well-timed extension of an established idea. In the example above, John's own efforts as a course coordinator evolved from the creativity of his predecessor, and his own creativity took the form of finding ways of building from the department's collective vision of what an introductory course might offer to students and the community. One of the most difficult parts of directing a course with many sections is the sense of burnout that can emerge from repetition that can seem, at its most negative, endless. Yet simple decisions can reframe and alter this feeling; the Speaker's Forum is always new each semester, and with this, the theme of the course is unique. No two semesters are the same, even if the core of what instructors teach remains consistent. Find ways of building a creative program that keeps you and your instructional staff engaged.

The question of creativity, of course, can be a perplexing one for course coordinators — What is/should be my contribution to this program? — but it is a useful way of thinking about the connections between vision and pedagogy. Creativity, or, we might say, the imprint of a particular coordinator on the course she or he supervises, does not need to be a large structural change (and certainly this should not be change solely for change's sake), but could, instead, be a matter of refinement, of shaping the program in small ways that make it more effective and more consistent with its values and mission. Selecting a course text that better meets the needs of students and faculty, or shaping major assignments so that they better meet course learning outcomes, are seemingly subtle changes that ripple outward through the students who complete the course and carry what they've learned into other classes and beyond. Or if we consider Kristen Treinen's revisions to instructor orientation, changes can involve a coordinator's research interests as they intersect with course mission, and changes may respond to the needs of instructional staff as they work to support course mission.

Adjustments to the course so that it is more consistent with and effective in enacting its mission not only benefit the introductory course, but also function to bolster and strengthen the department or program that houses it. Finding creativity in small ways can be an important step in feeling empowered and purposeful in your role as course coordinator.

Even Small Changes Can Have Meaningful and Lasting Results

Do what you can to build on the successes of the program you inherit. Small changes that build on the momentum of a program can make a big difference, investing in the continued life of the introductory courses on a campus. Whether in the form of a speakers' forum that invites students to hear their peers speak on issues of significance to the campus community or an assessment plan that helps your program grow and learn and communicate its effectiveness to other offices on campus, these small changes are consequential. For example, one of our former students who is now a tenured community college instructor explains this as giving as she can. In other words, she and her colleagues have no formal assessment or coordination processes for their introductory courses, though her program is facing considerable pressure to develop them. Working with her former professors and colleagues on other campuses, she has been able to make small contributions (such as developing a sample common syllabus with learning outcomes) that have helped the group move forward toward the development of a plan.

Another small change that can have meaningful and dramatic effects can be the decision to change the textbook for the course. When John got his first job as a director of an introductory course, he moved the book from one that centered on business and professional contexts for communication to a text that framed diversity as the focus. The new book brought the course more in line with the department's vision for the course and, most significantly, it made the course more connected to the departmental curriculum (including the training the graduate students were receiving in their own classes). In other universities, shifts from public speaking to introduction to communication (or vice versa) can have a dramatic effect in student learning and program vision. In one school, the move to an introduction to communication curriculum had no effect on the course's placement in the general education program, since the core syllabus did not change; what changed was the means by which those outcomes were achieved.

Encourage Instructors and Students to Assume Responsibility for Innovations

It is vital to support instructors' pedagogy in ways that are consistent with the program/course vision. Like all major changes or programs that anyone might start in relation to the introductory course, initiatives tend to succeed when coordinators help connect them to the logic and vision of the course itself. Perhaps a negative example would help clarify: Even the smallest, most sensible changes, like asking instructors to use a rubric for assignments or to follow a common syllabus or course text, can feel invasive and insulting to instructors if they do not understand why these are important changes to pursue and how they will benefit them and their students. As a course coordinator, whether directly or indirectly, you have access to students' and instructors' experiences with the course; finding ways to draw in these perspectives, whether through the use of instruments (like course evaluations or the SGID we described in Chapter 5) or in formal or informal discussions, can help you effect changes to the course that are meaningful and clearly grounded in others' experience (reducing the appearance that a given change is your "pet project").

There are other ways to increase responsibility for innovation in an introductory course. First, your work, and your instructors' and students' work, with the introductory course is important, not just to departmental or program support or perpetuation of the discipline, but to the vitality of civic discourse. The teaching staff is an important part of this initiative. When our own language ("basic course") minimizes the importance of introductory communication courses, course coordinators can have a difficult time helping their colleagues understand the larger purpose and function of our efforts. Through their efforts with the Speaker's Forum, John's community has shaped the course so that it advances complex ways of thinking about public speaking. In essence, they foreground the ideal that, when we speak in public, our communication has political, social, and cultural effects. Each semester the instructional staff challenges students to engage their peers, to research and develop a message for their fellow students and community members. The message they send to students is that this kind of intellectual work is important and matters.

Second, your colleagues in your department or program will often, whether they think of it in these ways or not, rely on the introductory course as an important means of outreach for the program (whether major, certificate, or concentration). Through your judicious development and promotion of your efforts, whether with a speakers' forum or a speech and debate event, you contribute to the development of a program or departmental identity on campus. This identity helps your program or department signal to others, on campus and off, that you are the "home" for communication studies instruction, questions, and opportunities. What might your program do to inspire a sense of departmental identity? As a potential source of outreach and new students, the introductory course is foundational to any department or program's reputation and civic identity.

ADAPTING TO EXIGENCIES

There are many different external forces that can affect your program; keeping your program vision in mind may help you weather these storms. Perhaps the most common sort of exigency is budgetary—this can appear variously as furloughs, layoffs, budget cuts, program restructuring, contract renegotiations, staffing changes, or other disruptions. However, there are other sorts of emergent circumstances that may affect the coordination of the introductory course, including national or local emergencies (such as environmental disasters or campus tragedies) and your own or other significant leaders' personal challenges (regarding, for example, health and wellness).

Because furloughs are increasingly common on college and university campuses across the country, and because there is so little guidance for how to respond to them, it is worth addressing them at some length. In the summer of 2009, Deanna learned that California State University was implementing furloughs as a means of responding to the impending fiscal crisis. Everyone would begin furloughs immediately, in her case nine days per semester for a total of 18 days, amounting to a nearly 10% income reduction. In addition to her own concerns as a faculty member, she also felt the challenges of navigating this difficult time as a GTA supervisor and introductory course coordinator; the conflicts she felt as an individual faculty member became magnified when she considered the effects of individual decisions across the many sections and hundreds of students in the course. She was acutely aware of the ways her colleagues — both more and less experienced — would read and assess (and perhaps even adopt) her actions.

Perhaps most perplexing to instructors was the question of whether and how to make a 10% reduction to their already robust workloads; many of Deanna's colleagues expressed this in terms of "furloughs mean I'm going to work harder even though I'm earning less." This became an increasingly complex debate as faculty implemented their respective positions on the furloughs — for example, whether they took furlough days on instructional days or would participate in faculty meetings or assessment activities. This became a matter of principle for many instructors, in that they would only perform work for which the State would pay or in that they would continue to do their jobs as they always had; in either case, these instructors would and could reasonably justify the value of their decisions in terms of what this would mean for students' learning. In planning her own response to the furloughs, Deanna considered both the mission and vision of the course and her own sense of professional commitment; in taking action, she focused on clearly communicating her rationale and trying to create a climate of dialogue and learning from one another by not demonizing others' actions, where divergent.

While budgetary concerns will often dominate any discussion of exigencies affecting the introductory course, it is important to remember that we will, from time to time, face other crises as well. Though it is unwise to assume that danger is lurking around every corner, we would be wise to prepare for foreseen and (as best we can) unforeseen challenges, whether in the form of natural disasters, personal and community tragedies, or other disruptions of our best-laid plans. Here, consulting with other offices on your campus (ranging from your supervisors' to the counseling program to facilities and beyond) will help you address and answer questions as they occur. Further, developing (or using an already established and effective) means to communicate with students, instructors, and supervisors during times of crisis will be essential. In the wake of campus shootings, many colleges and universities have now established efficient means to communicate with students on and off campus, as well as programs that can help students connect with community resources when they are in need.

As you navigate uncertain times, it can help to remember that course and program vision can help you remain consistent and transparent with colleagues and students. You can and should interrogate that vision as challenges arise; you can and should make decisions that help preserve your sense of vitality and efficacy; and you should not lightly abandon any of your program's past lessons, as challenges will always return.

Model Course Vision, Even (and Perhaps Especially) under Stress

As a coordinator, you should recognize that you will model your values and must be prepared to interrogate them. There will be times when, as a course coordinator, especially if you supervise GTAs or other less experienced colleagues, you will feel that your actions are under considerable scrutiny in ways you may or may not appreciate. Whether people are looking to see what path you take through significant organizational challenges or how you'll navigate family medical leave or how you lead a lesson about Aristotle's artistic proofs, whether or not they choose to emulate you, you will be modeling. Take care that you model values that you hold dear and that you are willing to examine and challenge in dialogue with others. This is not so different from the role you play ordinarily as an instructor, when you consider what to post in your Facebook status or wear on the first of classes, but it may feel more intense and consequential to you when circumstances are heightened or strained. It may be tempting to try to be as objective and impartial as possible, but you will make choices that are informed by your values and your sense of the vision of the course you coordinate; helping others understand how your decisions, both administrative and pedagogical, exist in relation to this vision is important for them to learn and interrogate too.

For example, furloughs became a teachable moment for many colleagues. Deanna worked with instructors, including and especially GTAs, in her department to better understand the communicative elements of the budget crisis and its effects on their campus, from the rhetoric they found in news reports and classroom conversations to the ways students' learning would be altered and made more complex by the experience. Like her colleagues on other campuses, she gently pushed back against some colleagues' assumption that they would, inevitably, work more for less, reminding them that they could reconfigure their workloads in ways that would make their teaching lives more meaningful to them (and that to assume that they would, inevitably, complete more work for less pay would only make that a self-fulfilling prophecy).

Colleagues on other campuses report a variety of strategies for dealing with imposed furloughs on their respective campuses, including working with unions on campus to protect graduate student assistants and other instruction staff that service the introductory course. Such an effort preserves the consistent instruction in foundation courses and serves to protect those most at risk financially at the university. Still others have included statements on syllabi or in class, noting how the pay cut has affected both the professor's ability to teach and, as a result, the students' experience. In all, most instructors and directors of foundational communication courses we talked to tried to find meaningful ways of incorporating the furloughs into their jobs in ways that protect the integrity and vision of their programs while still protecting their own interests.

Be Prepared to Examine Course Vision and Your Values

You must plan to address exigencies that affect the delivery and coordination of introductory communication courses through the program vision you have outlined and embraced. Most external influences are hard to predict; they are situations that arise, largely without much advanced warning. It is worth noting that you will, from time to time, find these situations deeply unsettling, and you will not always be happy with your responses in the moment. Your best bet is to be prepared to meet whatever comes with a consistent and thoughtful adherence to program vision. It will enable course instructors to recognize decisions within a framework with which they are already familiar.

Let's consider an even smaller, but still important, illustration of the importance of modeling: When you are ill (whether with a migraine, the flu, or something more serious), how you behave will teach others what is and is not appropriate about work in higher education. Even something as small as your decision to take a sick day or press on at work is pedagogical; discussing what informs your decisions with others and how those are linked to both program and personal wellness can strengthen your work together. Would you want your students or colleagues to do as you do? Opening your decisions and actions to consideration can be an important way to maintain the coherence and vitality of program (and personal) vision.

Career Vitality and Empowerment

Career vitality is, in part, a function of feeling empowered. With this, we don't mean to suggest that the power of positive thinking is all you need to succeed in university life. That said, it's wise to understand what you *can do* within circumstances that are not of your own making. Recovering a sense of choice, and affirming your values and working toward them in all aspects of your assignment, will help you avoid the sort of burnout that affects people who feel as though they are going through the motions. You may not be able to reverse a major campus decision like furloughs or layoffs, but there are actions you can take that will help you make meaning from that decision for your own purposes.

Value your colleagues and students as resources for your own learning. These people can help you make sense of experiences that are challenging to understand; even where you do not agree, the dialogue is usually heuristic, taking you in directions you might not otherwise think to travel. Moreover, you might find as much meaningful counsel from undergraduates as from your more senior colleagues; people with common interests and divergent experiences can be great problem solvers and troubleshooters if they work together as a team. You might discuss how to respond to students' feelings about a national tragedy, or you might consider ways to strengthen the curriculum. Whether about extreme or mundane issues, the colleagues you supervise can help you think through complex issues before and as you implement new policy or pedagogy. This does not mean you abdicate decisions that are rightly your own as coordinator, but it does mean that you can work with others to make sure the decisions you make are well informed, considerate, and consistent with program vision.

In the end, Deanna's goal was to teach and to learn from her colleagues how to reconfigure their workloads in ways that would be meaningful, keeping what is valuable and lessening or minimizing what is unnecessary or repetitive — for the period of furlough implementation, but also for the rest of their careers. In a sense, she was looking for ways to "work smarter, not harder." Further, she wanted to work with others and to do so in ways that were consistent not only with our disciplinary values, but with her own department and program visions. This meant exploring aspects of her work that Deanna had, until this time, considered sacrosanct. However harrowing (and painfully disruptive economically and emotionally), this difficult time helped her to understand that dialogue and collaboration with her colleagues are essential to the vitality of a program, department, and discipline.

Do Not Give Up Hard-Won Lessons

Where you and your colleagues have weathered a storm, it is tempting to minimize those struggles in favor of resuming your old patterns. We have probably all had the frustrating experience of trying to work with a faculty member who insists on defining the present moment by some isolated incident in the past (who believes that a department or institution cannot change or that each year is necessarily a decline from the previous), and we would not suggest that you pursue this course. However, if you and your colleagues work diligently to find meaning and purpose in an experience, you would be wise to make that a part of the department or program narrative in such a way that others who have not experienced the same circumstances can benefit by your insights. For example, even if your campus never experiences furloughs and layoffs again, if you have learned something about how to survive a budget crisis at your institution or how to make a complex and emotionally charged experience a teachable moment for yourself, your colleagues, or your students, sharing that as appropriate can help others learn from those lessons, too.

CONCLUSION

Education involves modeling; whether purposefully or accidentally, our actions and inactions share our values and beliefs with our colleagues and our students. To believe otherwise is naïve at best and dangerous at worst. While expectations of course coordinators vary from one program to another, in programs where they supervise less experienced colleagues like GTAs, their actions are consequential: Others will read their behavior for meaning. It is therefore important for you, to the degree you feel capable, to be open to discussion of your decisions and to be transparent in your reasoning. These discussions are potentially transformative moments for the community, especially as you model with them how they might engage in dialogue with one another, and through them, you will be able to work toward meaning and growth when even that feels very difficult to do. Your efforts at care—at self-care, at care for students and colleagues, at care for the quality of instruction in the course and what it does in the world—will distinguish you as a course coordinator.

Program vision and pedagogy exist in productive tension with one another. Without a sense of vision of the values and goals that link a community toward purposeful effort, pedagogy feels disoriented and lifeless; without pedagogy as a means to enact program vision, what purpose would it serve? What meaning would it hold for the community of students and educators who constitute a university? Your effort as a course coordinator to link vision and pedagogy, whether that involves large structural changes, small refinements, or personal actions or inactions, will matter—will become real—in dialogue with your colleagues and students. Their contributions, informed by diverse experiences and positions regarding university life and the introductory course, will enhance your own growth as surely as it will their own.

RECOMMENDED READING

Altbach, P. G., Berdahl, R. O., & Gumport, P. J. (Eds.). (2005). *American higher education in the twenty-first century: Social, political and economic challenges* (2nd ed.). Baltimore, MD: The Johns Hopkins University Press.

Altbach, et al.'s collection provides important context for the status—social, cultural, and economic—of higher education in the United States. Chapters by MacGuinness and Johnstone offer insights into the financial workings of colleges and universities and may help prepare coordinators and other academics for the cycles of fiscal expansion and contraction they face in the academy.

9

On Responding to Students' Needs

Pregnant Pause

> Week 12, the end of the first trimester . . . about time to tell your department chair. You want her to be one of the first people to know about your good news and your impending maternity leave. As you prepare your agenda for that conversation, high atop your list is the question of who should serve as acting course director during your leave and who will be poised to respond effectively to the students and instructors the course serves. In considering your predecessor as a possible replacement, you pause to contemplate how the program has changed — and more importantly, how the students have changed — in the eight years since you assumed this responsibility. Perhaps the most significant changes have been in the profound diversity of both the students and the instructors associated with this course, and in the new technology used to deliver and assess the course. You have had occasion to work with students and instructors who are working parents, first-generation college students, English language learners, or in recovery from illness or disability. You have helped advocate for restroom facilities for transgendered faculty and students with disabilities, and you have worked with your department chair to offer more sections of the coordinated class online and in the evenings. You've also learned numerous computer programs and skills to keep up with your students' needs and abilities, and your department's technological resources have gone through several iterations of change. The course, and your role, have evolved to stay relevant to the communities you serve.

* * *

Perhaps the most important role a course coordinator has on a campus is to ensure that all students have a meaningful experience in the course you supervise — they must, in the end, learn more about communication and fulfill the course objectives. While so much of the direct focus of a course coordinator is often on the instructors — the administration of training and direct observation of sections of the course — it can be hard to remain focused on the reality that these tasks are in service of the students who will be learning in these classrooms. Responding to the needs of these students, therefore, is part of effective supervision and, ultimately, a central part of developing a course that succeeds. In this chapter, we address two essential aspects of creating a classroom climate that will help students learn in meaningful and lasting ways — student diversity and the role of technology — in order to articulate an approach for how one may respond to the various and layered needs students bring with them to the classroom.

We acknowledge that one of the best aspects of being a course coordinator is the opportunity you have to interact with many different people from all quarters of university life. While what constitutes diversity for a given program can vary from campus to campus, it is the case that, as coordinators, we will inevitably teach (or supervise) people who are and are not like ourselves. This situates coordinators in a productive tension of sorts—we may have to confront our own assumptions and expectations in ways that may be discomforting, but that are intellectually and organizationally stimulating. Further, we acknowledge that technology presents new possibilities and new challenges to students and instructors. For some, the incorporation of technology is a blessing, a way to reinvest in their teaching and meet students in a form with which they are already familiar; yet, for others, technology use in and for the classroom may be complicated by lack of knowledge, experience, or resources. Here, we explore student needs and the implications they have for the course coordinator, the challenges and opportunities posed by these important issues, and, finally, how coordinators can play a role in responding to the difficulties that arise between the instructors and the students they supervise.

RESPONDING TO STUDENTS' NEEDS AS AN ETHIC OF CARE

We feel that one productive way of thinking about the students you work with in the foundational communication course is as an ethic: a disposition or direction toward students that enables you, as the coordinator of a course, to effectively work with the students under your supervision. As we noted above, it is easy to potentially stay too focused on the instructors you supervise; yet by crafting and refining this ethic toward students, you can remain dedicated to creating a valuable educational experience with students. An ethic suggests, of course, a moral attitude—in this case, of care and regard for students' learning; we embrace this as we proceed.

While a consumer model of educational practice reduces the complexity and significance of our relationship to students, our main purpose as course coordinators is to serve the learning of the students who study with us. As administrators of a course, this service can mean that we are attempting to meet the needs of upwards of 1,500 or more students a semester. There are some general principles that might aid in your thinking about this role and how you might orient toward the students you serve.

- **Curriculum:** While we have addressed curriculum in other parts of this book, it is important as you design and implement your course sections that you pay close attention to whether and how the curriculum is meeting the needs of students. This means attending to the campus culture and the role the course plays in the university. For example, on both our campuses, our coordinated introductory communication courses play a central role in the core or general education curriculum, and as a result, the course must meet overall oral communication skills requirements and contribute to campus goals of engaging issues of diversity and cultural awareness. This might not be the case for other campuses. If your course is part of a business college, then a stronger focus on business and professional communication would be in order, helping students develop public and small-group communication skills, including mastery of relevant communications technologies (such as PowerPoint or Elluminate), for an organizational/workplace context. Understanding and adjusting the curriculum of your course so that it better supports students' learning in future courses and beyond their time in school are an important part of course coordination.

- **Resources:** Shaping the coordinated course so that it helps students access campus resources that support their success is another important aspect of responding to students' needs as a course coordinator. For instance, perhaps your campus has a writing center, communication center or lab, or other supplemental instructional program that students can use to better meet the requirements of your course; connecting students to these offices can bolster their performance in the course. Including statements on these offices (as well as information about the campus disability resource center or counseling services) in course syllabi can raise students' awareness of campus resources. Further, apprising students of campus resource centers (like LGBTQ or women's centers) not only helps students thrive as members of campus life, but may also help them locate resources for certain class assignments. On both our campuses (and no doubt on your own and nearby campuses as well), there are several speakers series run by different offices and programs on campus; inviting students to attend these presentations helps students enhance their understanding of communication in public contexts and see it as an invaluable part of their learning.

- **More Effective Training:** While you, as the course coordinator, may already provide a multilayered series of trainings for your staff, we would encourage you to take advantage of the resources and training opportunities on your campus that could enhance your work in the course, such as "Safe Zone" training (a guided workshop on creating safe spaces for LGBTQ youth on campus), sessions on your college's or university's first-year experience programs, human resources presentations on policies affecting full- and part-time faculty, and the like. These sessions serve to keep the coordinator, as well as the instructors and students of the course, current on university opportunities, operations, and policies.

- **Policy:** As universities change and adapt, so do policies. From academic honesty to sexual harassment, it is vital that you are up to date on current policy matters that govern your work as a course coordinator. These matters will often be of central importance to the students who are in your courses. Where you work with instructors who teach across a number of different campuses, it is useful to remember that policies may vary considerably from one campus to another. For example, on one campus, it may be that instructors must grade students, in part, on attendance, while at another campus, the quality of students' participation may influence their grades, but instructors may not assign or deduct points from students' grades on attendance alone. If you are aware of these differences, you can help instructors who teach in a number of different schools better serve the students on your particular campus in ways that are transparent to them and consistent across their classes.

- **Keeping Current:** In order to remain vital and responsive in your role as a course coordinator, we encourage you to stay abreast of developments not only on your campus, but also in your field. This is true not only for our disciplinary knowledge—which inevitably shapes our textbook selections and our assignments—but also our understanding of effective teaching, in terms of technological aids, popular cultural texts, and other innovative pedagogies. For example, the vast majority of students have Facebook or other social media accounts; knowing this and having one yourself might enable you to be more fluent when talking to students and instructors about the role of these media in our lives. Making effective use of services like Turnitin.com can help you and the instructors of the course better prepare for and work with students on their needs surrounding academic honesty. Reading journals like *Basic Communication Course Annual* or *Communication Teacher* will keep you apprised of pressing developments in the teaching of communication and how you might enhance the experience of students and instructors associated with this coordinated course.

Rather than treating each of these bullet points as items for your "to do" list, recall that they interact in productive ways to form an ethic of care and regard for yourself and the people you support with this coordinated course. As an ethic, they help you remember that your position exists always *in relation to* students and their needs. Improving your own working conditions may well help you improve students' learning conditions. One of the ways in which this relationship may become troubling or difficult is when we must mediate, as coordinators or supervisors, in conflicts between students and instructors.

Mediation between Instructors and Students

There will be times when you, as a coordinator, must mediate in disputes between students and their instructors, though how this looks may vary, depending on how transparent your program or department's leadership structure is to students. In many programs that employ GTAs who teach stand-alone sections, the course syllabus, readings packet, or online materials indicate who the course coordinator or GTA supervisor is, and some even include instructions for how to appeal instructor decisions (perhaps most commonly, grading decisions) with this supervisor. Where this structure is less transparent to students, it may be that they approach the department chair, dean, division head, or some other campus leader first; in these cases, you will often need to share with these interested others your insights into the situation at hand. You may, still more rarely, learn from students how happy they are with their experience in the course or with their instructors, but, unfortunately, appeals and complaints will be far more common. In these conversations, one of your challenges will be to navigate the needs of all the people involved, and their varying perceptions and interests.

The sorts of challenges and concerns students bring to you will vary, depending on the policies and instructors in your program. For example, as we both teach in departments that rely heavily on GTAs, we find ourselves in conversations with students periodically; for Deanna, this may mean a conversation about a GTA's decision regarding a student's academic honesty or performance on an assignment, while for John this may entail a discussion about the course's attendance policy and a given instructor's interpretation/implementation of it. As someone who also works with part-time faculty and lecturers, Deanna must also, from time to time, navigate the difficult spaces created by students who may share troubling information about colleagues who do not enjoy long-term job security. The nature of the student's (or instructor's) concern will also affect who becomes involved in the conversation; in addition to students, department chairs, and deans or division heads, you may also find yourself speaking with academic advisors, athletic coaches, campus ombuds representatives, other instructors from within or outside your department, and, though more rarely, parents. Each of these people will have a different investment in the outcome of the discussion, and her or his access to all the available information — including information about what instructors do/do not learn in your department or program, department and course policies, and so forth — may vary considerably. Helping all parties navigate the situation at hand in a face-saving and productive way can be a significant challenge.

Many of the concerns that find their way to us as course coordinators are an expression of students' frustration with their own behavior and what they feel are unfair policies or decisions; put in their best light, these are conflicts of expectations — an instructor's actions are disconfirming of students' expectations for how that instructor should act. More rare, though this does occur, are serious instructor oversights or unprofessional conduct. In any case, as a coordinator, you may need to help a student understand or challenge an instructor's decision or help an instructor navigate a difficult situation involving a student or other colleague. In these instances, one of your responsibilities as a coordinator is to do so in a manner that is appropriate to your degree of authority in a situation (for example, for a GTA, you may serve in a supervisory capacity, but for a part-time faculty member or a long tenured full professor, a department chair or dean may have more authority to intervene directly) and that functions as a learning moment for all parties.

Mediating a dispute fairly, so that both parties feel you respect and understand them (even if you do not agree with them) is essential. Unless they are knowingly behaving unprofessionally, instructors deserve compassion and mentoring as surely as students do. In situations where culture may make this a more complex and difficult conversation (as in cases of sexual harassment or prejudice), you are likely to call upon other offices and administrators to weigh in on the situation (for example, in matters related to hate speech, sexual harassment, and other forms of prejudice, most universities have particular administrators, offices, and policies that must, by law, respond and document all levels of an institutional response). In such conversations, it is imperative that you act with discretion, take careful notes, consult with other offices as appropriate (i.e., as your university requires you to do) and mete judgments in a consistent way and in a reasonable time frame.

All of this seems clean and neat, compiled here in this chapter; however, in practice, the experience can feel frustrating, messy, and confusing. For example, let's say an instructor you supervise communicates to you that her classroom is a hostile and threatening environment and that the students are disrespectful and prejudiced against her for any number of reasons she can describe at length. If that were the case, you might consider observing in the classroom, engaging in more direct mentoring, and so on. However, let's also say that students from the class are coming to meet with you as this instructor's immediate supervisor. When you meet with each of them, you find that they appear reasonable and mature, considerate of the instructor's feelings, and capable of citing specific limitations of the instructor's pedagogy (e.g., that she is hostile and abrupt in responding to students' questions, that she does not prepare structured lesson plans, and so on). While they may well be prejudiced against this specific instructor, for her age perhaps or her cultural background, they do not appear to be any more so than other university students on your campus. This makes the matter quite a bit more complex; the truth, if we could say there is a truth in this situation, is likely somewhere in between the two positions, with weapons and wounds on both sides. Engaging in dialogue with each party may help you draw the two perspectives on the classroom environment into alignment; while they may not come to agreement, perhaps you can help them learn to listen to one another and admit and redress their respective limitations.

DIVERSITY IN THE COORDINATED COURSE

The difficulty of addressing issues of diversity in our coordinated communication courses lies in the reality that diversity will pose common challenges across campuses, even as the nature of that diversity varies. All campuses exist within structures of power and ideology and must, therefore, consider the role of privilege and oppression (such as racism, classism, sexism, heterosexism, ableism, and theism) in our individual and social lives. Communication course coordinators may feel this challenge and opportunity acutely, as communication functions to create, perpetuate, question, and resist inequality and oppression.

However, not all campuses experience diversity and difference in the same way, and because of this, it is important to find ways of meeting students' needs in different ways. Take, for example, a small Christian liberal arts college where students and faculty agree to participate in the same religious faith. Perhaps the number of *visibly* different students are few—less than 1 or 2% (though even seemingly homogeneous populations are rarely truly homogeneous when we consider aspects of human identity that extend beyond race/ethnicity to gender, sexuality, faith, ability, and economic class). Students and instructors may inadvertently assume sameness (in values, in experiences, in goals) where it does not really exist. Conversations regarding diversity are important for educating seemingly homogeneous populations about how power works across the country and in their own communities, and, perhaps more to the point, questions of diversity are important in helping students understand the value and meaning of diversity in their own cultures. Compare the diversity needs in this setting with an urban campus where each classroom may contain students from not only every race and ethnicity, but literally from all across the world. In this apparently profoundly diverse setting, students and instructors may assume difference (again, in values, in experiences, in goals) where there is also continuity and connection. Encouraging students to meaningfully explore diversity, without falling into relativism or a jaded sense that they are somehow savvier or better informed than students in other parts of the country as a result of the presence of diversity, becomes an important goal. Regardless, all campuses have an experience with diversity, and all campuses must meet the challenges and opportunities that such diversity engenders.

Inevitably, each campus must consider how to meet the needs of a diverse student body (as well as diversity within the instructional staff). To participate in this process, a course coordinator needs to address both the internal diversity of this specific community and prevailing notions of diversity on a larger, systemic level. All campuses must meet the needs of students who have challenges that require individual and institutional responses. The needs of students and instructors with disabilities exemplify one form of diversity that requires this sort of organized response (though we might also consider how campuses address the needs of students of color, nontraditional students or adult learners, and so on). For instance, John once taught in a room students could only access by stairs. He learned that if a student who used a wheelchair enrolled in the class, he would need to request a room change. His response would be individual, in that he would need to accommodate a particular student; however, he was also aware that the campus was in the process of removing architectural barriers so that it would be more in compliance with federal law. As a result, he chose thereafter to request accessible rooms routinely, especially in his role as a course coordinator, so that a student with a disability wouldn't feel like an exception that would relocate students to another, perhaps less desirable, quarter of campus. In this way, responding to student needs may require both attention to the local scene and understanding how to navigate power and privilege on a social systemic level.

However, not all students' needs are so easy to meet, and navigating questions of diversity in the introductory course can be quite difficult. Imagine that an instructor approaches you to say he's concerned about a disruptive student. After he reports several different encounters with this student (where the student has challenged the instructor openly in class over topics involving cultural diversity), you and the instructor are now concerned that the student is disruptive because he is uncomfortable with a Black instructor. Regardless of the "truth" of the concern, the instructor is now feeling uncomfortable himself with the student and has come to you for help. This becomes all the more concerning when the student approaches you with a request for a section change, noting problems with his instructor's teaching style, noting that he just can't relate to his instructor. Without a clear sense of what is happening here, this question of how to proceed is quite complex. As a coordinator, you weigh your concerns for the needs the student has articulated, the continued disruption the student may cause if he remains in the class, and your concerns with enabling his potential racism by granting the section change request. It may be that you attempt to mediate this conflict between student and instructor, hoping to reach a compromise and create a learning moment. Or, in the end, your concerns for the instructor's well-being and classroom control may well eclipse your concerns for social change, and you may sign the section change request. As is apparent in this example, issues of diversity (and the implications surrounding what diversity means) are a challenge that, as a course coordinator, you will negotiate from many angles, and in many surprising scenarios.

DIVERSITY: CHALLENGES AND OPPORTUNITIES FOR THE COURSE COORDINATOR

There are many challenges associated with meeting the needs of a diverse campus culture. A challenge is not necessarily negative; it surfaces the ever-present need to adjust your efforts in line with what you learn from students and instructors about what they feel they need. Taking these challenges seriously invites them to inform and perhaps even radically alter course curriculum and structure. These opportunities for change may result in small changes to assignments or course goals, or larger adjustments to the course in light of new laws that protect or increase access for certain populations (e.g., laws regarding protected identity categories like sexuality or disability status). These changes are important, as they ensure that the course proactively serves the needs and strengthens the values of the campus community.

Perhaps the most central challenge this diversity presents for a campus and, by extension, to you as a coordinator, is the need to understand how power and privilege undergird not only communication courses but also our work as professors. For us, this has meant engaging in research at the intersections of multicultural education, critical communication pedagogy, and cultural studies; we feel this work has enabled us, as coordinators, to develop an effective understanding of how power works, especially in its most mundane ways, to produce inequality (e.g., Fassett & Warren, 2004, 2005, 2007). However, there is a wide range of research both in our discipline (for example, in organizational communication) and beyond (for example, in sociology of education) that can help course coordinators better understand and frame for other instructors the problems associated with leaving abuses of power and privilege undertheorized (e.g., Ashcraft & Allen, in press; Buzzanell, Sterk, & Turner, 2004; Hendrix, Hebbani, & Johnson, 2007; Wink, 2011). Let's take an example that is unfortunately all too common: A female student comes to you with concerns about her male instructor, claiming that the jokes he makes in class are creating an uncomfortable environment for her and interfering with her learning. The male students in the class laugh loudly, and because, on the surface, there does not appear to be a problem, the student is afraid to broach the topic with the instructor.

In this case, knowing scholarship that can help you better understand how power, gender, and communication can intersect in the classroom, especially how small moments of sexism can re-create an environment that many others may perceive as violent, would be useful for a director (see, for example, Fotsch, 2008). In such a situation, the coordinator could not only address the issue of sexism as an inappropriate mode of classroom communication, but also explain the more concrete ways we create and re-create sexism through mundane talk (i.e., through gender-exclusive language like "mankind" or examples that frame men as powerful and women as irrational, emotional, or weak). Becoming versed in current theory and research regarding these sorts of issues could enhance the training and development of an instructional staff.

One way to understand the challenges and opportunities of diversity is to consider their effects on the major components of a coordinator's role. It may help to think of these challenges and opportunities more specifically in terms of how they affect our relationships with students, with instructors, with the curriculum for the course, and with the training we provide our colleagues who teach the course.

Diversity and Students

The students who enroll in introductory courses in communication are becoming more diverse each year. While some students remain "traditional" (i.e., white, middle class, aged 18 to 22, Christian), students from various races, nationalities, and class backgrounds (to say nothing of other forms of diversity) are entering our classrooms. We need to take this fact into consideration in both the training of our teaching staff and in our curricular materials. For instance, in a recent class, one of us identified two students who lived within 10 minutes of each other, yet those 10 minutes could not even begin to speak to the gulf that separated them economically. One student was from a wealthy suburb and had attended one of the finest high schools in the state, while the other was educated in an urban inner city and came from a struggling school. These students come into the classroom with different needs. Both need not only the content of the class, but also recognition of how their educations have prepared them differently. Perhaps the largest struggle for an instructor may be understanding that while one of these students' educations may be better in the traditional sense, they both have much to learn about how class privilege situates them differently in the classroom, often creating barriers in terms of their effectiveness at communicating with audiences who are different from themselves. Instructors need to meet these challenges with a varied approach that enables both — and all — students to learn and thrive in their classes.

The challenge of an increasingly diverse student body is also an opportunity to make the introductory course more vibrant and to highlight its importance. Sometimes in our efforts to allay students' fears regarding public speaking (and in seeking to create "safe" spaces in the classroom), we forget to ground public speaking in everyday settings where advocacy in the social sphere matters. Recognizing the challenge of diversity means challenging students to explore topics that matter to them and that can have a palpable effect on their lives, even where these topics are controversial, uncomfortable, or difficult to discuss. This is an opportunity to travel new terrain, to leave the shore of overdone speech topics and move toward the substantive and complex.

Our students are often, though not always, in our coordinated classes by requirement, not choice. In most cases, the communication course sells itself — students enjoy the interaction, the opportunity to speak on issues that matter to them; however, students still often attend because they feel they must. We have a significant responsibility to reach out to students across the disinterest divide. By contextualizing our mundane and public communication as deeply political and ideological, as constitutive of selves, relationships, and cultures, we can help students reflect on the relevance not only of their efforts to become more effective communicators, but of the course itself. In effect, we can inspire them to invest in their everyday lives, in the social and political realities that they help to create, by connecting the content of the course with their own lives and inviting reflection and possibility for change.

Diversity and Instructors

Each semester or year, we work with new instructors of the coordinated courses we supervise. These instructors come from all over the world and from all walks of life. This diversity is crucial to understand, as it affects how these instructors teach and how students will learn. As course coordinators, we always encourage instructors to use personal experience — to share their own cultural background as appropriate in their teaching. Such examples not only connect the instructor and her or his students to course content, and thus improve student learning, but they help teachers (especially first-time teachers) realize they have much to offer their students. Their backgrounds affect how students learn, shaping their understandings of communication. Knowing this enables you as a coordinator to talk with concerned instructors and students, helping them to see all communication as situated in cultural/social contexts.

For instance, John recently received a phone call from a parent about her daughter's instructor. This GTA was rather left-leaning, often spoke of his queer identity, and would draw on his LGBTQ activism in class as examples of public speaking. The parent was concerned not only because she felt that, as a Christian, queer identity was something that was against her faith, but also because she felt that such matters, especially the political and personal life of a gay man, shouldn't be part of a public speaking class. In this moment, John faced a challenge that was also an opportunity: to help this parent understand that this teacher was not doing anything inappropriate; that, in fact, he had encouraged this instructor to draw on his experiences as they would enable him to create a concrete context for communication that students could then use to connect the material in the book to his and their own lives. Culture, in all its many exciting and sometimes contradictory forms, is omnipresent in our lives; accepting that appropriate acknowledgement of our cultural lives may be an integral part of the classroom as well helps you to work with instructors to strengthen their pedagogy (as well as to work with students to strengthen their learning).

In contextualizing communication in substantive and nuanced ways even in introductory courses, we invite instructors to find ways of sharing their passions (activism, research, etc.) in the classroom, modeling passions (though not necessarily belief systems) they hope their students will embrace in their own communication. One way to do so is to explore thematic approaches to the course; another way could involve exploring the distinct features, challenges, and opportunities associated with diversity on your particular campus. In working with students to learn about communication in their everyday lives, instructors can learn more about the communities where they teach, discover what matters to their students, and engage in and practice communication as inquiry.

Diversity and Curriculum

As we have argued elsewhere (Fassett & Warren, 2007), and as we all feel perhaps every day of our instructional lives, what we do in the classroom is the real world, not some sheltered place devoid of conflict and divisiveness. We encounter many different kinds of people in the college classroom, and instead of filling us with fear, this prospect may fill us with promise. One of the challenges we may face, however, as course coordinators, is finding curricular materials that support engagement and analysis of culture in substantive ways. Unfortunately, it has been a tendency in our discipline to author textbooks that treat culture generally or topically, without providing space for or surfacing the sorts of interpersonal and intercultural challenges we face when our assumptions, stereotypes, and values collide. Creating space in the curriculum, through readings, reflective writings, values speeches, and other assignments, may make the classroom less "safe," but it also makes the conversations more real and lasting opportunities for learning. We have found that, in these conversations, students will help illuminate the limitations and the hypocrisies of our own work as educators, such as whether the textbook uses examples that routinely assume heterosexual romantic relationships. The diversity we experience in our colleagues and our students challenges us to revise and reinvent our curriculum to serve them in the most immediate and effective manner possible. Such efforts will not only enhance learning in the classroom, but put our students more directly in dialogue with contemporary disciplinary and social issues.

Choosing a textbook and/or other course materials that explore difference and diversity in powerful and meaningful ways will help you develop a progressive and relevant communication course for both students and instructors. However, course materials are only one place where you can make a difference. You might also encourage instructors to explore popular cultural texts like movies, television, media reports, and social networking sites as they emerge from students' interests and concerns. For instance, an instructor might explore how Facebook as a social networking site alters (both clarifies and obfuscates) our understandings of interpersonal communication and/or public communication.

Diversity and Training

In many ways, the training we provide to instructors is similar to what we received as GTAs some 15 years ago. This is significant in that our sense of how to train GTAs or other instructors is, as is the case with most of us, built from how we learned when we began our careers. This may be true for you as well. However, we diverge from the past in some important ways. For instance, we both focus, each in our own way, on what teaching means as a vocation; each of us teaches teachers in ways that place particular skills in the context of longevity, vitality, and advocacy. Because we believe communication is central to our and others' success not only as educators, but as members of a democratic society, we trumpet the importance of the introductory communication course. Further, because who we are as members of that society is inseparable from all the many different facets of our identity, we foreground in training critical cultural understandings of communication. As a coordinator it is important for you to explore approaches to teaching and learning that recognize that we all come from different social positional ties that are differently valued in this culture. To do so, you could invite conversations of power and oppression in the classroom through discussions of provocative readings (for example, bell hooks's "Confronting Class in the Classroom" or Alfie Kohn's "Grading: The Issue Is Not How But Why") and through performing and re-performing challenging hypothetical or actual classroom moments during forum theatre or role-play exercises. In these ways, you can work to heighten instructors' awareness of diversity and the challenges and opportunities it poses in the classroom.

Training programs are not just about survival for the instructor, but rather are a series of opportunities to join in dialogue about how we teach and to what ends. Orientations or staff meetings not only address the practicalities of the classroom, but do so in ways that invite consideration of how our classrooms may also be spaces of rigorous examination of communication as constitutive of power, oppression, resistance, and agency. Holding in mind a larger, sociocultural context creates space for students and instructors to prepare not only classwork or homework, but also work in the world, the work of creating a more just and compassionate world. This renewed sense of relevance—the notion that this course is part of the world and that we must, therefore, engage it meaningfully—helps reinforce an engaged sensibility in which all can explore the value and importance of our communication in all its forms.

Diversity and Safety

Perhaps one of the most pressing needs facing instructors and administrators of universities and colleges is the question of safety and security. Course coordinators, like other campus leaders, must take into consideration the diversity of their students and instructors in policy design and implementation; this is especially important with respect to safety and security. Most campuses now have committees that address these issues, ranging from emergency plans to review committees that assess various campus concerns and potential security risks—our campuses, and perhaps yours, too, are no exception. Many campuses have instituted emergency procedures for how to seek shelter or shelter in place; further, these campuses often have notification systems, whereby campus officials can readily contact students and community members via telephone, text message, and/or email. Many of these policies primarily address health concerns (e.g., chemical spills) and security (e.g., a suspicious, potentially armed person on campus) and are especially important to students who have disabilities and may need to work closely with campus representatives to evacuate or shelter.

In addition, many campuses have now established panels of faculty, administrators, and campus medical and safety personnel who review and respond to any students, staff, or faculty who appear to be a threat to public safety. Course policies on how to manage potential danger in the classroom are essential. It is important to remember, though, that it is not student, staff, or faculty diversity that brings danger. It is our responsibility, as course coordinators, to know campus policies and procedures and to work with diverse students and instructors to effectively navigate these policies and procedures in light of their needs. For instance, coordinators might work with students and instructors to develop policies on how to address student speeches that advocate hate and violence or speeches that include live animals or weapons as visual aids; these policies will help clarify for students their role in creating a collegial, respectful learning community. Part of the responsibility of the instructor (and, by extension, the coordinator) is to work with students to create environments where they will not tolerate violence or harassment. Clear policies and teacher training can aid in this preparation.

TECHNOLOGY IN THE COORDINATED COURSE

Addressing student needs also involves understanding the role of technology in your students' learning—from their everyday practices with technology to the integration of that knowledge with their classroom learning. Technology offers some of the most amazing and engaging possibilities for classrooms; it also gives rise to some complicated and thorny issues that will affect how instructors teach students. It is often in our efforts to respond to students' needs that we feel most pressured, as instructors, to embrace technology—as, for example, with "hybrid" or online instruction.

Key Considerations Regarding Technology

Because of the growing role of technology communication instruction, and the bright possibilities and real challenges it presents, it is essential that we better understand our own values with respect to technology in our classrooms, as well as the strengths and limitations associated with it, before making decisions that will affect us — students, instructors, and coordinators — alike. We address some of the most important considerations here:

Instructional Technology.   It is important to learn what is available to you as an instructor on your campus. For example, in many classrooms, instructors and students have access to technology that can enable innovative and productive educational experiences. On many campuses (though certainly not all, and certainly not in all classrooms on all campuses) instructors have access to "smart rooms," which typically include a computer, projector, and sometimes even a "smart board" that allows the instructor to write on a computer projection. These rooms make possible a wide array of learning enhancements, including screening sample or contemporary speeches and YouTube clips, drawing in various Web-based activities (e.g., online library modules), and such. PowerPoint is only one of a wide menu of options available to instructors in these facilities. It may also be that your campus has a distance learning facility, where through the use of video and teleconferencing features, you can interact with large numbers of students from across a vast geographic region. Large lecture halls are often technologically well equipped, complete with microphones and remote controls that enable a lecturer to engage with technology smoothly. Students in these spaces can purchase access to "clickers," making possible even more interaction. For instance, imagine showing a sample speech to the class and asking a series of questions: Was the speaker engaging, did the speaker have an important topic, did the speaker use ethical practices in delivery, and the like. Students with clickers could vote on the answer and immediately see the results on the screen, enabling a discussion of the speech with class feedback. Learning how to use the instructional technology on your campus is vital for meeting students' needs and facilitating instructors' use of such technologies as you and they feel is appropriate.

Textbook Technology.   Most textbook companies now offer interactive Web sites that students can navigate with the purchase of their textbooks. From watching sample speeches to taking practice exams to engaging chapter content through Web-based activities, students now have an ability to explore the potential of a text (and the content in that text) through multiple platforms. Instructors can take advantage of these technologies and incorporate activities and assignments online, changing how students study for and learn in their communication courses.

Students' Technology.   Students are often remarkably tech-savvy these days, in many cases more knowledgeable than their teachers. Taking advantage of students' interest in and experience with various forms of instructional technology can help instructors achieve learning outcomes in new and interesting ways. However, it is also important to acknowledge that technology can cause disruptions to learning as well. As a coordinator, you can encourage instructors to work with students to reduce non–curriculum-related use of smartphones, computers, or other technology in the classroom. Course policies that explicitly curtail personal technology use can mediate this a bit; however, increased effort may be needed in larger courses where observation of student behavior is more difficult. As textbooks begin to address this issue more, the communicative function of personal technology might move from simply a disciplinary issue to curriculum, enabling more sophisticated dialogues with students on the use and abuse of these technologies.

Distance Learning.   One of the fastest-growing enrollments in the country is in online courses, leaving many communication colleagues scrambling to meet the demand for distance education in a manner that preserves the integrity of traditionally delivered introductory courses. Compromises like hybrid (partially online, partially in-class) course structures that still enable public presentation of speeches have been created, with some success. Initial efforts in online learning should enable the field to learn more about the potential costs and rewards of such structures for learning; further, we will need to develop new modes of assessment to measure the learning benefits of such adaptations. It is most certainly true that online learning is here to stay, especially given the potential revenue such courses might garner in an era of decreasing state funding for public universities and growing interest in sustainability of environmental resources (e.g., fewer days in class on campus means fewer commuters, reduced power and facilities expenses for the university, etc.).

Social Networking.   Students, while at times unreflective of what kinds of information (and photos) they post to Twitter, Facebook, MySpace, and other social networking sites, are often very savvy users of community networks. Communication research is just beginning to account for the complexities of online communication; however, instructors in the foundational communication courses can use social network sites as meaningful pedagogical spaces. For instance, many instructors use Facebook as space for instructional communication, creating groups for classes as discussion boards, information dispensing, and course announcements. At SIUC, John and his team of instructors use Facebook as a site to advertise for program functions and events, communicating with students in a forum they already use and understand. Further, social network sites are a rich space for discussions of power and commodification.

Access to Technology.   While the joys and advantages of technology can be many, it is important to note that not all campuses, rooms, faculty, or students are equally equipped. The "digital divide" is still a very real phenomenon; even in technologically rich parts of the country like Silicon Valley, students may arrive in college classes without access to computing equipment, experience with common word processing software systems, knowledge of "netiquette," and so on. Similarly, instructors may struggle, especially if they do not have access to technology "refreshes," where they receive new office computing equipment, with learning management systems, projection equipment, or other resources.

In such cases, it may help for you as a coordinator to become knowledgeable about campus computing resources (both material and instructional) for students and faculty.

Instructor Resistance.   While certainly many instructors are technologically adept, it is certainly not always the case. More reticent instructors may resist technology because of the ways it can interfere with effective teaching and learning. That said, working with instructors of the coordinated course so that they understand the value of the different instructional technologies available to them will help them understand that technology in the classroom need not become a zero-sum game; instructors may choose what works best for their own and their students' learning.

Instructional technology is not a new phenomenon — while we don't typically think of them as such, our chalkboards, pens and pencils, and other traditional equipment for learning are technologies as well. In each case, we must consider the value of the technology to our students' learning (i.e., to the achievement of learning outcomes associated with the course), our own and our students' access to it, and the potential disruptions it might cause.

Online Courses

Online courses (in a variety of configurations — synchronous, asynchronous, accompanied by face-to-face meetings, etc.) are of particular concern in recent years for course coordinators. Such courses may well meet the needs of a broad array of underrepresented student groups (for example, students with disabilities; students who work full-time; students who are raising families or who are engaged in elder care; students who would otherwise have to forgo higher education because of their geographic location), and for that reason, we should consider their role in the courses we coordinate. But this can also raise a host of challenges for the coordinator, not the least of which may be personal or professional reservations about offering introductory courses in communication skills in computer-mediated, and not face-to-face, contexts.

This may be further complicated, especially for those of you who teach in community colleges, by institutional pressures to offer online instruction. In these cases, it may be helpful to meet with colleagues and articulation officers at nearby campuses so you can learn their own attitudes toward online communication courses. It may be possible to resist unwanted campus pressures by clarifying the stances of surrounding, articulating programs. Or it may be possible to resist unwanted pressures by discussing and invoking the intersections of the department or division and campus missions, allowing instructors' values to influence this issue. Finally, it may be possible to strike reasonable compromises, offering only certain communication courses in online formats, requiring online courses to hold a certain number of face-to-face meetings, or ensuring that there are "on-ground" classes in addition to the online sections.

CONCLUSION

Responding to the needs of the students we serve is an ongoing task. As campuses change, we must remember that a vital part of our role is maintaining our keen sense of what our students require. From their (and our) diverse backgrounds to their (and our) diverse relationships to technology, we should strive to create innovative and responsive introductory courses.

While there have been times in our careers where we wished culture was, at least in some ways, static and easy to logarithmically adjust for in our teaching and coordinating duties, far more often we appreciate and respect what we can learn from our students and colleagues about the role of culture, technology, and power in our lives. Sometimes change feels as though it is rushing at us headlong from all sides, and that is, indeed, the case; that said, communication courses afford us — students, teachers, and coordinators alike — opportunities to engage and alter our world in ways that matter to us, in ways that invite us to exercise agency.

REFERENCES

Ashcraft, K. L., & Allen, B. J. (in press). Politics even closer to home: Repositioning CME from the standpoint of communication studies. *Management Learning*.

Buzzanell, P. M., Sterk, H., & Turner, L. H. (2004). *Gender in applied communication contexts*. Thousand Oaks, CA: SAGE.

Fassett, D. L., & Warren, J. T. (2007). *Critical communication pedagogy*. Thousand Oaks, CA: SAGE Publications.

Fassett, D. L., & Warren, J. T. (2005). The strategic rhetoric of an educational identity: Interviewing Jane. *Communication and Critical/Cultural Studies, 2*, 238–256.

Fassett, D. L., & Warren, J. T. (2004). "You get pushed back": The strategic rhetoric of educational success and failure in higher education. *Communication Education, 53*, 21–39.

Fotsch, P. (2008). Race and resistance in the communication classroom. *Basic Communication Course Annual, 20*, 197–230.

Hendrix, K. G., Hebbani, A., & Johnson, O. (2007). The 'other' TA: An exploratory investigation of graduate teaching assistants of color. *International and Intercultural Communication Annual, 30*, 51–82.

Wink, J. (2011). *Critical pedagogy: Notes from the real world* (4th ed.). Boston, MA: Merrill.

RECOMMENDED READINGS

In recent years, the American Association of Colleges and Universities (AACU) has developed an excellent collection of resources regarding diversity; see, for example, http://www.aacu.org/resources/diversity/index.cfm. Of particular interest to course coordinators, faculty, and other campus leaders is their exploration of inclusive excellence and retention with students from across an array of marginalized groups.

Rendón, L. I., García, M., & Person, D. (Eds.). (2004). *Transforming the first year of college for students of color*. Columbia, SC: National Resource Center for The First Year Experience and Students in Transition.

Many introductory communication studies courses participate in or complement first-year experience programs on their campuses; further, even in cases where campuses do not have organized FYE programs, because introductory communication courses often enroll first-year college and university students, resources for FYE can be very helpful to course coordinators. In particular, this volume stands as an excellent collection of foundational readings and specific approaches for responding to the access and inclusion needs of students of color, including African Americans, Latinos, Asian/Pacific Americans, American Indians/Alaska natives, and multiracial/bicultural students.

As first-generation students attend college in increasing numbers, course coordinators have begun to consider how best to respond to these students' needs. An excellent resource for serving this particular student population is:

Rehangir, R. R. (2010). *Higher education and first-generation students: Cultivating community, voice and place for the new majority*. New York, NY: Palgrave-Macmillan.

Basic Communication Course Annual has published articles that address diversity in the introductory communication course in substantive and nuanced ways, including, for example:

Fotsch, P. (2008). Race and resistance in the communication classroom. *Basic Communication Course Annual, 20*.

Prividera, L. C. (2006). Suppressing cultural sensitivity: The role of whiteness in instructors' course content and pedagogical practices. *Basic Communication Course Annual, 18*.

Treinen, K. P. (2004). Creating a dialogue for change: Educating graduate teaching assistants in whiteness studies. *Basic Communication Course Annual, 16*.

Treinen, K. P., & Warren, J. T. (2001). Anti-racist pedagogy in the basic course: Teaching cultural communication as if whiteness matters. *Basic Communication Course Annual, 13*, 46–75.

Communication studies scholars have been working diligently to better understand and respond to the needs of English Language Learner (ELL) or English as a Second Language (ESL) students. For more information, we would recommend:

Hendrix, K. G. (2000). Assessment and skill development for ESL students in mainstream communication classes requiring oral presentations. *Journal of the Association for Communication Administration, 29*, 196–212.

An excellent collection of online learning activities that support student learning (both practically and conceptually) across a variety of disciplines, including communication studies. Whether an instructor teaches fully online, in a hybrid format, or otherwise supplements a course with online resources, this guide can spark interest, insight, and reflection.

Bonk, C. J., & Zhang, K. (2008). *Empowering online learning: 100+activities for reading, reflecting, displaying and doing*. San Francisco, CA: Jossey-Bass.

For guidance on how best to respond to the access and inclusion needs of students with disabilities, we recommend:

Burgstahler, S. E., & Coy, R. C. (Eds.). (2008). *Universal design in higher education: From principles to practice*. Cambridge, MA: Harvard Education Press.

Coombs, N. (2010). *Making online teaching accessible: Inclusive course design for students with disabilities*. San Francisco, CA: Jossey-Bass.

10

Self-Advocacy

Documenting Dedication

It's time for your first performance review as course coordinator. Knowing this day would come, you've prepared yourself by locating all the necessary forms and instructions and saving all your evaluations, appointment paperwork, and other important documents in a special file. But while the instructions for the performance review are clear and concise, they don't seem to address the complexity of your assignment. You know where to document your teaching evaluations, but is your role as course coordinator considered service? You recall a conversation with one of your graduate school buddies; he warned you to skip over basic course director positions because they are basically service positions, and, as he put it, "Nobody ever lost tenure for not doing enough service." You wonder if this is the case for your own position; because you are not a tenure-track hire, you are subject to a modified set of evaluative criteria. Is service to campus and community really such a low priority? Is course coordination service to the department or university? Or is it a significant part of your academic assignment? How will you share your contributions with the committees and individuals who will evaluate you?

* * *

Supervising and teaching within large, multisection communication courses can be a labor of love, something we undertake not because the work is glamorous or financially lucrative, but because our work feels meaningful and formative in our own and others' lives. This feeling of accomplishment and efficacy may wax and wane depending on the year, semester, or day; one day we may feel that others value our efforts and that we make productive contributions that improve people's lives; on another day, when we are feeling tired or overwhelmed, we might question whether what we do really matters all that much in the end. Any program that hopes to sustain itself, however, needs not only to grow professionally, but must continue to grow politically. This is to say, in an era of budget cuts, furloughs, and layoffs, foundational communication courses need to make the case for their survival. This chapter addresses advocacy efforts, beginning, as we believe one must, with the coordinator her or himself.

Periodic performance evaluations, while hassling in some respects (e.g., they may cause stress and anxiety about whether we will have continued employment, and they often involve paperwork, deadlines, and meetings), can be excellent reminders to take stock of our accomplishments, to respect ourselves and what we have achieved through our efforts. This is true not only for course coordinators, but also for instructors in introductory communication courses; if we are in the habit of teaching many, many sections of introductory courses over the years, when lessons and students blur together with the passage of time, it can be difficult to note and recognize what our effect on others may have been. Performance reviews, irrespective of one's status within the university structure or within the coordinated course, are occasions to reflect on what is working, why it is working, what we hope to accomplish in the future, and what we feel the value of those accomplishments will be to our students, our colleagues, and our institutions. In this chapter, we will discuss the importance of advocating for oneself during the review, tenure, and promotion process, or the review and retention process, and how both coordinators and instructors might best represent their accomplishments, strengths and limitations, in general, and at these important junctures in their employment, in particular.

PUBLIC PERCEPTIONS OF THE INTRODUCTORY COURSE

Our experiences as directors or coordinators of the introductory course have varied according to our places of employment. John still remembers that, very early in his career, one of his senior colleagues looked him in the eye and said: "You know, directing the basic course is not a life sentence." Confused, John asked this colleague what he meant. His colleague clarified: "Well, you are clearly a smart guy, and you should know that, really, you just need to do a good job on this until tenure; after that, you can give it up and move on to bigger and better things." Similarly, as a graduate student, Deanna routinely heard that being a "basic course director" was a thankless service assignment, something to do only until tenure; she was surprised that, when she assumed that role herself, her colleagues understood her work to be part of her academic assignment itself — her teaching and research — and not as an additional series of marginalized hurdles she would have to clear. Each program, even where we share similar disciplinary commitments, will vary in its commitment to and respect for the introductory course. Knowing the sorts of assumptions and values your colleagues associate with introductory course assignments will help you better determine when and how to represent yourself and your efforts with them.

   Work associated with the introductory course — whether for coordinators or instructors — is, at times, labor intensive; and depending on the institution, the reward or recognition for assignments associated with this course can vary. For some colleagues and administrators, the "best" introductory course is the one that faculty members never have to think or hear about; these programs define success as the quiet, smooth delivery of this course in ways that do not affect, challenge, or change the ordinary operations of the department. In these sorts of programs, the course coordinator can feel very isolated and, in extreme cases, used. These attitudes have consequences for instructors, as well, discouraging them from taking risks, from sharing their concerns in faculty meetings, and so on. In these sorts of programs, there may be very little recognition for efforts supporting the introductory course, and when a problem does arise, there can be a disproportionate focus on that problem and whether the coordinator or instructors did enough to prevent it. While there are other possible reasons for department colleagues to distance themselves from the introductory course (e.g., the faculty respect and appreciate people's work with this course and do not wish to interfere with a well-organized program), the routine absence of recognition can be taxing. In some ways, John's story of the senior faculty member is a classic example of this vision of the introductory course: Do your time in solitary "basic" course confinement until you can afford to escape it — and while John felt that his colleagues valued his work, the experience of doing the job as an untenured assistant professor was, indeed, isolating. One of our most important initial efforts at self-advocacy is questioning and challenging this pervasive understanding of the introductory course.

Unchecked, this attitude contributes to the overall burnout so common among long-term directors of these courses. For example, when he was at Bowling Green State University, John served a three-year term as course coordinator, one of the longest in recent memory; instituting terms of service helps to mitigate burnout and more evenly distribute labor (and empathy) across colleagues. While there are no statistics specifically regarding the burnout rates of course coordinators in communication studies, together we have often observed colleagues leave their positions on the end of their contracts or on receipt of tenure, never to return to the role.

Another model for understanding and appreciating colleagues' contributions to the introductory course is to recognize it as central to the department's mission — for example, in the preparation of a particular student population or in the training and development of graduate students. Often, programs that operate with this understanding of the introductory course recognize course coordination as an administrative assignment (with proper course reductions or reassigned time and additional salary income in the summer) that necessarily interacts with one's overall assignment (for example, with a coordinator's teaching or research). Key to understanding how to approach advocacy for your role as course coordinator is understanding what perception of the course and role your colleagues hold; once you know what they expect and assume, you can better strategize for how to productively support and challenge those expectations and assumptions.

STRATEGIES FOR SELF-ADVOCACY

Self-advocacy can feel, at times, like blatant self-promotion — awkward and uncomfortable. But, even though you *are* promoting yourself, seeing your efforts as exclusively self-serving would be narrow and unfair. In helping make your workload appropriately visible, you not only advocate for yourself, but also for the course, the people who will follow you in your position, and the discipline. As you reflect on your assignment in the introductory course, ask yourself: How can I help myself, my program, and the future of the course? When you help others see your work in these areas, you invite them into this shared vision.

Review Your Appointment Paperwork

Perhaps the most important part of self-advocacy begins with knowing how others will review your performance. Whether for tenure and promotion, contract renewal, or merit, you need to know how what you are doing corresponds with the expectations of the people who hired you. Review any documents that speak to the expectations of your role. These may include the following:

- Your appointment or hiring paperwork or contract
- Your union's bargaining agreement
- Your department's operating papers
- Any campus or department policies regarding GTA supervision or general education courses that speak to your role and what it entails

These documents can help you navigate what to take on and what to resist in your role; for example, you might choose to take on a particular assignment that is consistent with your appointment paperwork while politely declining responsibilities that exceed your role — or that belong properly to someone else. This review informs your decision making and makes it possible for you to protect the time you need in order to do your job well. More important, knowing these documents helps you understand what your employer considers successful performance in your assignment, making it a more achievable outcome for you.

Making sure your employer documents your workload in writing is important for all university employees, but especially for individuals who become course coordinators after already serving the department in some other capacity. Where your assignment changes from the parameters in your appointment paperwork or contract, it is important to document how this will also change how others will evaluate your performance. For Deanna, this was as simple as asking the chair to revise the description of her academic assignment for her dossier; this description clearly defined course coordination as part of her academic assignment (*not* as service) and indicated that she should seek peer and instructor review of her performance in that role. John needed a similar document, to clarify to others — both on campus and off — how to interpret the relationship between his administrative role and his research, teaching, and service duties. More specifically, for the merit review process, John and his chair identified in writing how his administrative role could affect his publication volume, the number and quality of his teaching evaluations, and participation in other service assignments.

It is also a good idea to document cases where a coordinator is supported by a stipend or other compensation. For instance, if your role as course coordinator is part of your departmental service and is not compensated in other ways, discuss with your chair, dean, or division head how this service will factor in during annual or other reviews. This is especially important on smaller campuses and at community colleges where your teaching load is considerable. For example, one of our community college colleagues is able to use time she spends developing materials that help coordinate the introductory course (such as a sample syllabus) toward her "flex time" — self-directed work she pursues as part of required service to her campus. Another one of our colleagues, who works at a small liberal arts college, has received other, perhaps less conventional but still somewhat satisfying compensation for course coordination activities he undertakes, including receiving modest travel support and a larger office space. These are important conversations to put in writing because they form the basis of whether you will be retained, tenured, promoted, or compensated and because they help make your efforts surrounding the introductory course visible to your colleagues.

A related issue that can sometimes affect the evaluation of a course coordinator is the question of who is responsible for the course during the summer months. What occurs during the summer varies from one program to another; while, on one campus, a coordinator may not assess general education courses or hire new instructors during the summer, on another campus, the coordinator may need to prepare and run a comprehensive training and development program. Compensation varies as well. At different times in our careers, we have not worked summers, have worked summers essentially for free, and have received stipend payments for our efforts. While you may never receive the compensation you feel you deserve for your efforts over the summer (or winter) months, it is important to meet with your department chair (and other significant department or college leaders) to discuss ways to make the course coordinator role equitable and livable. While you may feel tempted to take on uncompensated assignments during the summer months, take care that your willingness does not give rise to others' unrealistic expectations (about course coordinators, in general, and about you, in particular).

Make Your Efforts Visible

It is all too common for course coordinators and instructors alike to hear, from administrators and colleagues, that they should be able to do more and more with less and less; after all, once the course is "prepped," what more could you have to do? Of course, such assumptions neglect the ways maintaining a course can be challenging. For example, the course coordinator must work to make sure the course continually meets the needs of the discipline, university, department, instructors, students, and community by engaging in assessment, sitting on relevant governance committees, holding staff meetings and otherwise communicating with instructional staff, and so on. Similarly, even in "prepped" courses, instructors must continually adjust for the particular needs of the students they are teaching in a given semester, revising lesson plans, providing customized feedback for students, meeting with course coordinators and colleagues, and so on. When we engage in this maintenance work smoothly and effectively, addressing questions, conflicts, and challenges quietly, others may conclude that our work is easy. In a sense, our integrity and grace in this assignment help to render the course and our labor invisible to those who may supervise our workloads, leading to their sense that we can and should do more. Further, if you give the impression that you enjoy what you do, it is easier for others to conclude that you would, could, and should increase your workload responsibilities. However, we do not mean to suggest that you should strive for incompetence as a self-protective strategy; instead, we recommend finding ways to make your work visible for others.

An important way to responsibly and appropriately advocate for yourself within your department and university is to make the work you do apparent to others. However, visibility is not the same as whining; while whining will make your work more visible, it will also damage your reputation as a capable coordinator or instructor. Instead, strive for visibility as a means of documenting and clarifying for external audiences what you are doing with, to, and for the program.

- **Extend invitations to events you create or administer.** When you host public events (like a speaker's series, intramural public speaking competition, or additional skills-building workshops for students or instructors), consider extending invitations to your colleagues, department chair, division head, or dean.
- **Keep track of your efforts in the introductory course.** Record your work and share this information through annual evaluation documents, merit reviews, program reviews, and other means of department data collection. Besides the meaningful self-reflective space of a journal or diary of your efforts, you can include the following where appropriate:
  - Copies of the summer orientation schedule
  - Summaries of your responses to ongoing assessment questions and issues
  - Publications that evolve from your work with the introductory course
  - Coverage of course-related events in the campus newspaper or other media outlets
  - Letters of appreciation for your contributions as course coordinator to other programs or initiatives on campus

For each initiative you implement, clarify how you are effectively supporting program, department, and university missions. For example, if, as a coordinator, you transition to a paperless workflow, collecting teaching evaluations, syllabi, and other course materials in electronic form, you can help others understand that you are not only participating in national and local sustainability initiatives, but are showing commitment to keeping the course — and processes associated with it — current, and, perhaps most important to external audiences, are saving money. Or if, as an instructor, you enroll in a series of campus professional development workshops that support your efforts weaving service learning into the introductory course, you can help others understand that this is not only a passion of yours, but also a means to help students better meet the course learning outcomes. While you might share this information casually in the hallways with your colleagues, don't forget to include this in your performance evaluations and, where appropriate, to link your efforts in the introductory course to your other academic responsibilities (e.g., research and publication, travel and participation in academic conferences, etc.).

Show How the Course Is Integral to the Departmental Mission

In some programs, especially those at large public universities, work with introductory courses is cast as a service to the university, wherein coordinator and instructors promise "basic" attention to communication and civic engagement as part of a liberal arts education (sometimes even at the expense of their own disciplinary interests). At small liberal arts and community colleges, colleagues may take more shared ownership of the course, making it possible for coordinators and instructors to teach in multiple areas or take on other desirable assignments. In either case, those of us who work with the introductory course can feel marginal, as though we must sacrifice whatever we would rather be doing in order to meet this obligation. As coordinators, each of us has encountered both instructor and coordinator colleagues who feel as though they are "stuck" in the introductory course. Rather than bringing their passion to the introductory course, these colleagues may instead seek out other academic assignments, more "exciting" courses, and other opportunities they feel are better suited to their interests. As an advocate, it is important to find ways to challenge and complicate the reasoning that works against your course's vision; one way to do this is to show the centrality of the course to the department's mission.

There are many ways to create explicit connections between the introductory course and the department mission. A coordinator can do any of the following:

- Help create curricular offerings that support the course
- Modify the structure and delivery of the course
- Nominate instructors for teaching awards that acknowledge creativity and excellence in the introductory course
- Explore the parallels between the introductory course and the department's faculty expertise and curriculum; in this way, the course is a vital and essential preparation for the major, and faculty feel as though they can introduce their own passions and strengths to the content of the course

To the extent that the introductory course helps fill a recruitment function by drawing students into the major, our efforts to support the introductory course help strengthen and enhance the program overall.

Continue to Strengthen the Course

Even the most minor improvements can have a lasting effect on the overall vision of the course. From structural or curricular adjustments to textbook selection and assignment revision, our efforts with the introductory course can bring us rich rewards. In working to strengthen it, we ensure that the course is not stagnant but evolving (and that others perceive it as such too); our efforts to keep the course alive and in constant revision mean that we are better able to respond to student needs, disciplinary innovations, and economic constraints. Perhaps most important, your efforts, whether as a coordinator or as an instructor, to keep the course alive and responsive will help you remain engaged and excited about your role.

While others may mistakenly view the introductory course as a place where one's passions as an educator and researcher go to wither away, you can resist this negative attitude by exploring where your own interests intersect with the content of the course. The person who loves philosophy of communication can find ways of exploring constitutive, as opposed to representational, understandings of language; the person who loves performance studies can explore the ways our bodies are epistemic, complicating and enhancing students' understandings of nonverbal communication; and the person who is interested in how communication in the classroom functions to enhance or endanger learning has a living laboratory to bring theory to life in ways that can help empower students as they navigate a broad array of introductory college and university courses. While it is inappropriate to introduce doctoral coursework to first-year college students, there may be ways for you, as an instructor or coordinator, to find commonalities that are illuminating, challenging, and interesting.

Similarly, as a coordinator, you should strive to bring your strengths to the course. Even in already well-established programs, there is room for you to facilitate course revision, restructure or refine work flow, or work with others to develop and share best practices. Further, as we will discuss at greater length in the next chapter, your work with the introductory course may be a fertile ground for research, conference presentation, and publication. Data you collect routinely as part of course assessment may help you determine the effectiveness of particular assignments in meeting learning outcomes; interviews with instructors may grant you insight into the tensions and frustrations faculty face as they attempt to remain abreast of new disciplinary and pedagogical developments. Both, as well as many, many others, would be exciting lines of writing and research, and they are already a part of your work in the introductory course.

Invite Feedback

It is common for academics to give and receive a wide array of feedback in their roles; whether this is in the form of grades and evaluations of teaching or peer reviews of conference or manuscript submissions, this feedback often productively informs our efforts as teachers and researchers. It is also common these days to receive letters documenting the quality of one's service. Because course coordination is a central, and not tangential, aspect of your academic assignment, it is important to seek evaluations from others about how you are performing in this role. On many campuses there is no formal mechanism for evaluating course coordinators. We recommend and routinely practice seeking feedback from others, for the purposes of both strengthening our work as course coordinators and also documenting the effectiveness of our efforts for performance reviews. For example, every two years, Deanna asks an experienced colleague (e.g., her chair, her predecessor in the role, someone who holds a similar assignment on campus) to provide a peer evaluation of her work. Though the process the peer reviewer uses has varied from one occasion to the next, this usually involves reviewing materials associated with the introductory course, attending training and development activities, interviewing instructors, and perhaps even sitting in on some students' speeches. It helps if the person providing the review is already familiar with course coordination; then, in such cases, in addition to an evaluation, you also have access to someone's consultation, to a troubleshooting partner and mentor. In this way, you do more than document your strengths and areas for improvement with respect to this course; you also learn ways to make tangible improvements and strategize for the future.

CONCLUSION

Self-advocacy is inextricably tied to the success of the course you coordinate. Your ability to do good work is a function of your ability to correctly read and respond to others' expectations of your assignment, as well as to navigate which responsibilities you accept and when. While some of this advocacy will take the form of casual conversations with colleagues in and beyond your department (including, notably, administrators and other campus leaders), much of it involves quiet and diligent documentation, keeping people "in the loop" about improvements and challenges associated with the course, and maintaining an articulate and insistent stance about the role of the course in satisfying department, college, and university missions.

RECOMMENDED READINGS

Gunsalus, C. K. (2006). *The college administrator's survival guide*. Cambridge, MA: Harvard University Press.

Tina Gunsalus's survival guide is appropriate reading for any academic wishing to understand not only her or his role as a leader in the successful functioning of an institution of higher learning, but also the practical matters of how to address academic challenges (such as bullies, complaints, and allegations of misconduct). Even if you never intend to become a department chair, division head, dean, or other administrator, this work is an excellent primer for academic leadership skills.

Robertson, D. R. (2003). *Making time, making change: Avoiding overload in college teaching*. New York, NY: New Forums Press.

Written by the director of the Teaching and Learning Center at Eastern Kentucky University, this slim volume is a valuable resource for both instructors and course coordinators. Perhaps of greatest value are the practical suggestions the author shares for how, as academics, we can better spend our time in relation to our values. Particularly, the author shares advice for how to work toward balance of multiple, and perhaps even contradictory, academic assignments, helping the reader feel a greater sense of efficacy and empowerment in her or his role.

11

Research

Conflicting Interests

When you took on this role as an introductory course director, you knew it would take time and energy, not to mention inspiring you to think more explicitly about instruction and perhaps a little less about your areas of scholarly interest. When you left school, you sought out positions where you wouldn't have to be a researcher, first and foremost, but while your colleagues don't expect you to "publish or perish," they do expect you to be active. You're still trying to understand exactly what "active" means, but you know you don't have as much time these days to address your research interests. You're happy to coordinate the course and to help students and instructors engage in communication for civic action, but you wonder if you would have been happier, and perhaps more prolific, teaching rhetoric instead. This is a good job, and one you enjoy, but when will you have time or energy to write about the things that matter to you?

* * *

As educators, we often feel torn between a series of tensions — between teaching and other aspects of our assignments, between work and home, and so on. If we allow it to be, this can become a life of fragmentation and conflict. To the extent that we are able to reframe seemingly irresolvable tensions as connected and productive, we will experience our academic assignment as meaningful and rewarding. Spending our time in line with our values can be a challenging exercise, to be sure, but our efforts to this end are time well spent. A common tension that course coordinators experience is the sense that they give and give into a position that has little reward for them intellectually. At research universities, this can feel like a struggle to find time to write about one's area of expertise when we continuously grapple with a whole host of other administrative responsibilities, from gathering assessment data to mentoring instructors to intervening in students' complaints about the course or instructor. However, this can still feel like a tension even where research and publication are not at issue, at least not in terms of retention, tenure, or promotion. For example, over time, a course coordinator at a community college may also feel disengaged from the curriculum and alienated from what drew him or her to the discipline in the first place, and with limited or no support from his or her institution to engage in research or attend conferences, it can be harder to find mentors who face similar struggles or conversations that will enliven or enrich her or him. Research, for our purposes in this chapter, consists of the investigations we undertake as communication educators to enrich and enliven our lives as intellectuals, strengthening our roles as course coordinators and instructors and experiencing them as vital and rewarding. While this might include engaging in research studies and publishing the results, it might also include reading published works in the discipline, designing assessment activities that feel relevant and meaningful, or connecting with colleagues at local, regional, or national conferences.

RECONCEPTUALIZING RESEARCH

Research as a form of advocacy is more complex than it sounds. While someone working toward tenure might immediately think of research as publishing for job security or for personal fulfillment — in a sense, advocacy for one's status as a permanent academic — different people's positions in higher education will give rise to other, equally relevant understandings of what research as advocacy means. Living the academic life, irrespective of the institution, involves some form of research. This need not mean serving as the principal investigator of a funded research study, though it could; research also means undertaking modest projects you share at a conference, exploring developments in the discipline that change the structure of the course you supervise and how you teach it, or engaging in collaborations with students and colleagues that help you better understand the effectiveness of the course and how you might continue to strengthen it. Research, in this sense, keeps you vital and curious. As advocacy, it is a means to show your engagement in the course you coordinate and realize the course's vision in your own life.

Perhaps the most stereotypical understanding of research is best exemplified by our own experiences. In graduate school, we both taught an introduction to communication studies course entitled Speech, Self and Society. This course addressed communication theory, intercultural communication, and interpersonal communication in addition to public speaking. In the classes we were taking, we learned about critical pedagogy, educational philosophy, and cultural studies. While we didn't introduce articles from those classes to our students directly, our approach to assignments — our interest, for example, in discussing grading as ideology and trying contract grading, or in shaping assignments so that they challenged students to make connections between the classroom and the local community beyond it — was influenced by the conversations and debates we had in and out of our own classes as students.

Later, as we needed (and then wanted) to write dissertations and conference papers, and ultimately publications, we looked to our experiences as instructors in the introductory course as ways to learn about the discipline. We shared much of this work at conferences, where we formed relationships and collaborations with similarly curious colleagues. Whether in the Basic Course Division at the National Communication Association Conference, or the Communication and Instruction Interest Group at the Western States Communication Association Conference, or the Instructional Resources Interest Group at the Central States Communication Association Conference, these colleagues encouraged our interest in the introductory course and the ways that course informs our own interests in power and privilege, culture and community (and vice versa). These annual meetings and the conversations we had there made it possible for us to publish a range of scholarship, including books that serve the communities about which we care deeply—leading to this present volume.

The Basic Communication Course conference and listserv continue to be vital spaces where coordinators can dialogue about their shared interests and concerns (while the conference and organizers change, a Google search for "Basic Communication Course Conference" usually brings up the most recent conference; further, you can contact the chair of NCA's Basic Communication Course Division and she or he can connect you with the listserv administrator). However, your research might look similar to our own, in that it takes the form of papers and publications and focuses on how some aspect of the discipline speaks to or changes our understanding of the introductory course, or it might look different.

If we reconceptualize research as the work you do to remain engaged in the discipline, to strengthen and enrich your work with the introductory course, and to support and sustain your own intellectual vitality, then your research doesn't have to take the form of publications (though certainly this would be appropriate) or even conference attendance. For example, you might meet with instructors who share your interests in communication studies; with these people, you can discuss current writings and issues as they alter and deepen your understanding of the field. This could look like a reading group, or it could look like an assessment meeting that is informed by communication studies research. Or your research might look like quiet time in your office where you browse the NCA journal database for interesting readings, or it might mean connecting with friends from graduate school about what they are doing and how that is similar to or different from your own assignment. Are they involved in a study on campus? Did they just go to the state conference? Did they start sitting in on classes? Allowing others' insights and experiences to enrich our own is another way of remaining vital and connected to our field.

Don't forget the assessment efforts you undertake in your assignment. If you are gathering meaningful data about your experiences as an introductory course coordinator or instructor, the findings can influence your future efforts, and if you choose to share that information with colleagues on campus or around the country (for example, at a conference such as the Basic Course Directors Conference or through a publication like *Basic Communication Course Annual*), it can influence how others run similar courses. Sharing what you learn about your field can help encourage others to do the same, strengthening our collective work.

SHARING YOUR WORK

Finding ways to share your work with others, whether through publication, conference presentation, or other, less formal or structured mechanisms, is important for building the repository of collective insight that course coordinators share about introductory courses. Further, as we suggest in the preceding chapter, you should share your insights about the introductory course with the people who will evaluate your performance as coordinator. If you have implemented changes, and you can support these changes with sound reasoning, you will swiftly cultivate a reputation as someone who is professional and has integrity in this assignment. We would like to make a plea that you consider authoring published scholarship in this vein; while we have seen some pieces in the last few years surrounding introductory communication courses (in addition to what we see each year in *Basic Communication Course Annual*), many of the efforts at publishing on course coordination remain dated or anecdotal, local to particular campuses and coordinators. Like traditional recipes, our own best practices as coordinators will die with us if we don't share them with our heirs.

Often, what we are already doing as coordinators can form the basis of research we should share with others. For example, one of our community college colleagues holds a meeting at the start of the academic year where she reiterates the learning outcomes for the course and invites instructors to share best practices for how to achieve these learning outcomes. Over time, she has amassed a wealth of information about which activities and exercises are most useful with the students in this course; these insights could form the basis of published research that lends insight into effective communication instruction at the community college. In a similar vein, each year, John frames his GTA orientation in terms of a theme, an organizing concept that pulls a variety of different sessions of information into a common focus. He introduces this theme in a lecture at the start of the week, in hopes of creating a productive context for the teachers to invest (and reinvest) in their teaching. John also takes this talk as an occasion to model theory building as it relates to the introductory course. For the fall of 2010, John shared a theme of civic engagement and the role of the public intellectual. This theme attempted to establish a collective goal for instructors of the course while making possible multiple paths to achieving it.

Creating an annual theme and sharing it with the instructional staff is, in part, an effort on John's part to show his instructional staff his care and regard for their effort as educators — to show he is invested in their and their students' success. The 2010 theme encourages all instructors of the introductory course to see themselves as theory makers, even, and perhaps especially, in the classroom. Through this conversation, he is able to explain what steps he takes as a coordinator to build theory, to identify data-driven actions that will improve the course. In this talk, he not only affirms his investment in the introductory course, but he also begins work toward an essay for publication, one that documents his efforts to engage in research regarding the introductory course and share that research with the community that can profit most by it.

This particular theme of civic engagement takes up the question of how we, as teachers of introductory communication, are public intellectuals (Giroux, 2004), people whose responsibility it is to influence progressive change toward the common good. Giroux (2004) argues:

The power of the existing dominant order resides not only in the economic or material relations of power, but also in the realm of ideas and culture. This is why intellectuals must take sides, speak out, and engage in the hard work of debunking corporate culture's assault on teaching and learning, orient their teaching for social change, connect learning to public life, link knowledge to the operations of power, and allow issues of human rights and crimes against humanity in their diverse forms to occupy a space of critical and open discussion in the classroom. (p. 77)

In the scope of orientation, the talk that introduces this theme helps to conceptualize instructors' collective work in the course as part of larger social efforts to move toward social justice and greater equality. Particularly, John identifies mechanisms and avenues that instructors might pursue with students to make the course more relevant in their lives. John ends the talk with a call to arms, a challenge to teach "students by example the importance of taking a stand (without standing still) while rigorously engaging the full range of ideas about an issue" (Giroux, 2004, p. 72), to be models of social justice that might inspire others.

While this isn't the agenda all course coordinators would or should pursue, this does illuminate how one course coordinator incorporates his research interests, his interests in communication studies, into his administrative assignment. As you consider your own values and vision as a course coordinator, how might you do the same? How might your own interests — whether in service learning, leadership, or health communication — become heuristic ways of imagining how to strengthen and enhance the course you coordinate?

BUILDING CONNECTIONS BETWEEN YOUR INTERESTS AND YOUR ASSIGNMENT

One of the most important bits of advice we received as new educators was to build connections between our teaching and our research interests. In determining how to approach classes ranging from "introduction to communication studies" to "communication criticism," we found strength in grounding the course in concepts and readings about which we were both knowledgeable and curious. Even courses that seem thoroughly skills-based, like "public speaking" or "writing in the discipline," benefit from themes and questions that invite students into exploration of issues in communication studies that matter. For instance, Dr. Jonny Gray, the course coordinator before John at SIUC, developed the public/civic engagement focus of the introductory course. His efforts to develop the speaker's forum and to focus the course toward a more public speaking-oriented curriculum are directly in line with his scholarly work in rhetoric and activism. We have also worked to thematize courses, focusing them on particular issues in the discipline, community, or world, as in a writing workshop where students' work focused on working with the Silicon Valley AIDS Walk or in a rhetorical criticism course that foregrounded issues of culture and power in popular culture. We have from time to time used courses as occasions to learn with our students new areas of our field, delving into new readings and developing new ideas for writing, in general, or campus or personal improvement, in particular. Making courses our own has made these teaching experiences enjoyable and rewarding, and this is a skill that continues to serve us in our administrative assignment as course coordinators.

While many of us, as instructors, are familiar with the reasons why we would approach a new course preparation (or revisit a previously prepped course) through our interests and curiosities, we may forget to bring this same sound advice to our other administrative or service assignments. When a course coordinator is feeling overwhelmed, it is easier to see her or his assignment as a series of extra "to do" items on an already long list. In the stress of putting out fires, we often lose sight of the sorts of proactive measures, like attention to vision, that help us enjoy what we do. Our attention to program vision, to what we feel is important about our role as course coordinators, can help us make productive connections between our interests in communication studies and our assignment. Introductory courses, with their emphasis on skills, can feel distant from what made us excited about communication studies as a field in the first place; but by introducing examples and activities, themes and questions, that draw on our areas of interest and expertise, we can find continuity and a productive, mutually beneficial relationship between our intellectual growth and our teaching or coordinating.

As course coordinators, we can invite our areas of expertise to provide depth and nuance to the courses we supervise, but also to model a lifestyle of balance and engagement for our colleagues who teach these courses. A course coordinator who studies performance can, for example, introduce Augusto Boal's forum theatre into orientation or craft an oral interpretation exercise for the introductory course; one who studies public dialogue can model meetings on the works of Martin Buber or help instructors explore what it means to situate public speaking in the context of compassionate dialogue and mutual understanding.

Finding intellectually productive connections between one's teaching or administrative/service responsibilities and one's interests in the discipline is not only about engaging in research in the narrow sense of publishing; it is about asking and answering questions about our work with the courses we coordinate that help strengthen not only those courses, but also our own understandings of communication. It is important to remember different ways of understanding research and how it might function as advocacy for you, in terms of your leadership among colleagues; your continued interest in and commitment to your discipline; your contract renewal, tenure, or promotion; and your ability to secure resources for your program from the larger campus community.

FINDING AND MAKING TIME FOR RESEARCH

In the face of so many administrative, pedagogical, and personal commitments, the question of how one finds time to fulfill her or his scholarly passions is significantly individual, varying according to the nature of your assignment and your role and rank in your department or program. For instance, if you are an assistant professor or lecturer who has been assigned introductory course coordination as part of your assignment, you may be balancing your duties with completing your own dissertation, publishing for tenure, searching for other jobs, or starting a family. In any case, making time for research, for intellectual exploration and growth, is still essential. If you are a tenured professor, you may still be pursuing promotion or creating closure in your research program before retirement. If you teach in a program with significant teaching assignments, for example in the community college, then you may be grappling with developing multiple preparations, nurturing hundreds of students, as well as any number of life opportunities and challenges (like job interviews or family changes). In any case, the conditions that surround you will no doubt affect how you find research time. Further, research, while essential, may not always feel like your top priority.

Making time for what will help us grow and evolve as academics, in general, and course coordinators, in particular, is a challenging task. Here we share what we've learned over the years, from our own and our colleagues' experiences, for how to make research a reality:

- **If you are in a position to request release time or reconfigured time for your assignment, pursue opportunities that match your needs.** For colleagues in research universities, this may mean a summer stipend, allowing for relatively uninterrupted creative time, or a course release for a semester (timed, if possible, to the time of year that is most helpful for you) to enable you to catch up on your projects. For colleagues in community colleges, this may mean seeking additional credit toward service activities or a larger or more flexible allocation of professional development money; or it may mean working to link course coordination to a position that does carry release time — for example, in coordinating assessment activities for your division.

- **Coauthoring can enable productive dialogue and reflection as well as increase productivity.** While not all collaborations are equally positive (and not everyone is equally good at making them work), coauthorship can help encourage or make more feasible publication and continued growth and learning in relation to the discipline. As the saying goes, a worry shared is a worry halved; with the right coauthor, the same may be said for engaging in inquiry and writing activities through a division of labor. It can be reassuring to know that a given project is always in progress, even if you're not the one working on it at the moment.

- **Create schedules for research-related activities.** This is very similar to the advice personal trainers and professional athletes give people who want to become more fit; if you put exercise on your calendar, you will do it often — so, too, with research. This means blocking off chunks of time (as you do with class meetings or office hours) to go to the library or to meet with colleagues or to read or write in your office. It can also be helpful to create deadlines for particular projects — perhaps by setting a meeting to discuss a reading or share a draft, or by using conference submission deadlines to keep a project on track.

- **Write about pedagogy.** As the administrator of a course, you have in front of you untold opportunities for data collection and sharing. Whether this means using large classes as venues to administer surveys or studying how coordinators mentor new (or more experienced) teachers, your role is an avenue for engaging in meaningful conversations about how instructors teach and students learn. While it is true that in some departments, pedagogical scholarship is considered less valuable than non–teaching-related work, part of the job of researchers is to make the case for their labor (we would argue that this is true across the academic landscape). To this end, review your hiring papers and talk with your chair about how your research in pedagogy is directly connected with your job duties. Further, make sure your research is well grounded, well researched, and well documented. Part of making the case for pedagogical work being valuable and counting as "real research" is making sure it is good scholarship. Journals like *Basic Communication Course Annual*, *Communication Teacher*, *Liminalities*, *Communication Education*, and many regional and state journals are invested in research concerning pedagogy and research that may deal with the introductory course. Many of these journals are well established and have very solid reputations for rigorous peer-review processes.

- **Explore innovations in pedagogy.** Especially in assignments where you will teach a large number of courses and students each quarter or semester, making small adjustments to your courses that help keep them engaging and fresh for you and your students is key. Research, in this instance, may mean treating the classroom as a laboratory of sorts, where you study how students best learn communication. Your findings, whether you publish them or not, may inform not only your future classes, but also, should you choose to share them with colleagues, conversations about effective pedagogy in your program and on your campus.

- **Note the link between assessment and research.** From panel presentations at the National Communication Association, to regional conferences, to the Basic Communication Course Directors conference, many panels address questions of assessment, including not only the results of assessments based on innovative changes in programs, but also in terms of programs of assessment (measurements, indicators, etc.). The field of communication is in need of new assessment instruments, and we'd do well to invest our labor in this regard.

- **Seek balance.** While true balance is illusory, working toward some sense of dynamic equilibrium is useful. Sometimes administrators of introductory courses overinvest and allow the introductory course in all its many facets to consume their time. While certainly there will be times when this may be an issue, the best way to work toward balance is to give the role the time it deserves (and the time you've been compensated for) while keeping in play the other parts of your academic assignment that you find important and rewarding. There will always be work to keep you busy where it comes to coordinating an introductory course — finding balance and congruence between our roles and our other intellectual and personal pursuits will enable you to be better at both.

No doubt you have other ideas for remaining engaged and excited about your work in higher education; please don't neglect your own wisdom as you consider how research may be a means of advocacy. We recommend talking with your chair, dean, or division head about ways of managing the responsibility of course coordination with other aspects of your assignment. Creating congruence between your responsibilities as course coordinator and what excites you, generally speaking, about your work as an educator will help you enjoy a robust, rewarding, and stimulating career in this assignment.

REFERENCE

Giroux, H. A. (2004). Cultural studies, public pedagogy and the responsibility of intellectuals. *Communication and Critical/Cultural Studies, 1,* 59–79.

RECOMMENDED READING

Fullan, M., & Scott, G. (2009). *Turnaround leadership for higher education.* San Francisco, CA: Jossey-Bass.

This and similar readings help course coordinators better conceptualize functional and meaningful approaches to leadership in higher education. Fullan and Scott's work is particularly helpful in developing productive data-driven programs of publication and program improvement.

12

Campus Advocacy

Coordination on Campus

You have a meeting with the associate vice president of undergraduate studies this afternoon; since she's the person most directly concerned with the quality of general education on your campus, you're hoping she'll be able to help you understand and respond to something you're hearing your instructors share. As part of the new budgetary and enrollment challenges facing your campus, the university has introduced a new program for students who have repeatedly failed their English placement test and need additional remediation in writing. Rather than having to continue taking the test (and the remedial courses preparatory to the test) until they pass, these students are being asked to enroll in a new pilot course, one that the university hopes will make them better prepared for the coordinated course you supervise — a required upper-division writing as communication course. You knew that some graduates of this pilot course would be entering the sections of your course, and you assumed that the course would prepare them sufficiently for it. But over the course of the semester, you've met with first one instructor and then another, each wanting to go on the record with her or his concerns about these students' poor preparation for the course. You reminded each instructor to grade in accordance with her or his professional judgment; just because the university would like these students to graduate doesn't mean they should — not if they lack the skills necessary to do so. However, now that instructors have assigned the grades they feel are appropriate for these students — in most cases, failing — the students are starting to complain. In their frustration with a university process that has led them to feel first unprepared, then prepared, then unprepared again, they have turned against their course instructors, arguing that their standards are too strict. The instructors, most of whom teach part-time, are feeling unjustly accused and concerned for their positions, worried that these students' complaints will find their way into their personnel files. Equally concerned with respecting students' sense of transparency and fairness and instructors' sense of efficacy and autonomy, you consider what to say in your afternoon meeting.

* * *

As a course coordinator, you often have insights into the relationship between the work of the coordinated course and the campus community that course helps sustain. Because of your close contact with instructors, students, and administrators, you are uniquely poised to share insights with the campus community about the people and situations you and your instructional staff experience on a routine basis (for example, communicating with relevant others the relative preparedness of the students in the course or their frustration with campus furloughs, or assuming a leadership role in sustainability efforts on campus). In this chapter, we explore how the coordinator can work together with instructors and students to advocate for program needs within the larger campus community, including what campus advocacy means, why we engage in it, and how we can engage in it effectively. Often occasions for advocacy will emerge from assessment of student learning in the course, requiring and inspiring the coordinator to communicate assessment information to the offices and professionals on campus who can best act on your information, including those charged with the creation, identification, or modification of campus resources.

YOUR ROLE AS ADVOCATE

For however long you serve as a course coordinator, you will work to maintain and strengthen (and perhaps repair) the reputation of that course. Possibly without even knowing it, you became, in accepting this responsibility, an advocate. Advocacy, in the sense we mean it, is more than taking care of your own needs, though we do mean that as well; advocacy is also a matter of care and regard for the people with whom you work, irrespective of whether they are students, faculty, staff, or administrators. At some level, course coordinators may feel as though they have fallen into this sort of advocacy, in that they are in the right place at the right time to gather information that other offices and colleagues on campus need or desire; however, given that course coordinators are leaders who serve a diverse grouping of individuals who contribute to meaningful student learning and instructor professional development, campus advocacy is an important responsibility as well. In effect, you advocate for the students in the course, the instructors of the course, your department, your campus, and your community. This means that your advocacy makes possible professional development and continuity—i.e., your efforts to draw students and instructors into comparable and meaningful experiences with communication.

For instance, perhaps your campus, like so many across the country, is faced with reduced budgets and increased scrutiny about how monies are spent. Perhaps an administrator or office has targeted your program or coordinated course for significant budget cuts. Your role as advocate in this moment is not only to serve this course and the colleagues who teach it, but also to represent how this course fulfills the campus mission, how it meets students' needs as they prepare to graduate, and how the course is an essential part of what it means to be an educated member of your campus. Your argument for preserving the course cannot begin and end solely with the needs of the instructors who teach it, though those needs are surely real. You must also establish for audiences outside our discipline that successful completion of this course enhances students' success in future coursework, employment possibilities, and ability to create a supportive and respectful campus climate. In such times of crisis, it can be immensely helpful to be able to reach out to a community of your peers (for example, at NCA, or through the Basic Course Directors listserv) for their own experiences, insights, and success strategies.

In this way, advocacy cannot be an afterthought. While you will be tempted to focus exclusively or primarily on creating common syllabi or developing orientation programs, your role as an advocate means you must always proactively situate these activities in the context of your campus, department, and program or course visions. As in any teaching and learning, the *why* we do something is often just as important, or more important, than the *how*. Your goal should be to navigate the tension between setting personal and program goals and introducing and modifying those goals in the light of larger campus challenges and opportunities. The model we introduce here, of balancing an inward and an outward focus, helps illustrate the sort of productive tension coordinators must navigate on a day-to-day basis. This includes working with your colleagues and students to develop and revise a vision for your collective work that will help you navigate the tension between the practical and the philosophical, the internal and the external, the how and the why. By making meaning of this role in and beyond your academic assignment, you will feel challenged, relevant, and vital.

EFFECTIVE CAMPUS ADVOCACY

Part of your role as course coordinator involves understanding not only the microlevel, day-to-day operations of your course (such as scheduling or textbook selection), but also the macrolevel relationships between your program and others on campus. The coordinated course, while typically housed in a particular department or division, is nested within an array of other institutional systems from across the campus, including admissions, advising, assessment, cocurricular activities and events, initiatives (toward, for example, sustainability or inclusive excellence), services (such as campus counseling or student health), and so on. As a coordinator, you must be aware of how the communities in which your course is nested alter and shape that course, as well as how the course may speak to and challenge or change those "outside" influences. With this awareness comes a sense of empowerment and efficacy — the knowledge that your work is of consequence, that different aspects of the campus function together to give rise to students' learning, and that you can and should be a full participant not only in students' learning, but in how that learning takes place in a larger organizational context. Further, you build connections beyond your own department or program, helping you stay abreast of new developments on your campus and keeping you active in the decision-making process. Rather than feeling like a bystander to campus decisions, you and your program may have an important role to play.

We recommend here a model to help you, as a course coordinator, best advocate for your program, your students, your instructors, and your campus:

- First, engage in research. In any context, one of the most important contributions you can make is to share the data that inform your position. For example, in a case where your program is at risk of budget cuts, your informed reading of financial information, your knowledge of reports regarding campus programs and their relative effectiveness, and your understanding of the campus fiscal context will enable you to participate in a discussion with candor and credibility.

- Second, share your findings and your data-informed understanding of how a given situation will affect the campus and its ability to achieve its mission. For example, if your program is adversely affected by budget cuts, can you illustrate how the reduced number of sections will affect student graduation and retention rates? Can you show that students will seek those same courses elsewhere if there are not enough offerings on your campus? Is this course a service your community has come to expect, and, if so, will it harm the reputation of your campus if you can no longer offer it with the same level of success?

- Finally, promote positive change that responds to the issue in a proactive manner. Significant budget cuts are clearly alarming; helping find positive solutions that foreground campus interests (rather than local, departmental interests) may help you reach compromises that are mutually beneficial. To return to our example, you might consider how different course configurations or enrollment caps or other factors might influence how the course aids in responding to campus budgetary or enrollment exigencies.

Reading Campus and Community Cultures

There are important steps you can take, as a coordinator, to remain abreast of the developments that might affect the students and instructors of this course, including consulting news sources and networking.

News Sources.   Perhaps the most obvious means of understanding the social, cultural, and economic forces at work on your campus and in your community is reading (or viewing or otherwise remaining current with) news sources such as campus newspapers, reliable news media outlets, and even *The Chronicle of Higher Education*. These will help you understand (and anticipate your responses to) what is happening on your campus, the funding opportunities and challenges facing higher education in your state, and the purpose and value of education in communication. What you glean from these venues may help you shape training and development exercises or student assignments, determine relevant service learning opportunities, or even locate funding opportunities.

The campus newspaper can also help you develop insight into students' experiences on campus. How the news covers your program can inform you about how the community perceives the work you are doing in the course. Events and situations that cause the community to react with joy and celebration can be very informative — for example, your decision to participate in new textbook rental programs might appear in the paper, earning your program accolades and affording you insight into your community's perceptions of your decisions. However, your program might also receive coverage that shows how people are reacting to a decision with fear or frustration — these too can pose productive learning moments for people involved in a coordinated course. For example, students' frustration with a lack of effective campus recycling processes could give rise to a speaker's forum on sustainability at your school; or a student's alcohol-related death could be an important starting point for learning about campus mental health resources.

Networking. Another way you can learn about events on campus and in the community that may affect the coordinated course is through your service commitments. By participating on committees that help promote awareness of the learning needs of students with disabilities, for example, you are well positioned to adapt the course so that it better meets the needs of more students. By participating in your campus accreditation review process, you may develop a keen sense of whether your colleagues in other offices and departments are establishing important connections with campus neighbors through their service (for example, to schools, hospitals, senior centers) with community members. Choosing your service commitments wisely, so that they contribute to and create continuity across different aspects of your academic assignment, will put you in contact with key stakeholders on your campus — people who, often, can inform you about developments (for example, budgetary or enrollment) that may affect your program or assist you in sharing information with administrators, navigating difficult individuals or offices, and positioning your program for resources.

Speaking Into and Shaping Campus and Community Cultures

Perhaps as important as reading the campus climate and the place of the course in this setting and mission is finding ways of sharing your ideas and actively shaping your campus culture. There are important steps you can take to share insights from your experiences coordinating this course with appropriate campus and community groups.

Organize Your Thoughts. In order to properly represent your advocacy to others, it is vital to make sure your case is coherent, clear, and focused. Draw information from a variety of sources and allow the material to be, on some level, self-evident. If you are trying to build alliances with community organizations for internships or service learning, you can use data from assessment reports, communication scholarship, university/college mission statements, and/or testimonials from other such programs that support the relationship you are suggesting.

Share Relevant Findings from Assessment Reports. As a course coordinator, you routinely compile information about the effectiveness of the course, as well as form impressions based on the experiences students and instructors of the course share with you. If you are aware of the leadership structure on your campus (for example, who administers which office and with what leadership style or investment in your program, in particular, or student learning, in general), then you will be better able to share findings and insights with colleagues who can put this information to good use. Sometimes these can be significant (and thorny or complex) observations, involving making decisions about how courses articulate as prerequisites to or substitutes for your course, or communicating to others about the preparedness of students coming from particular programs or departments; others can be smaller and easier to fix, such as asking campus librarians to collaborate with instructors in responding to students' misunderstandings about academic honesty, or helping student government know how many students in the course are actively involved in state or local politics. It is tempting, with routine data collection, to file the report away in your computer, but if you have something that matters — whether troubling or celebratory — be sure to share it with someone who can act on it.

Serve on Important University Committees. Part of protecting both the existence of communication courses in the general education curriculum and the integrity of the program you are coordinating is to be present on central committees where the status of your course is involved. Decisions made by committees such as general education advisory boards, first-year-experience committees, college-level curriculum committees, communication/writing across the curriculum committees, and other related groups may affect your program, and your presence helps you advocate for your course with your colleagues. Further, it may be appropriate to establish partnerships with other, similar programs on campus (for example, first-year composition), not only to better understand one another's roles in students' learning, but to share common opportunities and respond to common threats.

Seek Community Connections. The instructors and students associated with this course are active in all manner of organizations, causes, and communities. If you invite them to do so, they will share their passions with you. Some of these groups (for example, Toastmasters, the local city council, a struggling non-profit) may well benefit from exploring connections to their neighboring communication studies program, and might invite students into their programs and offices to learn how to communicate effectively in those settings and to share what they have been learning in their classes.

Collaborate with Other Introductory Course Coordinators. Besides the Basic Course listserv, conferences and conventions, and other formal and informal contexts that enable colleagues to exchange stories, experiences, and strategies, it is important to foster connections with those who share your role locally, statewide, regionally, and nationally. Who are the other coordinators in your state? Who works in the foundational communication courses at the local community college or the university in your region? What can you share with others about your experiences? How can you learn from others about their experiences, and how can you advocate for each other? Such ties and connections will enable you to work collaboratively should state boards or other entities seek to interfere with communication course structures, curricula, or staff.

Create Relevant Professional Development Seminars. It may be difficult to keep your instructors associated with the coordinated course informed regarding your efforts to build up or participate in new relationships and new initiatives on campus. One simple mechanism for providing access to these developments is to create a series of seminars that help inform the staff and invite them to provide feedback that enhances the work you are doing or proposing. For instance, if you are considering a new service element to the foundational course or, in more advanced coordinated courses, an internship component, a brief seminar that shares both disciplinary research and community need may serve as a forum for instructors to discuss how it might work in their classrooms. Such feedback situations can help locate problems and proactively increase instructors' willingness to participate in this initiative.

Showcase Best Practices and Public Events.   As you bring guest speakers to campus or place students in the community, consider sharing this information with campus and local media outlets. This will help build a positive impression of your program, promote the good work students and instructors are doing, and invite community members to interact with students about their communication, transforming their classroom presentations into more public, powerful, and lasting learning occasions. If community members view the local college or university as a place where they can join in meaningful conversations about issues that matter to them, as a neighbor instead of as an ivory tower, they will more readily see themselves as participants in their own and other people's learning (and, one hopes, will vote as such).

Specific Advocacy Situations

Of course, not all course contexts are the same. Different situations call for different types and levels of advocacy. In what follows, we try to speak to some of the specific advocacy situations you might face and the important considerations that relate to them.

Staffing and Turnover.   Often the most common instructors of introductory courses are part-time faculty, whether GTAs or lecturers; for both groups, turnover is a challenge, but in different ways. Graduate student instructors are a fluid population; as one cohort graduates, another arrives. Here, while drawing on the energy and excitement new teachers bring to the classroom, the course coordinator must maintain a clear picture of how training occurs and how to prepare instructors for their assignment. This differs, necessarily, with an instructional staff of part-time and adjunct faculty. In many community college campuses, there is very little that draws part-time faculty together as a unified whole. Clear objectives and expectations can help generate a coherent set of courses. Further, encouraging formal and informal mentoring relationships can help create continuity across a large number of part-time instructors. Finally, the reality that many sections may be taught by tenured or tenure-track faculty can be quite challenging to a coordinator who may be trying to build a sense of cohesion. Engaging faculty in the continued development of a department or program mission can help draw them together in support of this course.

Budget Cuts.   Recently, a colleague noted that a change in her graduate assistants' contract with the university resulted in greater allotment of funds going to support health care. These significant increases (important as they are) were not absorbed by the administration that negotiated them, but were instead assigned to individual departments. Such a change meant that the department would have to significantly cut the number of GTAs they could hire. This resulted in a two-tiered response: First, the number of sections of the introductory course decreased, and many students could not enroll. The course coordinator was able to share figures with the dean and provost regarding the number of students the department could no longer serve in order to show the amount of lost revenue the cuts created. Second, the role of the coordinator as a spokesperson for the department and the course became abundantly clear. In contexts where campus colleagues addressed general education requirements, the director of the introductory course made the case for continued (and increased) support for the communication foundation course, using research showing that employers regard communication as an essential skill. At no time is the need for advocacy more essential than in lean budgetary times, and proactive participation in such conversations serves to further strengthen the reputation of the program.

Course Level.   Not all coordinated courses are, of course, introductory. In some ways, the introductory level is the most recognizable structure — many sections of public speaking or introduction to communication appear at campuses across the country. However, many other courses may be coordinated — for example, upper division general education courses, core courses in the major, and so on. The instructors who staff these courses may be equally diverse or perhaps more so than those who teach introductory courses, but often there is less structured support for their teaching. This creates a difficult situation for the coordinators who advocate on behalf of the course: Often, with less visible and less institutionally recognized labor, coordinators have to work against what others might perceive to be a shaky foundation from which to advocate. One reason for this is that often coordinators of more advanced courses do not receive course releases or other support, though they do receive recognition for this assignment in evaluation of their effectiveness in academic assignment. However, the need to build a sense of advocacy in and for these courses is just as important. Because these courses support the major or other aspects of university core curriculum (for example, advanced general education learning), it is important for course coordinators to clarify, with key constituents, the effectiveness of these courses in meeting the missions of these larger programs.

Course Organization.   Whether organized as large lectures with break-out groups or as stand-alone sections, the structure of a course may affect a coordinator's approach to advocacy. For a large group, it might mean finding ways of advocating for technology in the classroom, finding the right classroom that enables the kind of pedagogy you are seeking to implement, or testing sites that can meet the need for security. If you coordinate small groups, finding possibilities for either consistency or variation (depending on the guiding principles of the department/program) is essential. In large measure, it is important to consider what the needs of instructors and students are and to seek clear paths to meet them based in the organizational context of your course.

ADVOCATING DURING DIFFICULT FINANCIAL TIMES

Institutions of higher education move through periods of abundance and strife. As we write this volume, most colleges and universities are facing unprecedented economic challenges. It can be especially challenging for course coordinators to advocate for their programs when they know the entire campus may be hard hit by furloughs, layoffs, and budget cuts; however, these challenges mean we must do our best to make sure students are learning what is, in our professional judgment, their right and privilege. There are some strategies you can employ to strengthen your program so that it can better weather troubling times and perhaps even grow.

Perhaps the most important strategy for maintaining the quality of your program is to make it an essential part of the campus climate. That is, you should take steps, as a coordinator, to link the course to campus life in central and irreplaceable ways. It may be the case that, on your campus, the introductory communication course is relatively sheltered by public and campus perceptions that communication is a core or foundational skill that all students (and citizens) must possess; however, if your course is not academically sacred, perhaps you can shape it so that it contributes meaningfully to the campus first-year-experience program, serves as a model of effective assessment practices, or has a productive, mutually strengthening relationship with other programs on campus. Further, your own reputation will nurture and protect the course as well; for example, if you have a reputation for a rigorous and effective program, for competent and collegial service across different campus programs and offices, and for strong, well-written assessment reports, your program will, to some extent, share your good name.

It can be useful to link your program with other campus initiatives; this not only helps ensure that these programs do not encroach on your place in the university, but also, more importantly, creates a context for communication as an anchor for the university's general education mission. For instance, John's campus recently began a first-year-experience program dedicated to serving students who are just beginning college. The introduction to communication course he supervises has long been a course that first-year students take, and, as a result, much of the training has focused on enabling GTAs to assist with this transition, including material on academic honesty, citation formatting, and general writing and speaking skills. While initially concerned by the development of the first-year program — about whether and how it would affect the content of the introduction to communication course and, more significantly, disrupt its place in the general education program — John began talking with colleagues in the English Department and the first-year program to meaningfully link the courses. This has resulted in three new developments, including a common course reader that would help students with knowledge transfer between seemingly disparate courses, an attendance tracking system that helps identify and reach out to students who appear to be struggling, and an invigorated sense of commitment to the success of first-year students as they are enrolled in introductory communication courses. Other campuses, including Deanna's, are considering similar programs; by participating in the formative phases of the project, we are better positioned to shape their direction and scope, as well as our role within them. By contributing to a campus initiative that links fully to both campus and department missions, the course, its instructors, and its coordinator remain relevant to student success. Examining programs and initiatives on your campus could provide a much needed linkage to the campus and enable your program to enjoy further stability and growth.

CONCLUSION

This book has been a concerted effort for us to reflect on what we find to be the most pressing issues facing a communication studies course coordinator. We end this book with a discussion of advocacy purposefully, because we believe that advocacy holds the other aspects of this assignment together in powerful and meaningful ways. Leadership positions mean more than responding to the challenges you face, mean more than being reactive; becoming a course coordinator, becoming a campus leader, means becoming a visionary and an agent of change and innovation.

Each year we consider how to work with groups of new instructors, teaching them how to teach, asking them to consider, reflexively, the task they are about to undertake. We struggle a little bit each year as they focus on "students who don't read" or "the bad textbook" or "lazy students who won't come to class." In each instance, we work to balance their immediate needs and concerns against both our vision for what the introductory course might be and what they might, in the course of their careers, achieve. At least once each year we face a group of instructors who complain that their students can't outline. Their frustration is real, and it is meaningful as they struggle to help students meet their expectations. Our challenge in this moment is one of focus: What does it mean to concentrate on what students fail to do or on how students fail to produce what we expect from them? Is the point of our courses the ability to outline? Is that our most pressing concern? Should it be?

And each year we challenge these new instructors to consider: Who is the discipline? Who determines what is most important about communication, or about a communication class? In the end, what our discipline is and values and what our courses contain and emphasize are a matter of what instructors foreground in their classrooms. If an instructor wants students to master outlining skills, then she or he must center that concept, rewarding and challenging students as they match or depart from this expectation. If, however, the instructor wants students to become citizens of the world—agents of change in their communities, perceptive regarding the power of communication in shaping relationships—then outlining may not be the most important part of the class. Whether as coordinators or as instructors, what we do every day in the communication classroom is what the discipline is. To that end, our field emerges from even our most foundational courses and the instructors who teach them, not from the articles we find in peer-reviewed publications. Encouraging instructors to see themselves as creators and not just transmitters of knowledge is of the utmost importance for our work as course coordinators.

Advocacy involves creating the conditions for the possibility of empowerment; it is about building the ability and desire to make a difference in the lives of others. Course coordinators are, in their own way, primed to serve as advocates for a better world. As idealistic as that might sound, it also correctly identifies the core meaning of this position. Communication creates selves, relationships, organizations, cultures, communities—and, as players in how instructors and students develop that knowledge, it is incumbent on us to lead responsibly.